Brian O'Connell is President of INDE-
PENDENT SECTOR, a coalition of voluntary
organizations, foundations, and corporations
seeking to preserve and enhance the American
traditions of giving, volunteering, and nonprofit initiative.

Also by Brian O'Connell:
*Finding Values That Work:
  The Search for Fulfillment
Effective Leadership in
  Voluntary Organizations
America's Voluntary Spirit
The Board Member's Book
Our Organization*

PHILANTHROPY
in Action

BRIAN O'CONNELL

THE FOUNDATION CENTER

Copyright © 1987 by Brian O'Connell. All rights reserved.
Printed and bound in the United States of America.
Cover design by Apicella Design.

Library of Congress Cataloging-in-Publication Data

O'Connell, Brian, 1930-
  Philanthropy in action.

  Bibliography: p.
  Includes index.
  1. Endowments—United States—History. I. Title.
HV25.028 1987   361.7'632'0973   87–17729
ISBN 0-87954-230-6
ISBN 0-67954-231-4 (soft)

To
Ann Brown O'Connell
with
appreciation, admiration, affection

CONTENTS

FOREWORD

When I became president of the National Council on Philanthropy and later after INDEPENDENT SECTOR was formed, I found that I was called on frequently to write, testify, and speak about philanthropy. To try to make the statements interesting and persuasive, I was always on the lookout for good examples of gifts that had made a difference. It was frustrating how often even the leaders of the field would respond to me with something like, "Well, there's Carnegie's libraries and Rockefeller's yellow fever discovery and hundreds if not thousands of others but they don't come to mind at the moment."

The absence of ready references and good tales paralleled the difficulty I was having in finding some of the great literature describing the history, role, and impact of voluntary initiative in America. In that case, I found most people referred me to de Tocqueville and little else. Because it was particularly important to have fuller references, I went on the search that eventually resulted in the book of readings, *America's Voluntary Spirit*, published by The Foundation Center in 1983.

In the current case, an even fuller and much more difficult search of the literature was necessary to produce the examples that comprise *Philanthropy In Action*. Both efforts reinforce the conclusions of the committee that created INDEPENDENT SECTOR, that the voluntary sector is taken for granted, is seriously neglected in scholarship, and can be successfully challenged by skeptics who are made all the more suspicious by our generalizations.

One of the primary functions of INDEPENDENT SECTOR is to help Americans understand this nonprofit side of our country so that they will grasp how fundamental voluntary endeavor is to the maintenance of personal and national freedom, will be even more willing to support with time and money the causes of their choice, and will defend the independence of nonprofit organizations from undue governmental interference. This educational role requires a body of literature that is presently not at hand.

I don't pretend that *America's Voluntary Spirit* and *Philanthropy In Action* are scholarly works, but I hope these efforts to pull together some of what is known and to provide heretofore unassembled bibliographies will help stimulate the fuller research and writing that eventually will build an adequate literature. In the meantime, I hope these early books and The Foundation Center's willingness to keep them in print will provide some immediate resource for the growing number of people who are speaking and teaching about philanthropy and voluntary action.

It is important to prepare the reader that *Philanthropy In Action* is not a definitive record of grantmaking, or to borrow from Robert Bremner's introduction to *American Philanthropy*, ". . . is not an encyclopedia of good works. . . ." This effort is just one attempt to pull together some random examples of different kinds of grants that might be fun to know about and might help tell the story of what philanthropy does.

The book also does not represent a scientific sampling of grantmaking, nor have I attempted to verify that all of the grants have done what someone said they did. For that kind of empirical evidence we will also have to await more scholarly studies. For now, these several hundred examples, however random and anecdotal, do add up to rather clear lines of evidence that philanthropy has made, and continues to make, a very large difference in almost every area of human endeavor.

One limitation that even more thorough researchers will face and represents a fault we grantseekers must correct in the future, involves how maddeningly rare it is that published accounts of successes give credit to the financial backers. Repeatedly, we came across stories of wonderful breakthroughs that ignored the funding partners.

Initially we found the search of the literature very tough going. Philanthropy is not a topic of much contemporary interest. As we went back in time, we began to find fuller material. Prior to the 1930s and particularly from about 1800 to 1930, there was a great deal written about philanthropy and philanthropists. Our bibliography illustrates that during that period, books and periodicals gave a great deal of attention to the topic. Beginning with the depression and the New Deal, observers of the contemporary scene were understandably more interested in the growing role and functions of government. It was not until the 1960s that voluntary initiative and the philanthropy that supports it began to get much exposure again, and interest in philanthropy is still far less than it was a hundred years ago. As people of all political and philosophical persuasion have begun to realize the practical limitations of big government and the value of having both effective government and an effective voluntary sector, interest in philanthropy has reemerged.

Unfortunately, much of the best of the early literature is lost or buried, and we haven't really begun to resurrect it. Some of the best books are exceedingly rare. Many others are hardly known to the leaders of philanthropy and from my observation are rarely in their collections. If, indeed, "what is past is prologue" and we want students and the public to understand the role of philanthropy in our society, we need to be familiar with our own literature. For this reason, the reader is encouraged to review the bibliography at the end of this volume.

Fortunately, the Council on Foundations with its *Foundation News, Newsletter,* and special publications and The Foundation Center with its many important books and publications are now regularly supplying facts and information about grantmakers and the voluntary organizations they support. Both the casual reader and scholar should be familiar with their materials.

I continue to be grateful to The Foundation Center for its interest in my books and to Pat Read for her central role as editor of them. Thanks also to Rick Schoff for following up on all the publishing details. The head of the Center's Washington library, Margot Brinkley, has been helpful and patient with our heavy use of her valuable collection. At INDEPENDENT SECTOR, Sandy Solomon and Susan McConaghy have been wonderfully helpful.

Acknowledgment and appreciation are extended also to Barbara and Morton Mandel and their Premier Industrial Foundation, the George Gund Foundation, the 3M Foundation, and the Wells Fargo Foundation, which provided a small fund for research, editorial assistance, and preparation costs for this and other writings on the independent sector.

Without the participation of The Foundation Center, the fund to underwrite back-up costs, and the work of my Research Assistant, Ann Brown O'Connell, this very part-time writer with a very full-time job would have had absolutely no chance to add even slightly to the literature. In light of the size of the research task for this book and the undependable schedule of its harried author, it is especially appropriate that this book is dedicated to Ann.

With great appreciation,
Brian O'Connell
McLean, Virginia
August 13, 1986

PART I
Philanthropy: America's Extra Dimension

Philanthropy: America's Extra Dimension

Philanthropy plays many different roles in our society, but its central value is the extra dimension it provides for seeing and doing things differently. Philanthropy doesn't take the place of government or other basic institutions, but it does provide additional ways to address our problems and aspirations and to keep our basic institutions responsive and effective.

Philanthropy operates in thousands of different ways: many inspirational, some silly, and a few downright dangerous. Contrast the Rockefeller Foundations's "Green Revolution" which increased the food supply for millions with the Emma A. Robinson Christmas Dinner Trust Fund for Horses or Garrett Smith's funding of John Brown's raid on Harpers Ferry, and you have some feel for the scope.

Overall, America's philanthropy provides an enormously important extra dimension in our pursuit of happiness and protection of inalienable rights. Its impact is clear in just about every field of endeavor including fields as different as architecture, health, human rights, historic preservation, international understanding, the arts, neighborhoods, empowerment, patriotism, agriculture, rocketry, physics, the homeless, and astronomy. Most of the great movements of our society have had their origins in the independent sector: abolition of slavery, clarification and protection of civil rights, creation of public libraries, care and opportunities for the handicapped, and on and on. Some who led those efforts were viewed as unpopular, troublesome, rabble-rousing, and perhaps even dan-

3

gerous. It has been one of the hallmarks of philanthropy that it has offered support for unpopular people and ideas and protected their freedom.

Henry Allen Moe, long-time head of the John Simon Guggenheim Memorial Foundation, delivered the Founders Day Address at Johns Hopkins University in 1951 and gave it the appropriate title, "The Power of Freedom." He spoke of the genius of America—its freedom as a society and the freedom it allows individuals and institutions to be different. He quoted Elihu Root: "Freedom is the supreme treasure of our country." And he quoted Detlev Bronk: "Freedom is the grand ingredient of the great adventures of the human mind." Independence is in fact at the heart of the contribution made by philanthropic and voluntary organizations.

Occasionally, philanthropic support of unpopular ideas has led government officials and others to question the relative value of philanthropy's independence versus the need for public control over private expenditure of tax-free dollars. In 1953, the House Select Committee to Investigate Foundations and Other Organizations, popularly known as the "Reece Committee," held hearings on the use of foundation grants "for subversive purposes or for active political propaganda." During those hearings, *The Christian Century* published an editorial that presented a convincing argument for preserving philanthropy's independence:

> The central issue then is freedom. The foundations are not prepared to surrender to government the exclusive right to be concerned over the health, the education, the prosperity or even the safety of the people. They should be supported in their liberty to explore social questions. They uphold and practice freedom of enterprise in humanitarian concern for welfare, in intellectual concern for study and research. Having no faith in ignorance as a servant of democracy, they encourage independent inquiry and publication in politics and economics. Knowing that the more important issues, including survival, depend on right national and international relationships, they dig for and disseminate knowledge in these bitterly contested fields.

The historian Merle Curti, writing on "Tradition and Innovation in American Philanthropy: Growth and Present Status of American Foundations" (in the 1961 *Proceedings of the American Philosophical Society*), emphasized that the value of foundations and those they support is their freedom to be creative and that creativity is the quintessential character of nonprofit endeavor:

> This brief account of the way in which American philanthropy has developed from its Old World origins, of the newer methods and agencies that have been adopted or further developed in the United

States, and of the kind of private contributions that have been made
in various fields has done scant justice to the dedicated work of
many individuals and foundations. But it at least suggests the scope
and character of what has been done. And it gives support to the
thesis that, whatever its limitations, private philanthropy has played
a telling part especially in the America of the last seventy-five years
in opening the way to a larger emphasis on the esthetic and civic
components in the national life. In these respects, in the role that
many donors and some foundations have played, and in the
distinctive relationships with government that have developed,
American philanthropy has a record that is genuinely creative.

Speaking of the special role that philanthropy plays and of the freedom
it requires, John W. Gardner, one of the founders of the organization
INDEPENDENT SECTOR, observed:

Perhaps the most striking feature of the sector is its relative freedom
from constraints and its resulting pluralism. Within the bounds of
the law, all kinds of people can pursue any idea or program they
wish. Unlike government, an independent sector group need not
ascertain that its idea or philosophy is supported by some large
constituency, and unlike the business sector, they do not need to
pursue only those ideas which will be profitable. If a handful of
people want to back a new idea, they need seek no larger
consensus.

Americans have always believed in pluralism—the idea that a free
nation should be hospitable to many sources of initiative, many
kinds of institutions, many conflicting beliefs, and many competing
economic units. Our pluralism allows individuals and groups to
pursue goals that they themselves formulate, and out of that
pluralism has come virtually all of our creativity.

Institutions of the nonprofit sector are in a position to serve as
the guardians of intellectual and artistic freedom. Both the
commercial and political marketplaces are subject to leveling forces
that may threaten standards of excellence. In the nonprofit sector,
the fiercest champions of excellence may have their say. So may
the champions of liberty and justice.

There are many other statements characterizing the value of independent institutions. For a book describing the work of the Fund for the
Advancement of Education, Paul Woodring used the appropriate title,
Investment in Innovation. The Fund labeled its own ten-year report for
1951–1961, "Decade of Experiment." Paul Ylvisaker, who serves on the

boards of several foundations and is a consultant to the Council on Foundations, says that "Philanthropy is America's passing gear."

In light of the impact of philanthropy, there is some question whether it is accurate to describe it as an "extra dimension." Many champions consider philanthropy to be America's greatest institution or at least one of its most important. We need to be cautious, though, in putting it ahead of other aspects of our democratic way of life. It is important to remember the basic values of American society: freedom, worth and dignity of the individual, equal opportunity, justice, and mutual responsibility. Our fundamental vehicles for preserving and enhancing those basic values are

- Representative government starting with one person/one vote
- The freedoms of speech and assembly
- A free press
- A system of justice beginning with due process and presumption of innocence
- Universal public education

Philanthropy helps to preserve and enhance those vehicles, but it doesn't transcend them.

It's helpful to our perspective to realize that the philanthropic and voluntary sector is very much smaller than government or the commercial sector. In terms of National Income (NI), commerce totals 79 percent, government totals 15 percent, and the whole of the independent sector accounts for only 6 percent. Philanthropy alone, including all giving by foundations, corporations, and individuals, is but two percent. Subtracting individuals, the proportion for foundations and corporations is two-tenths of one percent.

The comparison becomes even starker when one measures the philanthropic dollars of foundations and corporations against the expenditures of government. As large and important as foundation and corporate giving are, they are not nearly as large as most people think. These two sources of philanthropy represent total annual expenditures of about $10 billion, while the combined expenditures of the three levels of government are about $2 trillion. Even if one were to subtract defense allocations from the government figures, lowering the total to $1.5 trillion, the combined grants of corporations and foundations are only one-half of one percent of what government spends. Even the whole of the independent sector, with annual expenditures of $150 billion, is less than ten percent the size of government.

When seen this way, it becomes clear that philanthropy is terribly small compared to government and that all such private expenditures have to be targeted carefully and uniquely or they won't be worth very much to society's needs and goals. There are ways by which that one-half of one percent and that ten percent can be spent to make a difference far beyond their relative sizes, but if these funds are not targeted carefully they would add an incidental rather than an extra dimension to our efforts to address major needs and aspirations.

A few years ago I attended a Ditchley Foundation Conference in England that had an ambitious title such as "The Future of Philanthropy in the Western World," and it became clear that for other countries, such as England, the total amounts represented by philanthropy are absolutely miniscule compared to government. In Britain, the total voluntary sector is about two percent the size of government compared with our ten percent. Even at that, representatives from those other countries argued that however small the percentage and the dollar figure might be, the sector provides absolutely vital elements of flexibility, innovation, creativity, and the capacity for criticism and reform, and therefore must be preserved.

One of the issues discussed at that meeting involved whether philanthropic dollars should be used to supplement government expenditures, particularly at a time of government cutbacks. At that time, both Prime Minister Thatcher and President Reagan were arguing that private philanthropy should be used to make up for some government retrenchment. Many U.S. mayors were also urging foundations and corporations to help government keep schools, libraries, and parks open and to maintain other public services. During those discussions and subsequently, it became clear that though philanthropy has a responsibility to deal with emergency matters, particularly those involving human suffering, in the long run the small amount that philanthropy represents must be reserved for unique *extra* purposes. If not, philanthropic expenditures will not represent anything very different or unique and therefore might not be worth preserving.

One of the lessons I've learned from this comparison between philanthropy and government is that one has to accept what philanthropy can't do and to realize and accept what government should do. In his article, "The Reputation of the American Philanthropist: A Historian's View," which appeared in the September, 1958 *Social Service Review,* Irving Wyllie put it this way:

> If America expected her philanthropists to be sensitive to current needs, she also expected them to be aware that there was a limit to what even the wisest and most liberal charity could accomplish. A college here, a soup kitchen there, did not add up to Utopia. Philanthropy was no substitute for social justice. There has been no period of time in which wealth has been more sensible of its duties

than now, wrote James Russell Lowell in 1884. It builds hospitals, it establishes missions among the poor, it endows schools. . . . But all these remedies are partial and palliative merely. It is as if we should apply plasters to a single pustule of the smallpox with a view to driving out the disease. The true way is to discover and to extirpate the germs. America preferred benefactors who did not view philanthropy as an antidote to reform but rather as an admission that reform was necessary. To give was to confess the need, and to confess the need was to open the door to change.

In his book, *Philanthropy's Role In Civilization: Its Contribution to Human Freedom,* Arnaud C. Marts describes philanthropy as a pioneering "minority movement," meaning that it represents activities that government will not or, because of its size or nature, should not undertake. He quotes Felix M. Warburg as follows: "The feeling was, and I think rightly, that experiments should be made by private institutions before the public's funds were risked in large amounts on schemes which have not been tried out thoroughly as yet. . . . I am quite sure the method has saved the United States a very large amount of money." Marts goes on to describe the pioneering roles of philanthropy in many fields of human endeavor.

It is unreasonable and even inappropriate to expect that all philanthropic organizations will be on the "cutting edge." While much of the good that philanthropy does is accomplished there, many funders find themselves encouraging organizations toward excellence, intervening where human misery is greatest, or nourishing the human spirit.

I've tried to identify several of the different though admittedly overlapping roles that philanthropy plays and have ended up with nine. At times in this exercise there were four or five and other times seventeen or eighteen, so clearly there is nothing sacrosanct in the delineation and enumeration of the roles. More important than the general outline are the illustrations that help show philanthropy in action.

I believe that philanthropy helps us:

- To Discover New Frontiers of Knowledge
- To Support and Encourage Excellence
- To Enable People to Exercise Their Potential
- To Relieve Human Misery
- To Preserve and Enhance Democratic Government and Institutions
- To Make Communities a Better Place to Live
- To Nourish The Spirit
- To Create Tolerance, Understanding, and Peace Among People
- To Remember the Dead

This latter may not seem to be a separate role—more a motivation—but in our research it shows up as such a pervasive factor that I chose to give it separate consideration.

I might have settled for just two roles—To Relieve Human Misery and To Maximize Human Potential—but the extended list allows a closer examination of the various ways that philanthropy makes a difference.

If I were really pressed and had to reduce it all the way back to just one role, it would be "To Serve as America's Extra Dimension."

PART II
Philanthropy In Action

1

To Discover New Frontiers of Knowledge

I. EXPLORATION AND DISCOVERY
II. THE SEARCH FOR KNOWLEDGE FOR
KNOWLEDGE'S SAKE
III. INVENTORS AND INVENTIONS

Exploration and Discovery

When I was growing up in Worcester, Massachusetts, we had a neighbor who was considered odd because he kept trying to put rockets in the air. Almost nobody thought he could do it, and the few who did were hardly enthusiasts. They worried that if he did succeed he would only cause perpetual rain or bring the sky falling in or shoot an angel.

Robert H. Goddard was known derisively as "the moon man." In 1920, he had made the laughable prediction that a rocket could go to the moon. For years the only money he had for research came from his own pocket. His first grant came in 1917: a $5,000 gift from the Hodgkins Fund of the Smithsonian Institution for "construction and launching a high altitude rocket." Nine years later his modest attempt to fulfill the terms of that grant rose 41 feet and flew for 2.5 seconds. This was just far enough to encourage Goddard and short enough to discourage funders.

In 1929, a larger model blasted off, literally and figuratively. The explosion did send his missile 100 feet up but started a fire several hundred feet wide. Most of the press attention focused on the fire, but a few stories marveled at the accomplishment. One of these was read by Mrs. Harry Guggenheim.

This history of Goddard's rocketry and the Guggenheim's support are beautifully captured in Milton Lomask's *Seed Money: The Guggenheim Story.* Lomask records that Harry Guggenheim consulted no less than

Charles Lindbergh on the practicality of Goddard's ideas. Lindbergh first satisfied himself and then the Guggenheims that Goddard just might be on to something big, then he made the case to Harry's father, Daniel Guggenheim. Mr. Lomask gives Lindbergh's recollection of their 1930 discussion:

> Mr. Dan: "Then you believe rockets have an important future?"
> Lindbergh: "Probably. Of course one is never certain."
> "But you think so. And this professor, he looks like a pretty capable man?"
> "As far as I can find out, Mr. Guggenheim, he knows more about rockets than anybody in the country."
> "How much money does he need?"
> "He'd like to have $25,000 a year for a four-year project."
> "Do you think he can accomplish enough to make it worth his time?"
> "Well, it's taking a chance, but if we're ever going to get beyond the limits of airplanes and propellers, we'll probably have to go to rockets. It's a chance but, yes, I think it's worth taking."
> "All right, I'll give him the money."

For the next two years, Goddard worked full time at a test site established in Roswell, New Mexico. When Daniel Guggenheim died, the last half of the grant could not be paid and the Roswell project had to be abandoned. Fortunately, once the estate was settled, and the Daniel and Florence Guggenheim Foundation was established, one of the foundations's first grants, renewed for nine successive years, was for $18,000 for the continuation of Goddard's work at Roswell. Of this period, Lomask writes:

> And here for a period of almost eleven years, he tested and refined the modern rocket. Sooner or later, "in one form or another," to quote Dr. (G. Edward) Pendray, "he tried out practically every one of the ideas that have since been developed successfully in large rockets and guided missiles, including gyro-controls, clustered rockets, research instrumentation, turbo-pumps for propellants, and gimbal-mounted tail sections capable of being moved in flight for steering. . . ." Pendray adds that the culmination of Goddard's work in New Mexico was a rocket that made a successful altitude shot of some 9,000 feet. . . .

Nine thousand feet in 1941 was quite a giant step from that flight in 1927 of less than 41 feet, but even that earlier launch was, according to Lomask, "the parent of all the 9000 mile Adases and Redstones that will ever fly, all the Sputniks that will ever circle planet earth, all the Project

Mercury, Saturn and Jupiter capsules that will ever soar to Venus, Moon and Mars. . . ."

Goddard's work was interrupted during the war and largely ignored by the U.S. government. The Germans took full advantage of it in developing their V-2 rockets. Goddard died in 1945 just about the time his pathfinding really began to show the way into space. Fortunately, Daniel and Florence Guggenheim carried forward their interest in Goddard's work and their commitment to space exploration by establishing centers for aerospace studies at California Institute of Technology, Columbia, Cornell, Harvard, and Princeton, and by funding various related projects and institutes.

There don't seem to be figures on how much Goddard received from various sources for his lifetime of research, but it probably was a good deal less than a half million dollars. Matched against what his work has led to, it is appropriate that the Guggenheim story is told under the heading, "Seed Money."

A quite different example of collaboration between funder and explorer is the case of Edsel Ford and Admiral Richard E. Byrd. Byrd dreamed of exploring the North Pole by airplane, even though most scientific and practical evidence suggested that such a venture would be foolhardy. But this was the early 1920s, when young minds were captivated by the potential of flight.

In his book, *From These Beginnings: The Early Philanthropy Of Henry And Edsel Ford, 1911–1936,* William Greenleaf describes the initial meeting of the two men and of their later friendship and partnership. Greenleaf records that they met in 1924 when Byrd was only a lieutenant commander and Ford was already president of the Ford Motor Company. Byrd had hoped for $10,000 but "twenty minutes after his visitor walked through the office door, Edsel had promised Byrd $15,000." Ford's grant was later increased to $20,000 and then to $30,000. In addition, Ford recognized that Byrd was a better explorer than fundraiser and took on the task of raising most of the remaining $140,000 that was needed. According to Greenleaf:

> On May 9, 1926 Commander Byrd and his co-pilot Floyd Bennett became the first to reach the North Pole by airplane. The feat gave indisputable evidence of the usefulness of the plane for polar exploration and awakened popular interest in the potentialities of aviation. It also showed that it was possible to navigate an airplane accurately under the peculiar magnetic conditions of the Arctic. Byrd made valuable contributions to aerial navigation, astronomical

observations and methods of exploration and to the compilation of scientific data on meteorology, seismology and polar glaciology.

Later, again with Edsel Ford's primary backing and fundraising assistance, Byrd organized a similar exploration to the South Pole. Greenleaf concludes the tale:

> Byrd was the first to circle the North and South Poles in a plane and, more than anyone else in this century, was responsible for extensive surveys of then unknown areas in the Arctic and Antarctic. The world recognizes his proving of the airplane as a reliable instrument of polar exploration. His scientific explorations may loom even more importantly if Antarctica becomes an area for technical development as man widens his search for fresh sources of mineral fuels. Byrd's expeditions to Antartica after World War II were financed by the U.S. Government as a matter of course.

Our knowledge of space was transformed as a result of the development of massive telescopes, most notably those at the Lick Observatory, and now the massive new instruments being funded by the Keck Foundation. The intervening history is a fascinating story of contribution and competition for the biggest and best. Actually, the story starts before Lick, when, as Howard S. Miller writes in *Dollars for Research*, "Upstart Cincinnati, not the older, richer cities of the Atlantic coast, built the first major American astronomical observatory. It was an incredible accomplishment for a back-country river town in the 1840s." Miller recounts that "Cincinnati's success, coupled with the growing capacity to produce evermore powerful telescopes, set off an intense competition between a number of cities to have the biggest and the best."

The drama moved next to San Francisco where the astronomer George Davidson was serving as the president of the California Academy of Sciences at a time when James Lick had been persuaded to donate "a valuable lot in downtown San Francisco in which to erect a museum and headquarters for the Academy." Lick had made his money initially in South America in the manufacture of pianos and then parlayed that stake into a fortune in real estate and other business ventures in California. However, he had no heirs and was on the lookout for a suitable memorial. According to Miller,

> Lick first considered erecting an immense pyramid in downtown San Francisco. Next he contemplated a million dollars worth of statuary, on behalf of himself and his parents, believing that they would survive for future civilizations to admire as antiquities. At

this juncture, Davidson and D. J. Staples, Lick's legal advisor, suggested that an astronomical observatory was at once a fitting monument and an active agency for the perpetual advancement of knowledge.

Over the next several years, Lick did everything possible to assure that the observatory was not only the largest and best, but the most visable. Miller writes:

> At one point he wanted to erect the dome in the San Francisco business district where it would be visible to all, and surround the building with statuary groups featuring Francis Scott Key, Thomas Paine, and himself. Assuring Lick that harbor fog, city lights and the vibration from passing vehicles would render the telescope useless in that locale, Davidson slowly guided the philanthropist to the mountain top observatory site.

Not surprisingly, Lick chose a different and far higher site. For a while the Lick observatory was indeed the biggest and the best in the world. Then, according to Miller, "Lick's astronomical monument spurred others to outdo him." Southern California was the first to try and came very close, but after a 40-inch refractor was ordered and in process, financial difficulties intervened and the project was halted.

The lure of such a refractor caught the imagination of the Chicago community, and after years of negotiation, the temporary millionaire Charles Tyson Yerkes became the donor, much to his own unhappiness and everyone else's. Miller describes Yerkes "as the model for Frank Cowperthwait, the robber baron protagonist of Theodore Dreiser's *The Financier and the Titan.* He thought that his gift would buy him acceptability and prestige. When neither was forthcoming, he left town and subsequently lost his money." But at least the University of Chicago had the biggest and best telescope, for a while.

At about that point, Andrew Carnegie stepped into the competition and put Southern California back in the picture. With Mr. Carnegie's help, the new "biggest and best" was established at the Mt. Wilson observatory with a 60-inch reflecting telescope! Subsequently, the telescope was expanded to a 100-inch refractor. As Miller reports:

> Carnegie's letter showed that enthusiasm for astronomy had motivated this latest gift, and that his sense of gratitude toward his adopted country had not diminished over the years. "I hope the work at Mt. Wilson will be vigorously pusht," he wrote, slipping occasionally into simplified spelling, "because I'm anxious to hear the expected results from it. I should like to be satisfied before I

depart, that we are going to repay to the old land, some part of the
debt we owe them by revealing more clearly than ever . . . the new
heavens."

Miller thought he was able to end the story with this concluding para-
graph: "Andrew Carnegie died in 1919, before the Mt. Wilson reflector
had begun full operation. Had he lived another decade, he would have
witnessed revolutionary stellar discoveries and might have contributed to
George Ellery Hales' last and greatest project, the Rockefeller-financed
200-inch reflector on Mt. Palomar."

In what I am sure is only the latest step in this healthy competition for
better ways to understand the universe, in 1985 the Keck Foundation
awarded $70 million for a telescope that will have a 400-inch diameter. It
well be known as the Keck Observatory, and will be built in Hawaii and
operated jointly by the California Institute of Technology and the University of California.

Edward Bromfield Phillips was a donor who made a different kind of
contribution to the development of astronomy. He had been one of several people to provide funding for a telescope for his native Boston, but he
also provided funds to ensure that there would be trained astronomers in
the future. Miller tells the story in his chapter, "The Works of Creators":

> Instruments, however, were only half the story. "Without practical
> astronomers." wrote Benjamin Peirce, "America can have no
> astronomy." The observer who spent his nights at the telescope
> could not spend his days earning a living. Because of the nature of
> his research, the astronomer had to be a full-time man of science.
> The matter of salaries was critical at Harvard, for William Cranch
> Bond had already served seven years without pay. Fortunately he
> had been a watchmaker by trade, and while acting as College
> Observer supported his family by regulating marine chronometers
> and doing contract work for the Coast Survey.
>   The promise of a new observatory heightened the need for
> permanent endowment, both for salaries and for ongoing
> institutional expenses. Already strained by fiscal problems of its
> own, the college treasury could do very little to help. Once
> committed, however, Harvard's patrons of science kept on giving.
> In 1846 thirty-three individuals subscribed $5,000 to meet current
> expenses. The next year, when the instruments were installed and
> the observatory commenced operations, David Sears added another
> $5,000 to his previous contribution. He earmarked the income
> from his second gift for salaries and the purchase of apparatus.
>   In 1848 Edward Bromfield Phillips unexpectedly bequeathed

Harvard $100,000 as a fund for observers' salaries. It was an astounding gift, "one of the largest in this part of the world to the cause of pure science."

The Search for Knowledge for Knowledge's Sake

Perhaps there has been competition to help build telescopes because they are so tangible. You can literally see the results, both in the equipment and in what it magnifies. Research is usually far less specific, and sustained support of it often involves an act of faith that the objectives will someday be realized. It's one thing to get a donor or board of trustees to buy a telescope, and quite another to convince them to go the long slow route of increasing the influence of a field of study or to invest in unexplored fields.

The Rockefeller Foundation's early and sustained support in the field of biology illustrates the accomplishments that can be realized through such acts of faith. In "Biochemistry, Chemistry and Private Foundations," from Warren Weaver's book, *U.S. Philanthropic Foundations,* Arne Tiselins, 1948 Nobel Laureate in chemistry, says:

> Beyond doubt one of the most striking demonstrations of what can be done is the Rockefeller Foundation program to promote unexplored fields in the basic life sciences concerned with the constitution, structure and function of living organisms and their component parts. This was a keen and unusually foresighted long-range project which was carried through in a most generous and successful way, with an investment of about $100 million from the beginning in the mid-thirties to the end [about 1951]. I mention the end because it would seem almost as difficult, and as essential to a foundation, to be able to terminate such a far-reaching project at a convenient time as it must have been to launch it. By "a convenient time" is meant, of course, a time when it was obvious to everybody that the field was so important that sufficient support was forthcoming through other channels. Today there is almost a competition among different organizations to support especially "molecular biology." The Rockefeller Foundation officers thoroughly examined the possibilities and the resources in the field and saw to it that support was directed to strategic points where the prospects of advance appeared particularly promising.
>
> It is a more rewarding task for a private foundation to help to start something new which appears promising. Thus, in today's perspective, it is interesting to find in the record of Rockefeller

Foundation grants from the thirties, research projects such as the application of isotopes to biological problems (for example, Niels Bohr, August Krogh, Georg von Hevesy, University of Copenhagen), biological ultrastructure (W. T. Astbury, University of Leeds), biochemistry of hormones (V. du Vigneaud, Cornell University Medical College), cooperative research in biophysics, chemical biology, cell physiology (J. Runnstrom, University of Stockholm), ultracentrifugation, proteins (T. Svedberg, University of Uppsala). Also we find among the early projects organic chemistry in relation to biology (Linus Pauling, California Institute of Technology), physico-chemical studies of serum proteins (Edwin Cohn, Harvard), further application of isotopes to biological problems (Harold Urey, Hans T. Clarke, and others).

Even less tangible and more farsighted is the Rockefeller Foundation's support of the broad range of humanities. For years, the Rockefeller Foundation has persevered in the almost endless, almost thankless task of encouraging greater attention to the humanities. Their point, so long-range that even a foundation with its record has a hard time holding the course, is that in the end, there will be more discovery, learning, and perhaps even peace if we strive now for stronger scholarship in such fields as history, philosophy, languages, and theology. Some of the foundation's critics yearn for the days of "instant breakthroughs" with penicillin, yellow fever, and "the Green Revolution."

One happy compromise—something tangible while remaining true to the basic building blocks of knowledge—was to provide the planning and start-up support for the National Humanities Center. The Center was established in 1978 to encourage research on the humanities and to ensure that such disciplines as sociology, history, and philosophy would influence the national and international debate on world problems affecting the quality and even the future of life. Recently, Rockefeller added $1 million to endow fellowships at the Center for junior scholars.

Here are some different examples of support of research:

- A long-term view and investment was involved in a grant by the Hill Family Foundation, now the Northwest Area Foundation, to establish the Hill Monastic Manuscript Library at St. John's University in Minnesota. A.A. Heckman, who headed the foundation, says that the library collects and microfilms "handwritten manuscripts predating the introduction of printing in Western Europe, . . . and today holds an extensive collection of microfilmed manuscripts dating as early as the 6th and 7th centuries and all illuminations in the

manuscripts are microfilmed in color film. . . . Scholars from
throughout the United States, Canada, and some from Europe visit
Hill Monastic Manuscript Library to pursue their research since the
Library is the only place in the world where they can probably find
in one place most of the information and source material they need
for their research."

The library is located in the Bush Center at St. Johns, donated by
the Bush Foundation, which adds another dimension to the relationship of philanthropy and scholarship.

• Heckman tells about another fascinating grant by Northwest that
involved a different aspect of exploration. "Some years ago, a grant
to the University of Minnesota supported early research on the use
of radio collars in tracking birds and animals. This research was
done long before such radio collars were used regularly by biolo-
gists and naturalists doing research on animals and birds throughout
the world."

• The Celanese Corporation provided close to a half million dollars in
1979 to the National Audubon Society for research on the habitats
of four endangered bird species: the bald eagle, California condor,
whooping crane, and Atlantic puffin.

• In 1986, H. Ross Perot provided a combination loan and gift of $15
million to enable the University of Texas to secure "a prized library
of classical English books, including the first words printed in English. . . ." The story by David Maraniss in the January 22 *Washington Post* added, "Derchard Turner, curator of the Ravsom
Humanities Research Center. . .called the purchase 'the major bib-
liographic acquisition of our time.'"

Maraniss also provides this personal glimpse of the relationship of donor
and scholar:

When he was first approached about purchasing the collection last
year, Perot said, he almost dismissed the idea, but decided to call
Turner.

I said, "How much are they worth?" and he said, "Twenty million
dollars," Perot recalled. I gulped and said, "What do they mean?"
and he said, "Ross, I would literally crawl to New York just to see
them." That's when I realized how important they were. . . .

Before this morning's news conference, Turner took Perot on a
quick tour of the display cases. They moved from the one showing
the copy of the first book printed in the English language, Raoul Le
Fevre's 1475 *Recuyell of the Historyes of Troye*, over to the case

with Shakespeare's folios and then to the one with *Comedies and Tragedies* by Francis Beaumont and John Fletcher.

"Look there!" an excited Perot said to Turner. "On the title page there it says, 'Never Printed Before.' There you are! Never printed before!" Perot and Turner, benefactor and curator, looked at each other and smiled.

One of the basic ways that philanthropy has attempted to seed and sustain scholarship has been to establish centers, departments, schools, or even whole institutions devoted to a particular subject of interest. The history of philanthropy has thousands of successful examples. For instance, Joseph Sheffield felt that in his time, the late 1800s, the sciences deserved greater attention, so he established the Scientific Department at Yale which for 100 years has provided enormous leadership in engineering and the other "hard" sciences.

On an even grander scale, the Sloan Foundation has concentrated on basic research in the physical sciences. Lee A. DuBridge in *U.S. Philanthropic Foundations*, edited by Warren Weaver, gives us these examples:

> The Sloan Foundation has provided major gifts for basic research in the physical sciences, mathematics, and engineering. These included: over $1 million to the California Institute of Technology to build a new laboratory for mathematics and physics; over $3 million to New York University to provide funds toward the construction of a building to house the Courant Institute of Mathematical Sciences and to support its continuing program; a $15 million grant to the Massachusetts Institute of Technology, and a similar $5 million grant to the California Institute of Technology, for the general support of basic research in the physical sciences, mathematics, and engineering; and $1 million to Stanford University toward the creation of a new mathematics center.

Very recently, Arnold O. Beckman gave $40 million to the University of Illinois "to establish an interdisciplinary institute to study human and artificial intelligence." Beckman, who made his fortune as head of National Technical Laboratories and Beckman Instruments, recognized that scientific exploration is becoming so complicated that it depends increasingly on new kinds of research and interdisciplinary cooperation. His Illinois grant will serve both purposes. The October 1985 issue of *The Chronicle of Higher Education* describes the Beckman Institute:

> The institute will house two centers—the Center for Biology, Behavior and Cognition and the Center for Materials Science, Computers and Computation.

The aim of the institute is to cut across the academic disciplines and bring together engineers, life scientists and physical scientists to study how humans think and learn and to use that research to make computers more powerful. Nearly 400 faculty members, graduate students and administrators will work at the two centers, a university spokesman said.

Research at the biology center will cover molecular biology, cell biology, neuroscience and cognitive science, while studies at the computer center will concern solid-state materials, large-scale integration and systems, computer science and information science.

"While we anticipate that some scholars may have exclusive affiliation with the Beckman Institute, most institute faculty members will also likely maintain active ties to their academic departments," said Stanley O. Ikenberry, the university's president. "In this way, we hope to achieve better communication and interaction among disciplines and between teaching and research."

Though Beckman dispenses his grants through the Arnold and Mabel Beckman Foundation, his is largely a personal philanthropy. A glimpse of his philanthropy is provided by Jule Flynn in a March 24, 1986 article in *Business Week:*

For scientists seeking research funds, mecca these days is neither the National Science Foundation nor the National Institutes of Health. It is a medical-instruments plant in Irvine, California. There, in a corner office overlooking a Japanese garden, tall, white-haired Arnold O. Beckman is doling out his half-billion-dollar fortune. The 85-year-old entrepreneur, who built Beckman Instruments, Inc. into a $618 million company before he sold out in 1982, is giving his money away with determination that recalls Andrew Carnegie's vow to run out of money and breath at the same time. . . .

Last year alone, Beckman gave away $75 million, an amount that probably ranked him second only to the Ford Foundation as the nation's most generous philanthropist. . . .

Giving away money has become a rewarding second career for this energetic octogenarian. He spends eight hours a day at his Irvine office, sifting through research proposals from a foot-high stack in his desk; during the past year he has received more than 1,300 of them. . . .

Beckman's largesse is distributed through an entity called the Arnold and Mabel Beckman Foundation, named for Beckman and his wife of 60 years. While other technological entrepreneurs, including David Packard and William R. Hewlett of Hewlett-Packard Co. and Polaroid Corporation's Edwin H. Land, rely on professional staffs and trustees to make philanthropic decisions, Beckman's foundation is largely a one-man show. It has three trustees in addition to Beckman and his wife, but they make few decisions. Beckman and his personal secretary, Jane Guilarte, are his operation's only full-time staffers.

Unlike big foundations, which he believes "just sit there and become sterile," Beckman uses his independence to target funds at the areas he knows best, such as the medical technology on which his company was built. He funds only institutions—primarily universities—that he feels can better identify researchers who deserve support. The son of an Illinois blacksmith, plainspoken and politically conservative, Beckman resents slick funding pitches. "If they knew me," he says, "they'd know to leave off the fancy covers. What I want is substance."

Beckman approaches each funding request with the care of a businessman. Before deciding to give U. C. Irvine $3.5 million to build Beckman Laser Institute, he toured the labs and quizzed researchers and outside professionals about the university's ability to handle new funds. It took Beckman several months to reach a positive decision. "I don't know of any contributor who is more sophisticated," says Simon Ramo, a co-founder of TRW, Inc. who, with Beckman, is a Caltech trustee.

Beckman's ability to pick winners is already showing results. One of his first projects was a seed-money grant for a supercomputing center at the University of Illinois. Now that school is widely regarded as a leader in supercomputing. Beckman has a "nose for technology," says the center's director, Larry Sharr. And he also clearly has a flair for philanthropy. "I'm conceited enough," admits Beckman, "to think I can do a better job allocating my funds than a faceless bureaucrat can." Andrew Carnegie couldn't have put it better.

The Howard Hughes Medical Institute—fast becoming America's largest private grantmaker—will focus its attention on basic medical research, including genetics, immunology, metabolic control, and neuroscience. The foundation will have an endowment of $5 billion and has already begun to make massive grants that will significantly increase exploratory work in the health sciences. For example, it has given $45 million to establish the Howard Hughes Institute in molecular neurobiology and behavior at Columbia University. The institute will focus on the study of the physical and chemical bases of development and behavior in animals and humans.

Earhart Foundation in Ann Arbor, Michigan, has had a long-standing interest in basic research. In Weaver's *U.S. Philanthropic Foundations,* George W. Beadle's chapter, "The Role of Foundations in the Development of Modern Biology," gives this example of Earhart's support:

> Until recently, most large-scale experiments with higher plants—for example, plant breeding, nutrition, physiology, ecology, etc.—were carried out under conditions in which the environment was inadequately controlled or not controlled at all. This is true of all outdoor experiments and most of those made in conventional greenhouses. Considering that every farmer, gardener, and plant lover knows that higher plants are extremely sensitive to environmental factors such as temperature, light, day length, humidity, water supply, plus physical and chemical properties of the soil, it is remarkable that not until 1937 was a greenhouse constructed within which temperatures were fully controlled. This was an important, but only partial, step. With funds granted by the Earhart Foundation, the Earhart Plant Research Laboratory, called unofficially the "phytotron," was constructed in 1949 at the California Institute of Technology. For the first time, temperature of air and soil, humidity, light, air movement, light-dark periods, mineral nutrition, and soil physical properties could be accurately controlled on a large scale. Many important discoveries have been made in this laboratory, thermoperiodicity, to name a single one. According to this, some plants will not develop normally if grown continuously at a constant temperature.
>
> Many phytotrons and "biotrons" are now in use or are being built. The first one would not have been built without foundation support.

The Wenner-Gren Foundation for Anthropological Research of New York is dedicated to "international support of research in anthropology and in closely related disciplines, so far as they pertain to the problems of the science of man." In one grant, the foundation joined with the University of Connecticut and the National Science Foundation to support a giant United States–Soviet Union project. As described in *The New York Times* (August 25, 1974), "a joint United States–Soviet discovery of 9,000-year-old Aleutian artifacts has led scientists to believe that the items are the first direct evidence that North America's original inhabitants came from Siberia."

Other grants made by Wenner-Grinn include "reconstruction and interpretation of Winnebago Indian songs, discovery of clay sources, research on factors influencing dental variations in man from Upper Pleistocene to recent periods, and study of political hierarchy and succession in Trobriand Islands."

Procter and Gamble has established a University Exploratory Research Program "to provide funds for exploratory research . . . in new areas of emerging science. The focus of this program is on the support of exploratory research which might not otherwise be funded because it is too speculative, even though it has intriguing potential."

The tale of James Smithson and the Smithsonian Institution is so well known that it doesn't need re-telling, but a few facts are perhaps not as well known and may add to the lessons of philanthropy. For most of this information I am indebted to *James Smithson and the Smithsonian Story* by Leonard Carmichael and J. C. Long, *Dollars for Research* by Howard Smith Miller, and *American Philanthropy* by Robert H. Bremner.

- Smithson left $500,000 "to found in Washington . . . an Establishment for the increase and diffusion of knowledge among men."
- The money arrived as 105 bags of gold sovereigns in eleven iron-bound boxes. (More impressive even than a check for a half million!)
- Smithson himself had never visited America.
- He had planned to give the money to the Royal Society in London but had a falling out with them when they refused to publish one of his papers.
- The income from the half million went to his nephew, Henry James Hungerford, during his lifetime and "the whole of the fortune to the children of his nephew, if he did marry." It was only in case that Hungerford should not marry that the secondary legatee was to be the United States.
- Congress almost rejected the bequest. In the *Money Givers,* Joseph Goulden reports, "Congress was suspicious of taking the mysterious Englishman's money, John C. Calhoun declaring it, 'beneath the dignity of the country to accept such gifts from foreigners.'"
- It took eight years to decide whether to accept the money and what to do with it. During this period there were four Congresses and three Presidents.
- During the delay, according to Bremner and Miller, the Treasury Department invested the money in speculative Western State Bonds for which the states repudiated their indebtedness in the early 1840s. When it came time to undertake Smithson's project, John Quincy Adams took the lead in convincing Congress that it had to make good on the half million dollars through a general appropriation.

• The Smithsonian Institution, though best known as a popular museum, has made its largest contribution to society through its support of research; the initial grant to Robert Goddard is one such example.

Inventors and Inventions

There is a category of philanthropists rarely recognized whose contributions are even more rarely acknowledged. These are the inventors and discoverers who donate their results for public purposes. One of the best of these philanthropists not only set an example through his own gifts, but established an organization to make it easier for others to follow suit.

Frederick Gartner Cottrell invented the electrostatic precipitator for controlling industrial air pollution and donated for the public good the proceeds of this enormously successful invention. He did so "in the belief that the laws of nature belong to all and should be discovered and applied to the common welfare." Cottrell first tried to give his invention to specific institutions, but interestingly none of them knew what to do with such an unconventional donation and all of them turned him down. Determined to dedicate the revenues from his research to fund other research efforts, he formed the Research Corporation in 1912 to provide "means for the extension of scientific investigation, research and experimentation. . . ." The current history of that foundation describes it this way:

> As a professor of chemistry at the University of California, Cottrell had first sought to donate his patents to existing institutions so that they could use the proceeds to support future research. After futile attempts to persuade any of them to undertake such a program of commercial development, he resolved with the help of the Secretary of the Smithsonian, Charles D. Walcott, to form his own institution to put his concepts of scientific philanthropy into practice.

Research Corporation describes itself as "one of the first U.S. foundations and the only one devoted exclusively to the advancement of science and technology." Cottrell established it in 1912 and today, long after the patent rights on the Cottrell electrostatic precipitator expired, the foundation is still one of the largest in the country with annual grants and program expenditures close to $10 million. During the early years, the Corporation backed Ernest O. Lawrence and the project that led to his cyclotron, as well as R. J. Van de Graaff and the Van de Graaff high voltage generator.

From the beginning, Cottrell and his associates encouraged inventors to contribute at least part of their patents. In "Science, Invention and Society," which tells the background of the Corporation, there are many examples of such generosity, for example:

> Aid from other inventors was indeed forthcoming. Outstanding were Robert R. Williams, Robert E. Waterman and their colleagues who, in 1935, assigned their patents on the synthesis of vitamin B_1, or thiamine, to Research Corporation. Beginning in 1942, Edward C. Kendall of the Mayo Clinic donated patents from his pioneering work on the steroid hormones, which ultimately resulted in cortisone. Yet another valuable addition was nystatin, the first successful anti-fungal antibiotic. This patent was donated in 1957 by Rachel Brown and Elizabeth Hazen of the Division of Laboratories and Research, New York State Department of Health.

Of the Brown-Hazen gift, the same publication adds:

> Fungal infections afflict a large part of the world's population, yet few clinicians are able to diagnose the disorders and there is little effective therapy. Appropriately, proceeds from the first effective antifungal antibiotic, nystatin, now support mycological research and training of research personnel, with emphasis on basic and adaptive research in medical mycology.
>
> The work is made possible by the Brown-Hazen Program, founded with patent rights donated by inventors Elizabeth Hazen and Rachel Brown. Until its concentration on mycology in 1973, the program had long aided a broad spectrum of research in microbiology, biochemistry and immunology.
>
> A 1958 grant to the California Institute of Technology aided an investigation of mutant genes in phage virus by Max Delbruck, a Nobel Prize winner 11 years later. A 1967 grant to Instituto Politecnico Nacional, Mexico, had the sought-for multiplier effect, launching independent research on enzymes in fungi by Carlos Casas-Campillo, a new faculty member. Within three years, the project had sparked a research group of 12 working in a well-equipped laboratory, and had attracted independent financial support.
>
> Other grants have strengthened whole departments in the life sciences at colleges and small universities, supported summer research programs, and stimulated much basic work in biochemistry, immunology and microbiology throughout the U.S., Canada and Mexico.
>
> Advanced training in medical mycology and a better understanding of fungal diseases were the targets of the largest

Brown-Hazen grants made in the early 1970s to Temple and Columbia Universities. By 1973, the patent on nystatin, in the 16th year of its 17-year life, had contributed over $8 million to such research and to the other grants programs of the foundation.

In more recent years, Research Corporation has added a College Science Program to identify and support promising teacher-investigators, both to aid in their own research and to generate the scientific curiosity and inventiveness of their students. Cottrell put it: "Bet on the youngsters. They are long shots, but many will pay off."

Several foundations and corporations participate in this effort, including the Olin Corporation Charitable Trust, the Bristol-Myers Company; the Atlantic Richfield Foundation; the Schering-Plough Foundation, Inc.; The Apple Education Foundation; The Greenwall Foundation; the M. J. Murdock Charitable Trust; the Northwest Area Foundation; The William and Flora Hewlett Foundation; and the Penta Corporation.

The Burroughs Wellcome Fund is a different example of an inventor/entrepreneur wanting a part of the financial benefits to be earmarked for philanthropy. The Fund is entirely separate from the pharmaceutical firm, Burrough Wellcome Company–USA, but receives a significant share of the profits of the company for health research, including basic medical sciences.

As one looks to new horizons, even beyond Goddard's moon, it is interesting that there already exists a Parapsychology Foundation "to advance understanding of psychic manifestations in man through research in psychology, chemistry, biology, physics, mathematics, philosophy, anthropology and related disciplines. Research areas include extrasensory perception, psychokinesis and related phenomena." There may be hope for all of us in one of the projects funded by the foundation "to study man's survival after death, principally through work on out-of-the-body experiences. . . ."

Perhaps we have a new "moon man" to smile at—*and* to keep an eye on.

2

To Support and Encourage Excellence

Supporting Leadership Institutions

When word reached the East Coast in 1885 that Leland Stanford was considering founding a college in the West to rank with Harvard and Columbia, a New York newspaper responded: "California needs a great university about like Switzerland needs a navy." Another New York paper predicted that: "For years to come Stanford professors would lecture in marble halls, to empty benches." Fortunately, the Governor was not dissuaded.

The Stanford tale could well be told under the heading "In Memoriam." Leland and Jane Stanford had only one child, Leland Stanford, Jr. He was born late in their lives, but soon became the center of their activity. He traveled with them on almost all their extensive trips. On a trip to Italy he contracted typhoid fever and died shortly before his sixteenth birthday. According to the history of Stanford:

> Governor Stanford who had remained at Leland's bedside
> continuously, fell into a troubled sleep the morning the boy died.
> When he awakened he turned to his wife and said, "The children
> of California shall be our children." These words were the real
> beginnings of Stanford University.

The original grant was worded, ". . . To promote the public welfare by founding . . . a university of high degree . . . to qualify its students for personal success and direct usefullness in life, . . . exercise and influence in behalf of humanity and civilization, teaching the blessings of liberty regulated by law, and including love and reverence for the great principles of government." Stanford wrote the following in a letter to one of the original trustees:

> To make our institution all that I want it to be, it must turn out students who shall be able to influence and direct thought in the way of elevating the masses. It seems to me that the great question for statesmen and for humanity is how shall the great body of the people be lifted up, made intelligent, able to avail itself of the advantages of its labor.

It is interesting to note that as they considered whether and how to establish such a great university, the Stanfords interviewed President Charles Eliot of Harvard who encouraged them to establish such an institution but warned that in addition to the land and buildings they would need to give an endowment of at least $5 million. Stanford responded: "Well, Jane, we could manage that, couldn't we?" The rest of the story is well known, except perhaps one often overlooked point that, from the start, Stanford University was to admit women, which brought one more response from the East: "Can you imagine such audacity as that?"

Vanderbilt University was also founded to bring the benefits of excellence in education to another part of the country that lacked a major educational institution, but Cornelius Vanderbilt's motives were somewhat different. Vanderbilt was concerned about what the Civil War had done to the country and was searching for some way to help revitalize the South and rebuild the nation's unity. Sarah Knowles Bolton tells the story in *Famous Givers and Their Gifts*:

> In February, 1873, Bishop McTyeire of Nashville, Tenn., was visiting with the family of Mr. Vanderbilt in New York City. . . . Both men had married cousins in the city of Mobile, who were very intimate in their girlhood, and this brought the Bishop and Mr. Vanderbilt into friendly relations. One evening when they were conversing about the effects of the Civil War upon the Southern states, Commodore Vanderbilt, as he was usually called, expressed the desire to do something for the South, and asked the Bishop what he would suggest. The Bishop had immediate concern for a struggling college in Nashville but also a larger design to use higher education as a means of building the leadership necessary to both reconstruction and the country.

According to Bolton, the idea struck Vanderbilt as exactly what he had been looking for, and he immediately pledged a half million dollars. In making the initial gift, Vanderbilt said: "If the school, through its influence contributes even in the smallest degree to the strengthening of ties which should exist between all geographical sections of our common country, I shall feel that it has accomplished one of the objects that has led me to take an interest in it."

Vanderbilt continued to take an interest in the college, urging the Bishop to become its president and donating an additional half million dollars so that it could afford to meet the standards of excellence he wished for it. In this way, Central University of Nashville became Vanderbilt University and from the start was destined for excellence.

There are similar, fascinating tales relating to the establishment and development of hundreds of American colleges and other institutions. The gifts of John D. Rockefeller, Jr., which totaled $35 million, to build the University of Chicago constitute one of the most prominent examples. That sum would be worth more than $500 million today which makes it the largest gift ever provided to education. In constant dollars, Robert Woodruff's gift of $100 million to Emory University probably stands as the largest, though other pledges to other institutions are coming close.

A related aside—shortly after the Woodruff gift was announced, I said to Boisfeuillet Jones, who oversees the Woodruff related trusts and funds, that I thought it was wonderful that Robert Woodruff had given this money and could enjoy seeing the results during his lifetime. With his courtly southern charm Boisfeuillet corrected softly: "Brian, that wasn't Mr. Woodruff's money, it was his daddy's." Just a few years later, Woodruff died at the age of 95, with no heirs, and left his vast Coca-Cola related fortune to transform The Trebor (Robert spelled backwards) Foundation into the new and very large Robert W. Woodruff Foundation. The Woodruff family has had a major role in establishing other institutions of excellence in Atlanta and throughout the South.

Grants may fund institutions or they may serve to transform them. An example drawn from the earliest years of the Republic is a little known gift of $10,000 by George Washington to save Washington and Lee University from closing. Examples of other direct gifts are common among many foundations and corporations today; they range from the "bricks and mortar" emphasis of the Kresge Foundation to the "humanizing education" efforts of the Hazen Foundation. Increasingly, too, the larger corporate giving programs are focusing on development of excellent institutions in areas of mutual interest, whether education, arts, conservation, or other fields.

The history of American philanthropy is rich with examples of gifts that have built institutions that have enormous influence on the educational, cultural, and scientific life of the nation. My files are stocked with wonderful tales about the generosity and vision of the Vassars, Dukes, Colgates, Dartmouths, Tufts, Hopkins, Cornells, Browns, Bards, Mudds, Mills, Smiths, and Wilsons—and the list goes on and on.

Most of these institutions and hundreds of others have been assisted in their building efforts through the unusual "bricks and mortar" support program of the Kresge Foundation. In 1983 alone, this foundation provided $35 million in challenge grants to institutions for construction and renovation of facilities.

Most of these gifts are given more directly than that of Eleanor Ritchey to Auburn University. A U.P.I story on January 6, 1984 put the tale this way:

> The death of Musketeer, the last of 150 stray dogs that lived off the $12 million estate of an eccentric oil company heiress, has cleared the way for Auburn University to inherit the fortune.
>
> The late Eleanor Ritchey, an unmarried granddaughter of Philip John Bayer, who founded the Quaker State Refining Company, adopted the pack of dogs, most of them stray or unwanted, before she died in 1968 in Fort Lauderdale, Fla.
>
> Miss Ritchey's will stipulated that the money would go to Auburn when her last dog died or 20 years passed, whichever came first.
>
> Auburn officials learned Monday of the death of Musketeer, a 17-year-old stray.

A lesser gift to an important college, but one given even more from the heart and with great sacrifice, involved Mary Johnston who "lived on an annual retirement pension of $4,500 while contributing $1,000 a year to Oberlin . . . and left her entire estate, earned from a lifetime of hard work that included teaching and domestic service, to the College for scholarships on her death at 91 . . . ." Johnston had enrolled at Oberlin, but had to drop out because of financial difficulties. Through perseverance she pursued her degree on a part-time basis, completing it 25 years later. She was always grateful to Oberlin for bearing with her.

College officials felt that Mary Johnston represented such an important model that they commissioned a brochure to be written by Ellen Lawson of the Women's History Project about Johnston's life and generosity. It begins with words from a sermon that had become the guiding credo of Mary Johnston's life: "We are the inheritors of the past, the possessor's of the present, and the makers of the future." The pamphlet observes that Johnston, "true to these words, accepted the conditions of her birth, used them to possess the possibilities of the time in which she lived, and continually worked to make a better future for those who would follow."

There is a wonderful quote from a note Johnston wrote: "I was born like everybody else—maybe. I was born a woman—can't help that, I was born poor—can't help that, and I was born black—can't help that." She added that she "wanted to prove that regardless of color, sex or material conditions, you can achieve." Lawson writes that: "Johnston inherited family values enabling her to possess the best her era had to offer a poor black girl and to make a better future for generations born in similar circumstances."

Encouraging Organizations and Professions to Excellence

There are many other grantmaking programs that devote their attention to helping organizations, professions, and programs move toward excellence. The Blandin Foundation established a "Principals Fellowship Program . . . to conceptualize the school as an influential part of a community and as a component of a larger social system. To provide positive leadership and interact positively with individuals and groups in school and community. To lead personnel and use technology efficiently and effectively." Christopher Wagner, principal of the Albrook High School in Saginaw, Minnesota, participated with 23 other principals in the nine month, part-time experience. When necessary the program even paid for substitutes during his absences. Wagner credits the program with bringing him to "the cutting edge of developing and implementing change."

A number of innovative grantmaking programs have been established to encourage excellence in the teaching profession.

- The First Interstate Bank of Arizona Charitable Foundation awarded the Arizona Educational Foundation a $40,000 grant to create a teacher of the year "Ambassadors for Excellence" program.
- The General Electric Company and the Bridgeport Area Foundation have established a "Teacher Award Program" to stimulate and reward teachers for "innovative math teaching ideas."
- Eastman Kodak has a "Teacher Incentive Program" to attract and retain talented young teachers.
- The Burlington Northern Foundation developed a Faculty Achievement Award Program ". . . to honor outstanding college and university teaching." According to Donald North, president of the foundation, "Our purpose is to reward teacher and faculty–scholar excellence to become better teachers, to help address the problem of low faculty compensation . . . ."
- Amoco is one of the leaders among companies providing fellowships to encourage development in neglected sciences. For example,

Amoco contributed more than a million and a half dollars for a three-year Ph.D. Fellowship in Engineering Program. Exxon has followed Amoco's lead on a far larger scale by supporting 60 to 70 doctoral candidates each year. One farsighted aspect of such programs is that they promote faculty development and retention even though in the short term they encourage colleges and universities to compete with sponsoring companies for the best students.

- Amoco has also committed $12 million to a University of Chicago program to improve the teaching of math.

- With seed money from the Hearst Foundations, Phillips Academy at Andover established the "MS2 program which offered especially skilled minority students the opportunity to study science and math at the Academy campus to help prepare them for these fields in college. Working with educators and guidance counselors, students are selected to participate in three consecutive tuition-free summers and a four-, six-, or ten-week spring term of study at Phillips Academy. Thirty new ninth-grade students enroll each year. The MS2 program is designed to complement and fortify the students' public school education and is highly successful in correcting the underrepresentation of minorities in competitive colleges and universities throughout the country."

The Exxon Education Foundation began a program "that helps good teachers help each other." In the November/December 1984 issue of *Foundation News*, Richard R. Johnson of the foundation wrote:

The report of the National Commission on Excellence in Education calls for sweeping changes to improve education in the United States. Many of the recommended changes, however, seem to require expenditures with a price tag beyond what this society is currently willing to underwrite. The question is, where should we start?

Anthony Alvarado, chancellor of the New York City Schools, asserts that "Our most valuable assets are not measurable in dollars and cents, but rather in terms of human ability. The creative strength of our teachers, their remarkable resilience in the face of massive cutbacks and their need to foster excellence despite funding limitations is the real capital in the educational bank."

Rather than starting from scratch to rebuild this extensive base of human capital, we can improve the system more efficiently by locating and building upon existing strengths.

Starting with this premise, in 1979 the Exxon Education Foundation worked with the New York City public schools to

design a program to improve teaching. The IMPACT II program
has cost approximately 27 cents per student while affecting teaching
in scores of schools in—and now beyond—the New York City
system.

An outside evaluation of the program concluded that "The
success of IMPACT II comes from trusting teachers, supporting
their judgement, honoring their commitment, and then carefully
crafting and nurturing a network to facilitate the changes they
undertake."

The objective of IMPACT II has been to pass along information
about examples of effective teaching so that other teachers could
incorporate these ideas into their own classrooms.

The Sloan Foundation has also exercised leadership in helping institutions develop their education and training programs. Warren Weaver
notes:

> In engineering education, a $5 million grant from the Sloan
> Foundation has made possible the creation of a Center for
> Continuing Education in Engineering at M.I.T., providing for a new
> building and for operating expenses. The Sloan program of
> fellowships in engineering has provided critical assistance.

On the general subject of philanthropy's support for the physical
sciences, Weaver says:

> The private foundations have assisted excellent universities to
> become better and good universities to become excellent. It is this
> policy, combined with the policy of understanding support of
> individual scientists, which has enabled the private foundations to
> be key factors in the extraordinary uplift in the status of the United
> States as a leader in scientific and engineering progress during the
> past forty years.

Many donors attempt to encourage institutions and professions to
excellence through helping to strengthen the basic operations. The
Esmark Company, now part of Beatrice, established an "Excellence
Award" which goes to nonprofits for excellence in management. Esmark's
program to encourage and honor individual agencies builds upon an effort
by the Chicago Community Trust to honor and assist individuals who are
singled out for their leadership performance. The organizations of each of
the Esmark winners receive $10,000 for special activities.

A different but important example of encouraging institutions, professions, and society as a whole to move toward excellence is the support of
John D. Rockefeller, 3rd and Elizabeth Dollard to help launch the Hast-

ings Center which has done the pioneering work on medical ethics. It's officially called the Institute of Society, Ethics and the Life Sciences.

The Commonwealth Fund is among the leaders in a wide variety of programs designed to achieve excellence in medical education and health care. In her 1985 President's Report, Margaret Mahoney, the Fund's president, spoke of the merit of fellowships and other awards:

HOW CAN PHILANTHROPY HELP?

Major improvements in fellowship support could slow this drain and increase the numbers of young gifted people in scientific and medical research. The National Institutes of Health Career Development Awards are a model to attract the best minds. Such support should aim at neglected areas of research—both basic and applied—where younger people can make their mark, given the significance of the problems to be solved and the numbers of people who could benefit from the solutions.

As an example, Alzheimer's Disease research some five years ago had relatively few research dollars or fellowships to battle a disease potentially affecting millions—with the numbers expected to soar as the population ages. The same shortage of support existed for two other important problems affecting sizable groups of people— alcoholism and incontinence. In these three areas, The Commonwealth Fund, over recent years, has given support in the belief that the dimensions of the problems and the need for research called for a new cadre of scholarship. The Fund's support for research relating to senile dementia is basic scientific inquiry; research on incontinence seeks a suitable clinical intervention; research in alcoholism tries to determine the effectiveness of various ways to help. In each, spirited, daring and persistent young researchers have taken leading roles, with distinguished mentors in the background.

The success of recruiting some of the best younger minds to work in these areas indicates that financial support does make a difference. It can be crucial in determining careers and producing the future scientists-clinicians-inventors who will carry on the search for answers to some of the most complex medical problems. These individuals will have the possibility of a hero's recognition.

Support for younger people through grants or fellowships is something philanthropy can do well. Both are visible signs of recognized worth. So are prizes and awards. These bring pleasure to the recipient, but their real value lies in bringing professional and public recognition of such heroes and confirming the importance of their striving.

The Albert Lasker Medical Research Awards have frequently come even before recognition within a discipline—Oswald Avery was so honored. Sometimes, the Lasker Awards have honored discoverers who would otherwise have been all but unrecognized. One recent Lasker Award winner said simply, "It brought dignity to the work."

For more than 80 years, American philanthropy has encouraged new and flexible educational pathways to attract and support talent. For example, some years ago, The Commonwealth Fund joined with the Carnegie Corporation in developing a new concept, the clinical scholar in medicine. The intent was to provide highly intelligent young physicians—potential risk-taking researchers in medicine—the opportunity to change the architecture of clinical research in order to improve the availability and quality of medical care. The program, now funded by The Robert Wood Johnson Foundation, has attracted some of the most gifted young physicians. They may develop new insights into such diverse and sophisticated issues as the nature of illness, the process of disease, the variations in medical practice, and the effect of medical decision making on the cost and organization of care.

They feel the call—and challenge—to open up new approaches in medical research. They put self second to the pursuit of new knowledge and, with careful concern for providing proof of their findings, dedicate themselves to a difficult unexplored path that can lead to improving patient care.

Some of these clinical scholars in medicine may one day receive a hero's recognition for their contributions to improving human health or perhaps for their findings on the organization of health care. And they will deserve this recognition for having broken with tradition to do something important for the benefit of others.

Betting on People and Leadership Development

One of the routine ways that funders attempt to support and encourage excellence is to identify and back talented people. This involves spotting the achievers and those who might become so.

For more than 100 years, the Rotch Traveling Scholarship has been awarded to architectural students, providing the winner with funds for a year's travel to study different branches of architecture. The program was endowed by the family of Benjamin S. Rotch of Boston who had been inspired by his son's architectural interests and accomplishments. A glance down the list of winners reveals such major figures as Louis Skidmore and Edward Durrell Stone. As early as 1920, *American Architect* published this observation: "The scholarship can fairly be called one of the most important educational factors in the professional life of this country." In 1938, the distinguished architect Charles D. Maginnis, then the president of the AIA and a former winner, said:

> The ambitions that in the years have been excited by the glamour of the "Rotch" are beyond count . . . but the actual vision of mellowing cathedrals, the touch of fingers on the marbles of the Parthenon, the release from the provincialism which dimly perceived Europe in the books—these were the full gift of it.

Reports from recent winners reveal that the award is still enormously important to the intended broadening of a young architect's perspective. For example this letter was written from Russia by the 1971 scholar John Sheehy:

> . . . The architecture that is most Russian is that of the beautiful onion-dome churches throughout the country, many of which are now museums, few of which are used for services, but for the storage of farm machinery, but the structures with their forms and colors, really come across as magnificent pieces of architecture seen against the sky.

In the 1980 program report, "The Rotch" was described this way: "A first-hand experience of a people, its past, its present, its problems, hopes and architecture; and opening up of the mind and the spirit . . . this is what the Rotch does for its scholars and through them for the profession." The program continues, administered by the Boston Society of Architects.

At a recent gathering of college presidents, I was fortunate to sit next to Dick Wood, the new president of Earlham College. In the course of conversation, he mentioned that he had been a Danforth Fellow, and when I asked about the experience he responded emphatically that the fellowship had been the most profound influence on his professional development and one of the most important on his personal life. He said he was not alone in feeling this way: he and a very large number of Danforth and Kent Fellows had long ago created the Society for Values and Higher Education so that they could maintain their contacts and thus sustain their mutual growth.

Personal and professional growth have been hallmarks of the Danforth Foundation since its establishment by William H. Danforth, the founder of the Ralston-Purina Company. One of the first programs of the foundation was the American Youth Foundation, a summer program for leadership training. In Keele and Kiger's *Foundations*, there is a description of many of the programs initiated by the foundation including:

- the Danforth Associates Program "to encourage the growth and development of college teachers"
- the Danforth Graduate Fellowships Program "to encourage the leadership and character development of women college graduates"
- the Danforth Teacher Grants "to provide graduate fellowships for competent young teachers who had not yet completed a doctoral degree"
- a fellowship program "to provide graduate study for those pursuing a career in college teaching"
- the Danforth College Project Fund "for working with administrators, students and other faculty members for the improvement of learning and teaching"
- the Dorothy Danforth Compton Fellowships "for minority college seniors and graduate students to study for doctoral programs, in preparation for college teaching"
- Danforth Seminars for Federal Judges and Educators
- Danforth School Administrators Fellowship Program "for senior high school principals" and
- Danforth Community Seminars "on issues for educators and leaders in metropolitan St. Louis."

Other excellent programs serve the dual purpose of betting on people and encouraging professions to excellence. The Markle Scholars Program of the Markle Foundation focused on "assistance for physicians in academic medicine" during the years 1947 to 1969 "to enable physicians to work in academic medicine and research rather than in private practice." During its 22 years, the program awarded 506 fellowships in 90 medical schools.

The Robert Wood Johnson Foundation currently operates several professional and institutional development programs also related to health, including

- the Clinical Scholars Program "to help young physicians-clinicians acquire special skills in certain non-biological disciplines such as epidemiology, demography, economics, management techniques and other related fields that can better prepare them for leadership in new and more complicated systems of health and medical care," and
- the Fellowships in Public Policy "developed under the auspices of the National Academy of Sciences' Institute of Medicine and the American Political Science Association for mid-career health educators to spend a year of intensive work on health policy issues."

The Mellon Fellowship in the Humanities, administered by The Woodrow Wilson National Fellowship Foundation, provides encouragement and assistance each year for more than a hundred outstanding students for "graduate work in preparation for a career of teaching and scholarship in a humanistic field. . . ."

As with the establishment of educational institutions, the story of philanthropy past and present is studded with examples of special efforts to identify and encourage talented people from almost every field of endeavor.

- Westinghouse has a Science Talent Search "to discover at the high school senior level and support with scholarships those who have the potential to become the research scientists and engineers of the future."

- Eastman Kodak has a Kodak Scholars Program ". . . to inspire the pursuit of educational excellence" and a Kodak Fellows Program ". . . for doctoral level students."

- The Winston-Salem Foundation, continuing a tradition begun in 1889 by the H. Montague Medal Fund, presents an award "to the student who attains the highest scholastic average in his or her senior year at each area high school."

- The Century III Leaders Program of Shell Companies has been in existence since 1976. Each year, approximately 350,000 high school seniors compete nationally, beginning at the school level, for the Century III Leaders award. Two seniors from each state and the District of Columbia are selected as finalists to meet in Colonial Williamsburg each spring for a leadership meeting. Each of the 102 national winners is given a $1,500 scholarship. Century III Leaders combine leadership training scholarships and an opportunity to meet and talk with others of equal talent from across the nation.

- Another field of activity covered by an honors program involves the Hearst Journalism Awards program for journalism students and their schools of journalism.

- The National Merit Scholarship Program established by the Ford Foundation, remains one of the very best examples of spotting and assisting young people whatever their later career choices.

According to Keele and Kiger's *Foundations*, in 1957, the Edward John Noble Foundation:

. . . initiated a large new program to finance the graduate training of students who had demonstrated outstanding leadership potential by the time they had reached their senior year in college. Convinced that such potential could not necessarily be determined by any conventional academic measurement, Mr. Noble instead selected a group of colleges and universities across the country and asked the president of each to nominate one candidate a year for a National Leadership Fellowship, with personal leadership qualities rather than academic distinction as the principal criterion for selection. The number of institutions involved in this successful experiment eventually reached nearly fifty. In all, more than five hundred young students participated in the program, which was later merged with a new International Fellows Program initiated by the foundation in 1960 at Columbia University.

One of the largest current efforts for the development of leadership is conducted by the Bush Foundation through the Bush Leadership Program, which since 1965 has provided traineeships and internships to more than 300 individuals in these categories:

- *Bush Leadership Program* (Bush Leadership Fellows, Bush Summer Fellows): "To enrich, through academic and/or internship periods, the experience of emerging leaders and prepare them for high-level responsibility. Emphasis on administrative training in midcareer."

- *Bush Public Schools Executive Fellows Program:* "To improve management skills of highly motivated public school administrators in midcareer."

- *The Bush Foundation Fellowships for Artists:* "To assist selected artists to work full-time in their chosen art forms. Not for academic training. Students not eligible."

- *Bush Clinical Fellows Program:* "To encourage personal and professional development which will contribute to advancement of health care in the community through self-directed study or project."

- *Bush Principals Leadership Program:* "To assist principals in the development of leadership skills, and to help participants to design and implement a plan for school improvement."

One of the longest running leadership development efforts is run by the Kellogg Foundation, which conducts and supports both national and international fellowships covering health, education, agriculture, government, and nonprofit management. The national fellowships program is designed to "equip them to deal in those complex decision-making areas where expertise in the single discipline is insufficient." The foundation's long-standing and growing interest in community education is also related to its investment in people. Very recently, the foundation awarded a major grant to Virginia State University to establish a Virginia Rural Leadership Development Program.

For many years, the John Hay Whitney Foundation supported "Opportunity Fellows" for "men and women who, because of racial and/or economic barriers, encountered unusual difficulties in carrying on graduate or professional study or study for the arts."

It should be acknowledged that not all efforts to encourage and reward excellence pan out. F. Emerson Andrews points out that in 1930 the Samuel G. Davis Fund was established in the Mashpee Massachusetts schools to reward young men "for good, kind manners," but in 1983 town officials petitioned the court to let them use the money for school construction "because they couldn't find enough mannerly boys to reward."

Recognizing Excellence

Backing winners and honoring them has always been one of the investments of philanthropy. John W. Gardner has said that "The best philanthropy is money wedded to talent and imagination."

The MacArthur Fellows Program is now the giant of these efforts to recognize talented people. It provides recipients with five years of support amounting to hundreds of thousands of dollars. Initially there was criticism of the program because so many of those chosen were already well established. Though the age and name-recognition levels of Fellows have dropped, the foundation still concentrates on recognizing people who already have achieved substantial results and who they believe might well, with further encouragement, broaden their reach. The foundation honors and supports these extraordinary individuals.

If the Rotch architectural award recognizes unusual potential in architecture, the Pritzker prize goes "to an architect for his or her contribution to our society through a substantial body of built work. It is given for architecture as an art." The annual prize of $100,000 and a sculpture by Henry Moore are awarded by the Hyatt Foundation. Winners since the award was established in 1979 have been Philip Johnson, Luis Barragan, James Sterling, Kevin Roche, I. M. Pei, Richard Meier, Gottfried Boehm, and Hans Hollein.

For many years, the Rockefeller Public Service Awards, funded by John D. Rockefeller, 3rd, provided recognition and encouragement, first to civil servants and then to a broader array of leaders including community activists. The award was established to raise the stock of government civil servants. For years, it was the most prestigious of honors recognizing the public efforts of individuals.

The awards of the Lasker Foundation have repeatedly zeroed in on people who have already made important contributions in the health fields and who are destined for even greater accomplishment. I've heard people tease Mary Lasker that she has a way of knowing who's going to get the Nobel prizes even before the King of Sweden does, either that or she has influence with the Selection Committee, because so many of the Lasker winners have gone on to become Nobel Laureates.

General Motors provides three major prizes in the area of cancer research and control: the Kettering, Sloan, and Mott awards which provide each winner $100,000, a gold medal, and an optional $30,000 to sponsor a conference or workshop.

One of the most unusual awards is "given annually to one scholarly book and one book of imaginative literature that promote interracial understanding and the abolition of racism." These awards were established in 1935 by Edith Anisfield Wolfe. The Council on Foundations' *Newsletter* reported that in 1985 the awards went to:

> . . . exiled South African writer, Breyten Breytenbach and David S. Wyman, an American expert on 20th Century Jewish history. . . . Breytenbach's winning book, *Mouroir: Mirrornotes of a Novel* is a collection of essays written during Breytenbach's seven years imprisonment in South Africa on charges of anti-apartheid terrorism. Wyman's *The Abandonment of the Jews: America and the Holocaust, 1941–45* is a scholarly expose of the failure of Western democracies to aid the Jewish victims of Nazi persecution. . . . The award is administered by the Cleveland Foundation and carries a $3,000 cash stipend.

The San Francisco Foundation also "encourages excellence through recognition." It runs three public service award programs "to recognize the important work of individuals and community organizations."

In almost every field there is likely to be some award for deserving individuals and institutions. Many grantmakers include at least one such award. There's even a book, *Winners: The Blue Ribbon Encyclopedia of Awards*, which is four times the format and size of standard books, extending 915 pages and describing more than 600 awards and their recipients. It includes architecture and design, aviation and aeronautics, public service, heroism, visual arts, and twenty-one other categories.

In his 1951 Founders' Day address, "The Power of Freedom" at John Hopkins University, Henry Allen Moe spoke of the support of excellence:

> My theme . . . is that man's temple of achievement has been built by individual men—men of eager questing minds and devoted spirits—thinking and visualizing and feeling through all the ages. Most of them were journeymen—good craftsmen entitled to our honor—but here and there stands out one who exemplifies, in

Bertrand Russell's words, "all the noon-day brightness of human genius."

. . . Doubtless all developments of the human mind and spirit, had they enjoyed in the past the precise reportage of modern science, similarly could be tagged with the names of individual persons. Including developments in the arts, it ought to be affirmed; for there is no distinction of kind or quality between so-called scholarship and so-called creative work in their highest exercise; and the reason is, of course, and very simply, that both in their highest exercise are creative performances. John Livingston Lowes has explained it in *The Road to Xanadu:* ". . . the imagination voyaging through chaos and reducing it to clarity and order is the symbol of all the quests which lend glory to our dust."

All the quests, be it noted; and be it noted also that the imagination voyaging through chaos and reducing it to clarity and order is what makes all scholarship and all art worthy of their proper pride.

To develop and bring to their highest possible exercise the capacities of individual persons to make that voyage is, quite obviously, the world's most needed result. Only thus shall we add that knowledge and understanding which is our best hope for survival and progress. All universities and all foundations should know that they miss all their best opportunities if they fail to recognize that this should be their one goal, and that it is the *only goal* within their reach.

3

To Enable People to Exercise Their Potential

I. LITERACY
II. LIFETIME OPPORTUNITIES FOR LEARNING
III. EQUAL OPPORTUNITY AND EMPOWERMENT
IV. MAXIMUM FUNCTIONING FOR THE
DISABLED AND ELDERLY
V. EXPANDING HUMAN POTENTIAL

Literacy

In a 1935 history of the Anna T. Jeanes Fund, written by its President Arthur D. Wright, there is this account of a 1907 meeting of Miss Jeanes, Hollis B. Frisell, President of Hampton Institute, Booker T. Washington, head of Tuskegee Institute, and George Peabody, an officer of the General Education Board:

> "Dost thee remember that thee didst call upon me and that I gave thee a check?"
> "Yes, well do I remember, Miss Jeanes, your fine generosity," said Mr. Frisell.
> "And dost thee remember that I gave thee a like sum, Dr. Washington?" Booker T. Washington assented in like manner.
> "And dost thee remember that thee didst write me about making a gift to the General Education Board?"
> "Yes, indeed, I do," said Mr. Peabody, "and I am grateful for the privilege of sharing in this rich opportunity for service."
> "Thee dost not need to thank me. It is I who needs to thank thee,"—and with a flash of spirit she added—"and I didn't do it to save my soul from Hell either!"

With that introduction to their discussion, Anna T. Jeanes, an elderly, plain living, plain talking, Philadelphia Quaker turned over a million dollars in securities establishing The Negro Rural School Fund to help the poorest and most isolated black children in the South to read and write. Just as Cornelius Vanderbilt felt that education was the solution to reconstructing the South and healing the nation, Jeanes believed that education would eventually truly free a people just released from slavery.

Anna T. Jeanes was, in her own words "guided by a God of love and peace." She had written a book, *The Sacrificer and the Non-Sacrificer*, tracing the teachings of religions throughout the world, and when she responded to George Peabody, "it is I who needs to thank thee," she really meant it. She believed that what the best of religion teaches is that giving is not a sacrifice but the happy extension of a generous diety. Thus she also meant "and I didn't do it to save my soul from Hell, either!"

Peabody himself was a giant in philanthropy, a champion of the freed slave, and a believer in education as the second step of the ladder to freedom. He was central in the establishment of the General Education Board. As early as 1867, Peabody, a Northerner, had formed the Peabody Education Fund "for the purpose of stimulating educational development for the people of the Southern and Southwestern states according to their existent needs and opportunities."

In *Philanthropy in Negro Education*, written in 1930, Ullin Whitney Leavell credits, in order, the Quakers, the Peabody Education Fund (1867), the John F. Slater Fund (1882), the General Education Board (1902), the Anna T. Jeanes Fund (1907), and the Julius Rosenwald Fund (1912) as the principal early contributors to Negro rights and education. Of their philanthropy Leavell says,

> The appearance of the large educational foundation at the close of the Civil War with special emphasis upon the educational development of the south, constitutes an innovation in the history of philanthropy. The broader motive of the newer philanthropy, that of stimulation to self-help, sets it apart from prior philanthropic organizations which established educational institutions and maintained them.

Today, education is still one of the most basic ways to provide people with the tools they need to exercise their potential. For example, the Babcock Foundation recently gave a large grant to the University of North Carolina to study adolescent illiteracy in the South, while the Gannett Foundation and the B. Dalton subsidiary of Dayton Hudson are devoting a large part of their philanthropy to projects aimed at increasing literacy.

Literacy, as a first step toward self-sufficiency, is at the heart of the rapidly growing program and organization, "Reading Is Fundamental" (RIF), which had its first major funding from the Ford Foundation and later sizable help from the Edna McConnell Clark Foundation. After RIF's book

Why Johnny Can't Read was published, the federal government began to fund the program and now RIF has 3,300 project sites.

In the January/February issue of *Foundation News,* Barbara Bush explained why she chose literacy as her special project during her husband's tenure as Vice President. She reviewed the work of such groups as RIF, Lawbach Literacy International, the National School Volunteer Program, and the March of Dimes Reading Olympics. She also reported on important collaborations between funders and projects including Atlantic Richfield and the Joint Educational Project of Los Angeles; United Technologies/Aetna and Literacy Volunteers; and World Book–Childcraft and Parents and Teachers Helping (PATH). Many other corporations are involved with literacy programs, including Grumman whose employees work extensively with Literacy Volunteers; Time Inc. which operates "Time To Read" using Time employees as tutors; and Hallmark which funded "Play and Learn," a project involving Kansas City's School Board and Art Institute.

For 35 years, the Rosenberg Foundation has given high priority to its Early Childhood Development Project, which emphasizes populations whose children "are at risk," including migrant farm laborers.

Literacy is one of the first steps to opportunity. Access is another. One of the fifty or so people who responded to my request for examples of gifts that have made a difference was George Penick, then of the Babcock Foundation and now head of the Jessie Ball duPont Religious, Charitable and Education Fund. Penick said:

> Some rather daring ideas seem to have made a difference in the long run. . . . Back in the 1960s John Ehle (a man well known in his own right as a writer, a dreamer, and a doer) received a small grant from Anne Cannon Forsyth through her personal foundation to search out and find the gifted but hidden talent that was buried in the minority children of the South and to give those children an opportunity to attend private secondary schools that otherwise would maintain a lily-white complexion. Through his own personal efforts and with an intuition of an individual's potential that many say is transcendental, John found children that would never have been recognized as exceptionally talented, and even if they were so recognized in their own, local, segregated communities, would never have had the opportunity to pursue the education that was made available to them through this program. This was more than just a "merit scholarship" program, because most programs of that ilk reward those who already have shown themselves to be of exceptional potential and who probably will be able to unlock the doors of success whether or not they receive the assistance. This program found children in an underdeveloped part of the country

and in a race that, at the time, was widely perceived as being "inferior" by the Southern society that failed to provide the educational opportunities that were needed to enter a first-rate prep school. Today these students are in numerous positions of leadership in our country, and in addition, the schools in which they were placed acknowledge that this was one of the most beneficial grants that was ever made because it provided them valuable students and proved to the skeptics that minority children could indeed achieve success in a highly competitive academic setting.

Lifetime Opportunities for Learning

> The great object that I desire to accomplish by the erection of this institution is . . . to unfold the volume of nature, that the young may see the beauties of creation, enjoy its blessings and learn to love God from whom cometh every good and perfect gift.

With that dedication, Peter Cooper established Cooper Union "to serve the intellectual wants and improvement of the working classes." Later, at the opening of the School of Science and Art, Cooper said, "It is now my privilege enjoyed to welcome the youth of the city and country to the benefits and privileges of this Institution."

The "stewardship of wealth" obviously stems from Andrew Carnegie's "Gospel of Wealth," and nothing did more than Carnegie's libraries to provide most Americans with early and lifetime exposure to knowledge and learning. Carnegie's library crusade is probably the best known illustration of the impact of philanthropy. If it were not already so well recognized, it should probably have been the banner story of this book. Indeed, it is already the subject of many good books, one appropriately entitled *The Best Gift* by Beckman, Langmead, and Black. *Carnegie Libraries: Their History and Impact on American Public Library Development* by George S. Bobinski is another excellent account. That book provides the following details:

> Andrew Carnegie, often referred to as the "patron saint of libraries," in his lifetime made new library buildings available to hundreds of communities all over the world. Very few towns which requested such gifts and agreed to his terms were ever refused. He donated $56,162,622 for the construction of 2,509 library buildings throughout the English speaking parts of the world. More than $40 million of this amount was given for the erection of 1,679 public library buildings in 1,412 communities in the United States.

Carnegie decided to focus his domestic philanthropic efforts on the creation of libraries for the public because he felt that the people in libraries in Scotland and Pittsburgh had an enormous influence on his life and success by allowing him to read books, and he wanted to provide similar resources for others.

These gifts had an enormous impact on millions of people. Yet many are no longer aware of how Carnegie influenced life in their communities. Bobinski notes the disappearance of the Carnegie libraries:

> Carnegie public library philanthropy in the United States began more than 80 years ago in 1886. Many of these library buildings are now being replaced, and the originals either torn down or used for non-library purposes. At times, perhaps, a plaque marks a wall of the new library with a brief statement that this building superceded an earlier one built by Andrew Carnegie, but just as often there is no reminder.

It is a reminder that knowledge lasts longer than buildings and that philanthropists should accept and take encouragement that the impact of their gifts will be felt long after they and their buildings are forgotten.

Carnegie was not alone in his commitment to libraries and learning. In *Famous Givers and Their Gifts*, Sarah Knowles Bolton devotes a chapter to "Philanthropists and Their Libraries." She starts with Enoch Pratt who gave more than a million dollars in 1882 to establish what is still the main library in Baltimore, and she goes on to tell of the gifts of James Lennox to New York, Walter L. Newberry and John Crerar to Chicago, and Mortimer Fabricius Reynolds to Rochester, New York. She also mentions gifts by John Jacob Astor and others to the New York Public Library.

One aspect of these library gifts was not very popular; a usual condition was that the community had to agree to maintain the library. As explained by Arnaud Marts in *Philanthropy's Role in Civilization:*

> We protested long and vigorously against voting support to libraries, but because philanthropy patiently led the way we have today something like 11,000 free public libraries, with 162,000,000 volumes on their shelves, which circulate 340,000,000 books a year to 20,000,000 borrowers. The major part of the cost of operating these libraries now comes from tax funds.
>
> Benjamin Franklin and his associates created the first library, in 1731, in Philadelphia; other philanthropists gave voluntary funds to establish libraries in Charleston, Providence, New York City, Baltimore, and elsewhere. It was not until 117 years later that the state—Massachusetts—passed an act permitting a municipality to tax itself for the support of a library. Even with this permissive act, the citizens of our most enlightened communities were slow to vote funds, and the free library long continued to be regarded as a luxury. The son of a president of Harvard, for example, published a

book in 1875 in which he endeavored to dissuade his fellow
citizens against a certain appropriation for a library. He asks: "Upon
what principle can a citizen who has the power to cast his ballot
justify himself in voting increased taxation upon his neighbor for
the purpose of establishing a library?"

Philanthropy gave 150 years to the patient demonstration of the
social value of public libraries before the general citizenry was
ready to vote any considerable tax appropriations toward their
support. And it might still be providing the major support had it
not been for the canny generosity of Andrew Carnegie, who began
to offer handsome library buildings to thousands of cities on
condition that they would thereafter support the institution.

It was this offer of something for nothing which suddenly turned
the scale of public opinion in many a city. In Edinburgh, Scotland,
for instance, the voters were induced to reject a proposal to
establish a public library there by the display of sandwich signs with
the following inscription:

> Ratepayers!
> Resist this Free Library Dodge
> and Save Yourselves from the Burden of 6,000
> of Additional Taxation!

A more recent vehicle for extending knowledge and learning to a large
number of people is the community college. The Kellogg Foundation has
been the largest national backer, literally and figuratively, of the effort to
create and expand community colleges across the nation. Kellogg's dollars, leadership, and inspiration have put higher education within reach of
the majority of Americans. James Richmond, formerly with the foundation
and who got his start in community colleges in Missouri, Kansas, and Ohio,
tells this fascinating tale: "In 1958, shortly after Edward Gleazer was
appointed executive director of the American Association of Junior Colleges (AAJC), Gleazer attended the organization's annual meeting in
Grand Rapids and found the experience terribly disheartening." As Richmond tells it:

Thirty years ago AAJC was a very limited organization. Its main
purpose was to conduct the annual convention. I was told its
patriarchs were 34 eastern, private junior colleges whose nominal
dues barely covered postage on the *Trade Journal* . . . which was
printed by Dr. James Reynolds in the basement of his home in
Austin, Texas—when he could spare time from teaching at the
University of Texas. So with these financial problems on his mind,
Ed Gleazer decided not to come directly home from the convention.
Instead he transferred from the train in Port Huron, Michigan and

stopped in Battle Creek hoping to just talk with the Kellogg Foundation people. When the train pulled into Battle Creek, he telephoned the Foundation and received an appointment within the hour.

People tell me that the meeting began alone with the Foundation's president, Dr. Emory Morris. Ed Gleazer told his story so well and so convincingly, however, that he was stopped—again and again—as Dr. Morris asked other Foundation officials to join them. By noon, six Kellogg Foundation officers were in the room. They accompanied Gleazer to lunch and by the end of the day had become interested in both the problems and potential of the junior college movement.

Richmond indicates that Dr. Morris and other leaders in Battle Creek had already been "struggling to identify and chart the future of the local junior college which had been opened on a one-year, trial basis only." Since the time of that visit, Kellogg has helped build the capacity of what is now known as the American Association of Community and Junior Colleges so that it could be a major force in stimulating creation and expansion of community colleges throughout the country. By 1975, Kellogg had provided support for the development of 66 community colleges and added to earlier grants to many colleges to expand facilities, curricula, and faculty. By 1985, Kellogg had provided 175 grants totaling $34,471,929 to more than 100 community colleges. These efforts in turn attracted support of a far greater level from other funders, particularly those in the areas where the institutions were being developed. Obviously too, they have had enormous influence on government's commitment to this aspect of education.

Kellogg's favorable experience with this program has led it to expand its contributions to other aspects of continuing education—now one of its largest endeavors.

Libraries, community colleges and other aspects of continuing education have helped millions of people to exercise their fuller potential. So too the Carnegie Corporation's interest in Sesame Street and public television opened new learning possibilities for youngsters in particular and for the public in general. The Ford Foundation's massive investment in public broadcasting took us a giant step further.

Equal Opportunity and Empowerment

In the past, present, and most likely in the future, a large part of organized philanthropy has and will be aimed at building the capacity of people to help themselves. As far back as the Twelfth Century, Maimonides described the highest order and benefit of charity in the Mishna Torah:

The highest degree; than which there is nothing higher, is to take hold of a Jew who has been crushed and to give him a gift or a loan or to enter into partnership with him or to find work for him, and then to put him on his feet so he will not be dependent on his fellow man.

One of the largest players in the effort to provide public education for minorities and the poor was the General Education Board. During its lifetime, from 1902 to 1964, GEB concentrated on the particular educational needs of black children in the South. The positive example it set and the criticism it received for failing to deal with such underlying problems as segregation and racism per se, both set the stage for the efforts of those who followed.

In 1942, a group of black leaders joined together in what is now known as the Durham Conference which declared that "compulsory segregation is unjust." Together they set forth the specifics of reform they considered the most important: "political and civil rights, jobs, education, agriculture, military service, social welfare and health." A year later, the Conference of White Southerners on Race Relations met in Atlanta, agreed with the Durham Statement, and pronounced its objectives just. Three months later, a joint committee from both groups met in Richmond, Virginia, to organize the Southern Regional Council:

. . . for the improvement of economic, civic and race conditions in the South in all efforts toward regional and racial development; to attain through research and action programs the ideals and practices of equal opportunity for all people in the region; to reduce race tension, the basis of racial tension, racial misunderstanding and racial distrust; to develop and integrate leadership in the South on new levels of regional development and fellowship; and to cooperate with local, state and regional agencies on all levels in the attainment of the desired objectives.

(These quotes and the full statements from the Durham, Atlanta, and Richmond Conferences appear in *New South: The Southern Regional Council 1944-1964.*)

The Southern Regional Council had had its origins in The Commission on Interracial Cooperation, established in 1919. Principal funding originally came from the Rosenwald Fund and a diverse group of church bodies, labor unions, individuals, and smaller grants from foundations. In a summary of the Council's first 30 years, the *Atlanta Constitution* reported:

They wanted a regional organization, not from a provincial desire to separate the South's problems from the nation's, but from the conviction that such an organization has unique advantages. It can express the best and often neglected elements of Southern thought and conscience; it can serve as a convincing demonstration of Southerners working together as fellow citizens, without regard to race and can tap local resources and initiative often inaccessible to agencies outside the region.

These efforts were, of course, just a prelude to the advocacy and activism that were soon to follow. In a piece published a dozen years ago, I traced the evolution of the impact of voluntary organizations under the title "From Service to Advocacy to Empowerment." While earlier groups, like the General Education Board, felt they "must operate within the restraints of segregation," later activists and their funders insisted that empowerment was the liberating stage necessary to enable people to exercise their potential.

The Carnegie Corporation took the lead in support of the Law Students' Civil Rights Research Council and of the NAACP Legal Defense and Education Fund/Earl Warren Legal Training Program which were trying to increase the number of black lawyers in the South. Eli Evans, then a program officer for Carnegie and now president of the Revson Foundation, reports that: "Ultimately, 38 foundations and 30 corporations invested $7 million in the same project which increased the number of [black] students in Southern universities from 22 students in 1969 to 427 seven years later. This became the talent pool for elected officials, university trustees, school board members, etc." A special report, "A Step Toward Equal Justice," contained an evaluation of the program and included a case study that began:

> On opposite corners of the intersection of Second Avenue and Ninth Street in Columbus, Georgia stand two structures, each intentionally functional and unintentionally symbolic. Outwardly, the more impressive of the two is the 11-story Government Center, which houses the only consolidated city–county administration in Georgia. It is so new that the concrete still smells damp. The other, far less prepossessing, is a modest, rambling frame building that once was a notorious local "sporting house." The gold-lettered sign suspended over the door announces "Bishop and Hudlin, Attorneys at Law."
>
> To the 170,000 residents of Muscogee County, the Government Center is a glass-and-concrete embodiment of change. Rising out of a fountain-studded plaza on the site of the late, unlamented old courthouse, the Center soars gracefully above a montage of sagging Victorian homes, colorless commercial buildings, and mighty churches.
>
> To Sanford Bishop, 26, and his partner Richard Hudlin, 27, the white frame house opposite is the embodiment of an opportunity.

> For Bishop and Hudlin are both young, talented and Black, and they
> have accepted the challenge of proving that Columbus can move
> into a new era as easily as it moved into a new courthouse.

That was written in 1972. Today, 15 years later, Sanford Bishop and Richard Hudlin still practice in Columbus.

Similar efforts on behalf of other minority groups have also been initiated through private funders. The Ford Foundation has taken the lead in establishing many legal defense and education funds; for example, it awarded a $2.2 million grant to help found the Mexican-American Legal Defense and Education Fund (MALDEF) which provides legal services to Mexican-Americans and helps in the education of Mexican-American lawyers.

The Ford Foundation also provided funding for a pilot project that developed into the Native American Rights Fund (NARF). NARF was started "to provide to poor and disadvantaged people access to lawyers and the legal process." Unlike other legal and education defense funds, NARF devotes primary attention to the rights of Indian tribes. In a report, funded and issued by the Lilly Endowment, John Folk Williams writes of "The American Indian: An Overview of the Issues":

> Fundamental to the unique aims of the Indians is the fact that theirs
> is not a movement of individuals but of peoples. Indian legal rights
> depend on the historical existence of the Indian nations long before
> the formation of the United States. The legal implications of that
> origin give Indians tribes the status that no other group in the
> country possesses, and the enforcement of those group rights is an
> essential Indian objective.

Speaking of the Ford Foundation's support, NARF's Executive Director John Echohawk says:

> . . . it cannot be stated strongly enough what a difference that
> backing meant to the Indian rights movement. For the first time
> Native Americans were guaranteed quality advocacy for a sustained
> period to successfully advance their rights. What a difference that
> knowledge makes in the legal arena—both to our opponents—as
> well as to Native Americans . . . . For the first time, America's
> Indians are being assured that the white man's system can work for,
> and not just against them.

The Syntex Corporation has also taken a keen interest in educating lawyers because, according to Frank Koch of Syntex: "We felt it would provide solid long-range benefits for the Mexican-American community . . . [and because] our company was more sensitive to this situation than other firms, since Syntex began as a small research organization in Mexico City."

On another front, in 1984, CBS Inc. pledged $1.25 million to the Hispanic Policy Development Project:

> . . . to support studies on the urgent needs and problems confronting Hispanic communities in the United States; to identify and evaluate policy options for dealing with such specific needs and problems; to communicate the results of these studies to policy and decisionmakers, the media and the general public; to include broadly representative non-Hispanic and Hispanic leaders in the activities of the organization, in order to increase their involvement and strengthen the impact of the organization's efforts; and to work closely with Hispanic institutions and scholars to build bridges between them, to increase the visibility of Hispanic policy leadership, and to develop opportunities for young Hispanic policy and analysts.

Another dimension of empowerment is voter registration. The Stern family, picking up where Mrs. Edgar Stern's father Julius Rosenwald left off, has been in the forefront of voter education efforts, beginning in Mrs. Stern's home state of Louisiana. The Stern Family Fund was a rarity with its early and steadfast support of the unpopular effort to register blacks in the South and minorities throughout the country. The Field Foundation has a similar record. When Lester Dunbar, former President of the Field Foundation, was executive director of the Southern Regional Council, SRC conducted a large Voter Education Project (VEP) which later spun off and was headed by Vernon Jordan before he went on to the United Negro College Fund and the National Urban League. Charles Rooks, now head of the Meyer Charitable Trust, worked with VEP and said:

> While the "revolution" in Southern politics caused by the emergence of Black political power is due to many factors, the role of the Voter Education Project (earlier a project of the Southern Regional Council) is an important part of this story. Ford, Rockefeller Brothers, Carnegie, and some other large foundations made important contributions, but the real "heroes" in the foundation world were a group of small foundations (Taconic, Norman, etc.) that supported VEP at the outset, when it was a much riskier undertaking.

Other illustrations of support of voters' rights include:

• The Northwest Area Foundation supported research by the Native American Rights Fund to analyze violations of the voting rights of Indians in Montana and North and South Dakota.

- The George Gund Foundation provided funding to the Midwest Voter Registration Project "to increase Hispanic participation in the American electoral process."
- Cummins Engine was one of the first companies to fund voter registration efforts.

The women's movement is an even earlier story of disenfranchisement, the struggle for suffrage, and of the few courageous souls who provided financial support. The principal benefactor was Mrs. Oliver H. P. Belmont of New York who, at enormous personal sacrifice and risk, even from rival factions in the movement, was the steadfast supporter of a number of women's groups credited with passage of the Suffrage Amendment. She provided the New York headquarters and made regular lifesaving grants to the National American Women Suffrage Association, was for years the anonymous supporter of the Southern States Woman Conference, supported the Jail Bond Fund of the Women's Trade Union League, and was the main financial backer of Congressional Union.

Another surprising stalwart was Mrs. Frank Leslie, the publisher of *Leslie's Weekly.* She had been a modest, regular supporter of the National American Woman Suffrage Association, but stunned and delighted the organization when she left $2 million in her will for "furtherance of the cause of Woman Suffrage." An earlier bequest also fanned life into the movement. In the 1880s, Elizabeth Eddy left $50,000 to Lucy Stone and Susan B. Anthony which was used in part to publish the initial volumes of *The History of Woman's Suffrage.*

One of the most poignant fundraising efforts is told by Eleanor Flexner in *Century of Struggle.* She writes of Susan B. Anthony's declining health and the need to keep the President of the Association, Dr. Anna Howard Shaw, on the lecture circuit to keep generating interest and support:

> She (Anthony) was in harness until her last illness during the Annual Suffrage Convention in 1906, held in Baltimore; even then, ill as she was, she held out long enough to win a promise from M. Carey Thomas and her close friend Miss Mary Garrett that they would raise a fund of $60,000 which would support Dr. Shaw for a five-year period, so that suffrage work would not suffer from her lecturing for a livelihood. One month after this last service to the cause which had been her life, Miss Anthony was dead. Her passing marked the end of an era. She was the last of the giants who had launched the struggle to improve the condition of women to leave the scene. She had lived and worked, without respite and without discouragement, through the years of ridicule, vilification, and apparent hopelessness, which today are all but forgotten. When she

died, few thinking people denied either the logic or the
inevitability of woman suffrage. The only question that remained
was, "When?"

Thanks to Anthony, Paul, Shaw, Stanton, and so many other courageous
activists and the support of Belmont, Eddy, Leslie, and others, the end of
that stage of the battle was only a few years away.

A few years earlier, on another battleground, the same Mary Garrett
who helped raise money to fund Shaw's lectures took up the cause of
establishing a medical school at Johns Hopkins that would admit women.
A large part of the effort to establish that now famous medical institution
stemmed from the determination of women in the region to have a prestigious school that would train women physicians. According to Sarah
Knowles Bolton in *Famous Givers and Their Gifts:*

> The Trustees accepted the gifts from the Committee of Ladies, a
> sum which with its accrued interest, amounted to $119,000, toward
> the endowment of a medical school to which "women should be
> admitted upon the same terms which may be prescribed for men."
>
> This gift was made in October, 1891; but as it was inadequate for
> the purposes proposed, Ms. Mary E. Garrett, in addition to her
> previous subscriptions, offered to the Trustees a sum of $306,977,
> which, with other available resources, made up the amount of
> $500,000, which had been agreed upon as the minimum
> endowment of the Johns Hopkins Medical School.

Foundations and corporations have been generally slow in funding the
vast roster of urgent issues relating to gender equality. Recently however,
a growing number of organizations are taking more appropriate interest.
The Geraldine Dodge Foundation has begun to fund research including a
four-year longitudinal study at Emma Willard, the oldest girls' school in
America, "to examine moral and cognitive development in young
women." Scott McVay, director of the foundation, says: "I expect that it
will alter the education of women and our perception of their indispensable role on matters not only of local but regional, national and international import." The William H. Donner Foundation began a "women in
management" program in 1974 which, according to Keele and Kiger's
Foundations, provides "support for programs designed to prepare women
for successful managerial careers in corporations and academia."

A major new push has been added with the expansion of the Rockefeller
Foundation's interest. In his 1984 "President Review," Richard W.
Lyman outlined these plans by quoting from the report of a Task Force he
had established on the subject:

> In general terms, a rationale for broadened and intensified RF work
> in this area can be derived from egalitarian ideals and from

economic justification for fuller investment in women. The basic lines of argument can be roughly summarized as follows:

- increased attention to women's roles and opportunities is warranted in that the Foundation is dedicated to promoting the well-being of *all* mankind, and there is growing evidence that women and men worldwide are not sharing equally in gains in welfare;
- the achievement of equity-oriented economic development depends not only upon balanced allocation of goods and services between social classes and ethnic groups, but between men and women within such divisions;
- existing program efforts to promote self-sustaining social and economic improvements can be made more effective by enabling women to increase their productivity and, thus, to contribute more broadly to the achievement of societal goals; and
- whereas women's issues are gaining widespread salience and credibility and many governments are discovering their female constituents, the Foundation has a legitimate role to play in responding to the needs of women outside the U.S.

Lyman added:

Three principal objectives were noted in the memorandum: Increasing the number of grants directly concerned with women's activities; ensuring that women are involved as participants in activities aimed at accomplishing broader objectives; and examining grant impacts on women, especially to ensure that they will not be affected adversely.

The need for greater attention to women's issues was highlighted by a 1985 survey on the worldwide state of women funded by the Rockefeller Foundation, Carnegie Corporation, and Ford Foundation to coincide with the United Nation's International Decade for Women. According to the Council on Foundations' May, 1985 *Newsletter,* the survey concludes:

Whether in the economy, education, health, or government, there is no major field of activity in any country in which women have attained equality with men . . . the influx of women into the paid labor force has not significantly narrowed the gap between men's and women's pay; nor has it stemmed the rising tide of poverty among women. Despite the key role that women have in third world economies, they have been largely bypassed in development strategies.

One of the increasing numbers of funders that devotes all of their attention to women's issues is the Women's Foundation, which states its mission as: "For the fulfillment of the many dreams and aspirations of young girls and for the continued strengthening and empowerment of all women." To achieve this mission, the Women's Foundation has funded such diverse programs as the Alliance Against Women's Oppression, Big Sisters, California Coordinating Council for Domestic Violence, Children's Council of San Francisco, Comparable Worth Project, Displaced Homemakers Center, San Mateo Advisory Council on Women, Shasta County Women's Refuge, Stepping Stone Growth Center, Women Against Violence-Emergency Services (WAVES)/Advocates for Women, Womenspace Unlimited, and Women's Voices.

Other examples of funders with a primary focus on women's issues include: the Business and Professional Women's Foundation, which has provided "Career Advancement Scholarships, Loans for Women in Graduate Business Studies, Loans for Women in Engineering Studies, and Fellowships and Research Grants for Women's Issues"; the Ms. Foundation for Women, whose grants have addressed such issues as nonsexist textbooks, women's shelters, domestic violence, low income child care services, and sexual harrassment; and the Bette Clair McMurry Foundation, whose funding program has included a Women in Film series, media grants such as a video documentary on "The Managerial Woman" and a directory and workshop for women in films, theatre grants such as women playright residencies, and general grants such as the Texas Women's History project and policewomen management training.

Beyond empowerment of minorities and women, many grants focus on the unemployed and underemployed; for example:

- "Putting It All Together" in St. Paul, Minnesota, supported by Dayton Hudson and others, links volunteers with welfare women who are trying to find work.
- The Bilingual Clerical Skills Training Program of the National Puerto Rican Forum was launched with funds from Aetna.
- The National Hispanic Business Agenda was begun by Coca-Cola which set aside a portion of its marketing business for placement with Hispanic banks, ad agencies, and other businesses.
- "70001 Ltd," a pilot job program for high school drop outs was begun by Thom McCann and is now launched as a national organization with 46 corporate sponsors.
- "Training Inc." was established by the Indianapolis Foundation and the YMCA to train and place long-term unemployed.

Other grants relate to workers rights; for example:

- Support from National Community Funds/The Funding Exchange for pesticide hazards, migrant workers' rights, asbestos hazards, mining hazards, and research on labor negotiations; and
- Support from the Haymarket Peoples' Fund for hiring of minorities and women in the construction industry, job safety, worker counseling, secondary labor force organizing, and organization of low-income and unemployed workers.

George Penick offered a second nomination of grants that have made a larger difference. This one relates to economic opportunity:

> Several million dollars granted by the Mary Reynolds Babcock Foundation and the Z. Smith Reynolds Foundation was combined with major grants from national foundations, such as Ford that created a five-year experiment called the North Carolina Fund. The Fund ran from 1963 through 1968. It was the prototype for OEO and was a major effort to enable poor people to take control of their lives. The unique combination of private support (led by Paul Ylvisaker at the Ford Foundation and Charles Babcock in North Carolina) combined with enlightened government leadership (led by Governor Sanford, John Ehle, Joel Fleishman, and others) made for a truly innovative and forceful pioneering effort to affect a change in poverty in this state. The North Carolina Fund was directed by George Esser and was designed to end after five years, which it did. Interestingly, both "gifts" grew from the mind of a unique individual, John Ehle, who also was the father of both the North Carolina School of the Arts and North Carolina School of Science and Mathematics.

Many of the community foundations, such as the one in St. Paul, have provided assistance to specific populations in their geographic areas and have attended to the general matter of community and neighborhood economic development. In testimony before the House Ways and Means Committee in 1983, Dang Her, Director of the Lao Family Community in St. Paul, Minnesota, said:

> At the time Hmong/Lao people began to arrive in St. Paul, the St. Paul Foundation took the financial risk to get our organization started, advocated for us with other foundations, enabled us to leverage funding from several public and private sources, and served as a community convenor of discussions on important issues for refugees.

Her went on to list several grants that permitted establishment of the community center, a driver's education program for refugees, establishment of a sewing business and the development of local and national markets, the establishment of a community garden and farm project as a training and marketing venture, and other general and special project grants as well.

The needs and aspirations of minorities, women, and others have frequently been the focus of "alternative funds," a newer phenomenon in philanthropy. These funds have been springing up in many communities and regions. The July/August 1984 issue of *Foundation News* carried a feature on "alternative funds" which it says were initially called "change-oriented" or "radical" funds. The article quotes David Hunter of the Stern Fund as follows:

> . . . the alternatives share a firm commitment to a redistribution of wealth and power. They're all concerned with furthering democracy in American society; and *economic* democracy—widespread participation in the economy—may well be the tripping point. They do not believe, as the more conservative foundations do, that the goal is simply to train underprivileged so they can get a piece of the action. The goal is to change the action itself.

The article's author, Roger M. Williams, adds, "If that is the goal, the method is grassroots 'empowerment,' a Sixties phrase that means enabling the most downtrodden of Americans to 'gain control over their own lives.' "

Williams describes the Funding Exchange which is made up of nine regional member foundations: "Haymarket Peoples Fund—New England; North Star Fund—New York City; Bread and Roses Community Fund—Greater Philadelphia area; Common Capital Support Fund—District of Columbia; Fund for Southern Communities—the Carolinas and Georgia; Crossroads Fund—Chicago and northern Illinois; McKenzie River Gathering—Oregon; Vangard Public Foundation—San Francisco Bay Area; and Liberty Hill Foundation—Los Angeles." He notes that the "Vangard [Foundation] pioneered more than the concept of the alternative fund. It also introduced a novel method of financing: amassing capital from young people with inherited wealth and what used to be called a social conscience. All but one of the Funding Exchange members operate with that base . . . ." He quotes a conversation with Obbie Benz, the founder of Vanguard: "It was obvious . . . how wealth exploits non-wealth, and the only way to resolve the contradictions of wealth was to give some of it away—not to ordinary, safe charities that perpetuate the white, wealthy world, but to organizations striving for social and economic justice."

The Hunt Alternatives Fund, which operates primarily in Dallas, Denver, and New York, was founded by heirs of the Hunt fortune. A sampling of their grants for 1984 provides an indication of interests of such change-oriented funds. Support went to the Dallas Tenants Association, Housing and Economic Development Corporation of Dallas, Women's Way Back House, Access Institute, Cornerstone Center for Justice and Peace, Center for Immigrants' Rights, Minority Rights Group, and Physicians for Social Responsibility.

The Youth Project, formed in 1970, has its own distinctive approach. They describe themselves as:

. . . working for social justice and peace by supporting grassroots groups and building citizens' movements. We seek to identify effective local, state, regional, and national organizations and to provide them with the financial and technical assistance necessary to help them succeed. We also support the development of coalitions toward the goal of building broad national constituencies for change. Consistent with our founding mission, the Youth Project is committed to developing progressive leadership, in particular, supporting opportunities for young people as social change activists.

In addition to its own granting efforts, the Project helps other grantors identify national and community groups worthy of support. It attempts to broker the needs of relatively unknown community groups with funding sources eager to locate groups that work effectively for change.

Not all of the change-oriented foundations are new or technically described as "alternative." Such groups as Ford, Gund, New World, Rosenberg, Whitney, Norman, Taconic, Joyce, Babcock, Beldon, Field, Needmor, Stern, and many more have been on the cutting edge of social change for a long time.

The Rockefeller Foundation and the Midas-International Corporation Foundation provided the start-up grants for Saul Alinsky's Training Institute for Community Organizers to:

. . . turn his extraordinary energy and experience . . . to full-time, intensive training of community organizers for American communities . . . . The explosive growth of the urban crisis in America has enormously increased the need for effectively organized urban slum communities and has correspondingly magnified what Mr. Alinsky calls the "apalling dearth of persons who know how to organize in and for a free society." He has concluded that he and his small staff in the Industrial Areas Foundation can do too little to meet this urgent need by their own direct community organizational efforts. They can accomplish far more by turning their knowledge and experience to training potential leaders to become effective community organizers.

Corporations are beginning to move in this direction, too. In addition to CBS, Midas, and Syntex, there are Amoco with its housing and minority engineers programs, American Can with its hunger projects, Exxon with its founding support of Harlem Prep and neighborhood groups, Aetna with a string of leadership efforts involving community and neighborhood economic development, Equitable with its Times Square redevelopment, and the combined efforts of Metropolitan Life, Mutual Life, New York Life, and TIAA to fund the Legal Aid for the Poor Project of the Bar Association of New York City.

Maximum Functioning for the Disabled and Elderly

In 1817, private benevolence stimulated the first organized work in this country for the education of the deaf. The Reverend T. H. Gallaudet founded the Connecticut Asylum for the Education of Deaf and Dumb Persons. Personal gifts provided most of the funds, although the state legislature was induced to appropriate $5,000. Later, Congress gave 23,000 acres of land and the name was changed to the American Asylum for the Deaf. This personal pioneering by Dr. Gallaudet led to important changes. By 1880 there were 61 such institutions serving 8,000 deaf students. More than half of these facilities were tax-supported, and a number of those which were privately financed also received some state or municipal aid.

One college for the deaf—Gallaudet College in Washington, D.C.— was founded in 1857 on the private initiative of the philanthropist Amos Kendall, although the United States Government soon joined in its support. Alexander Graham Bell used the $10,000 he received as part of the Volta prize, awarded him for the invention of the telephone, to establish the American Association to Promote the Teaching of Speech to the Deaf. One of the greatest schools for the deaf is the privately endowed Clark School at Northampton, Massachusetts. The young Grace Goodhue taught there before her marriage to Calvin Coolidge. In 1927, the friends of President and Mrs. Coolidge honored them by making voluntary contributions of $3 million to the endowment of the school as a Coolidge Memorial Fund.

For the above history, we're indebted to Arnaud C. Marts and his book *Philanthropy's Role in Civilization.* The same resource records that:

> Our first three schools for the blind were founded and maintained
> by private efforts. In 1832, Dr. S. G. Howe (husband of Julia Ward
> Howe, who among other things wrote "The Battle Hymn of the
> Republic"), valiant young crusader of Boston, established the
> Perkins Institute, the first educational institution in America for the

blind. Two similar institutions were founded shortly thereafter, one in New York and one in Philadelphia.

[Marts indicates that Dr. Howe], recognizing that some of his blind pupils were also subnormal mentally . . . opened an experimental school for the feeble-minded in Barre, Massachusetts. The results were so convincing that within a few years New York established a state institution for the feeble-minded . . . . The school established by Dr. Howe was also the forerunner of modern developments in the general fields of psychiatry and mental hygiene.

Dorothea Dix, like Howe, donated her own funds to pioneer programs serving the mentally ill. Later Clifford Beers, author of *A Mind that Found Itself*, contributed his own modest funds and went heavily into debt to form the National Committee for Mental Hygiene, now the National Mental Health Association. As told in Norman Dain's *Clifford W. Beers: Advocate for the Insane*, philanthropist Henry Phipps "came to the rescue" with a grant totaling $100,000 and later the Falk, Grant, Ittleson, and New York foundations followed suit; but the cause to which Dix and Beers gave so much has remained grossly underfunded by comparison to the personal and national consequences it represents. Newer interest by MacArthur and Hughes is beginning to change that.

Much of the story of support for handicapped and disadvantaged groups is covered under Role Four, "To Relieve Human Misery," but some stories belong here because the underlying purpose of the giving was to help people grow into their potential:

- The Carnegie Corporation gave the initial funding for "Talking Books" through the American Foundation for the Blind. Robert Bremner in *American Philanthropy* writes, "The venture offered a classic example of the way philanthropy is supposed to work, because in 1935, after the foundations had perfected the program, Congress began to appropriate money to the Library of Congress to permit nationwide extension of the service."

- The New England Life Insurance Company, in cooperation with the New York Association for the Blind, installed a large-print typewriter in its headquarters. During spare moments on the job, employees type books for the vision-impaired. Xerox has also helped improve resources for the blind by donating 200 reading machines.

- The Louise W. Keasler Fund of the California Community Foundation provided sophisticated transmitters and receivers for hard-of-hearing children in Southern California.

- The Cabot Corporation's division in Indianapolis devotes its charitable efforts to the deaf. Among the projects it has funded are "closed-captioned" facilities for theatres, volunteer services at the Indiana School for the Deaf, and fellowships in accoustical research at Indiana University.

The Rogg Memorial Foundation and the Taylor-McHenry Foundation, along with the Rotary Club and its foundation, funded a project developed by Albert Hingley, Jr., the parent of a learning disabled child. This project experimented successfully with a "learning team" to help the learning disabled acquire new skills. According to David Mitzel of Ohio University–Zanesville:

> This combination of foundation support brought together Ohio University–Zanesville, Ohio University–Athens, and a city and county school system in a cooperative venture that has resulted in two successful summer programs involving learning disabled students, their parents, their teachers, school psychologists, university faculty, consultants and prominent citizens in "the learning team."

In the 1840s, Theodore Lyman gave the large sum of $75,000 to establish the Lyman School in Massachusetts, the first state juvenile reformatory. The William Penn Foundation, founded by the Haas family of Philadelphia, has pioneered in support of programs to assist unemployed minority youth, and to provide vocational guidance and services to younger persons newly released from prison.

The Ray Foundation funds a rehabilitation project called "A New Oregon Trail" which they introduce this way:

> There is a new Oregon Trail which winds its way through a labyrinth of modern problems. This road leads through the tragedies of child abuse and neglect, of murder and assault, of alcohol and drug abuse, of robbery and rape, within young lives poised on the brink of a lifetime of disaster. A journey along this trail through the Oregon juvenile corrections system is at once both an educational experience and a challenge, some of these adolescents appear jaded and scarred to a degree that seems overwhelming, their consciences seared into insensitivity. If this were the end of the road, this would indeed be a sad and depressing story—but it is not the end, it is only the beginning, for there is hope that lives can be redeemed. There are many dedicated individuals working with these young people from a variety of perspectives and approaches—educational, physical, emotional and spiritual. This is a story not only of the kids

with whom they work, but of their commitment, of their
frustrations, of their dreams and of their needs.

The Ford Foundation made the so-called "grey areas" grants, which,
according to Mitchell Ginsburg, former Commissioner of Human Affairs
in New York City, "led almost directly to a major federal program against
juvenile delinquency and subsequently played a key role in the development of the Community Action Program." Aetna provided early support
for development of the program that has become Elderhostel, a program
that broadens educational opportunities for older citizens. According to
Robert Roggeveen, formerly of Aetna: "It was seed money in the purest
sense. Our grant put in place the first structure, the necessary structure,
that made it possible for Elderhostel to develop into the first-rate, important national program that it has become."

In a *New York Times* story of September 15, 1985, Kathleen Teltsch
wrote about another project serving the older population:

> Convinced that frail and elderly Americans are often better off
> living at home, seven charitable foundations have agreed to work
> together to develop new alternatives to institutionalized care.
> The seven philanthropies have together provided an initial $4.2
> million to develop model projects offering a combination of medical
> and social services in at least a dozen cities . . . .
> The program grows out of planning by the New York Center for
> Policy on Aging which was set up by the New York Community
> Trust and the program will be conducted by the Cornell Medical
> College.
> . . . besides the New York Community Trust [the funders] are the
> Commonwealth Fund of New York, the Pew Memorial Trust,
> the Arthur Vining Davis Foundation, the Duke Endowment, the
> John A. Hartford Foundation and the Cleveland Foundation.
> Each foundation has had some previous involvement in trying to
> assist the elderly, according to Margaret Mahoney, President of the
> Commonwealth Fund, which contributed $1.6 million to the
> program.

Teltsch reported separately that the Commonwealth Fund also gave $5
million for "a commission to develop model projects to help older people
cope with isolation and insure easier access for them to health and long-
term care services. Other projects will expand alternative living arrangements, such as sharing homes, and opportunities for earning income."

For many older people, the uncertainty of their living situations can
hamper their ability to lead full, productive lives. A number of philanthropic efforts have been undertaken to address this issue. For example:

- In 1984, Allied-Signal Inc. initiated a major Program on Aging which emphasizes support for research relating to the elderly. This program also includes an "annual achievement award presented to recognize outstanding individual accomplishments in the field of aging."
- The Greater Essex Community Foundation and the Department of Health and Human Services organized a project on home equity conversion, a form of reverse mortgage for the elderly—an important strategy in the effort to stabilize the living situations of the nation's aged.
- The J. C. Penney Foundation established Penney Farms in Florida for aged and retired ministers and their wives or widows.
- The Pittsburgh Foundation supported a project of Council Care Senior Adult Day Center to "help elderly people stay in their own homes."
- Westinghouse has been heavily involved with a Surrogate Grandparents Program to help both generations help one another.

Expanding Human Potential

From the start, philanthropy has been interested in encouragement of the gifted. The Spencer Foundation was recently honored by the Association for the Gifted as "the foundation supporting the most research on giftedness." A review of the foundation's annual reports reveals increasing attention to this neglected seed crop and points out that much of the research on gifted people provides greater understanding about how all people develop intellectually and how everyone can be assisted toward greater intellectual growth.

More recently, the Sid W. Richardson Foundation has taken a significant interest in this area of learning, including funding of the research for and publication of *Educating Able Learners: Programs and Promising Practices* by June Cox, Neil Daniel, and Bruce Boston. The Oregon Community Foundation and the Northwest Area Foundation teamed up to fund a gifted child program in the Oregon public schools.

The Hogg Foundation, with its emphasis on mental health, has been a pioneer in human development. It funds programs ranging from Project ABC (Any Baby Can), which seeks to increase the functioning of "developmentally delayed babies," to its long-term radio series on mental health, values, and personal development. The Stone Foundation publishes Clement Stone's ideas on Positive Mental Attitude (PMA) and other funders are increasingly interested in Transcendental Meditation and other schools and theories of expanded awareness.

In Boston in the late 1800s a very different approach to increasing human performance took hold. In her chapter on John Lowell, Jr., Sarah Knowles Bolton recounts this tale:

> Mr. Henry C. Hardon of Boston tells of this conversation between two teachers: "Name some one thing that would enable your boys to achieve more, and build up the school." —"A plate of good soup and a thick slice of bread after recess," was the reply. "I could get twice the work before twelve. They want new blood." Mrs. Hemenway knew that in many homes food is poorly cooked, and health is thereby impaired, so she started cooking-schools in Boston, which she called school kitchens; and when it was found to be difficult to secure suitable teachers, she established and supported a normal school of cooking. Boston, seeing the need of proper cooking teachers in its future work in the schools, has provided a department of cooking in the city Normal School.

The wealthy and influential Mrs. Hemenway did the same for school exercise classes. With cheers or jeers she must be recalled as the first to promote required physical exercise in school. About 100 years later—in 1941—the Nutrition Foundation was established. Fifty businesses provided the initial $1.5 million that resulted in the development of many of today's fortified foods.

Many of the largest obstacles to human growth relate to illness and other barriers to full health. Therefore all of the various examples of health-related projects covered elsewhere in this book should really be included here also. From the smallest effort to help an individual achieve physical and economic independence to mass efforts to help people grow as human beings, philanthropy has played a large role in enabling people to exercise their potential. To some extent, these efforts are at the core of relieving human misery, and therefore the next chapter and role are an extension of this one.

4

To Relieve
Human Misery

I. DIRECT INTERVENTION AND ASSISTANCE
II. SEEKING CAUSES AND CURES
III. SUPPORT OF BASIC INSTITUTIONS FOR ONGOING
RESEARCH, PREVENTION, AND ASSISTANCE

Direct Intervention and Assistance

The Helping Hand Mission for Homeless and Destitute Men was established in Detroit in the mid 1800s, and when the founder's son, who had been brought up in the work of the mission, became well-to-do, he remembered those people and those lessons. Tracy W. McGregor expanded the size and the scope of the effort but kept it targeted to those in greatest need, who were, as reported in Keele and Kiger's *Foundations*, "homeless men, needy children, underprivileged mothers, epileptics and feeble minded children." McGregor also used his contacts to interest other influential Detroit people to become active in service to the most downtrodden.

The Mission was renamed the McGregor Institute and the McGregor Fund was established to support it and to initiate other projects with similar objectives. By the 1930s, the examples set by McGregor's organizations began to have influence far beyond Detroit and Michigan, culminating in one of the most significant social welfare developments of this century. As told by Keele and Kiger:

> As the economic depression of the 1930s worsened, the McGregor
> Fund increased gifts to the McGregor Institute to support the
> feeding and housing of Detroit's destitute men. Welfare agencies
> across the country noted large increases in the number of transient

71

and homeless people. Guided by McGregor's interests, the McGregor Fund provided seed money for a National Committee on Care of Transient and Homeless. Representatives of fifteen national welfare agencies, along with interested individuals such as McGregor, formed the initial committee. Through local census surveys of transients, sponsored by the McGregor Fund, the Committee was successful in influencing legislation, in 1933, establishing the Federal Emergency Relief Administration (FERA). Through the efforts of FERA Administrator, Harry Hopkins, federal programs and resources were used to address the plight of the homeless.

The same city has produced a more recent example of concern for the vulnerable. The Conference Board's 1983 survey of corporate contributions reports, "A recent study commissioned by Michigan Bell Telephone to determine Detroit's most critical needs, led Michigan Bell to commit $100,000 to a food distribution program for the city's hungry."

The December, 1985 Council on Foundations *Newsletter* reports: "Hundreds of families affected by devastating disaster have received support from the Weingart Foundation during the last three years. The Foundation has awarded $795,000 in grants to or through the American Red Cross for families affected by floods, fires and earthquakes in America and Mexico." The same publication reported in March 1985:

> Victims of Ethiopia's massive famine will receive food and other assistance under an emergency relief effort initiated by the J. Howard Pew Freedom Trust. Grants totalling $935,000 have been awarded to four organizations—Africare, Catholic Relief Services, Lutheran World Relief and Oxfam America—to provide emergency relief in the drought-torn country.
>
> The immediate needs in Ethiopia extend beyond emergency food relief, explained Robert I. Smith, President of the Trust. They include transportation of food, the purchase and distribution of medical supplies, blankets, tents, fuel for cooking and heating; and the establishment of sanitation facilities in refugee camps. In addition to emergency food relief, Smith explained that rehabilitation and development efforts would be undertaken to help surviving populations attain self-sufficiency.

During the human service budget crisis of the 1980s, many corporate funders provided emergency support for food, shelter, health, and other services. Some examples are:

• The Metropolitan Atlanta Community Foundation and its corporate members created an emergency fund to provide temporary help to agencies adjusting to funding cuts.

- Beatrice Foods took the lead in supporting what is now the large Greater Chicago Food Depository jointly funded by several corporations to provide surplus food to shelters.
- Mellon Bank and the H. J. Heinz Co. provided the funding for Pittsburgh's "Great Tomato Patch," an activity of the Greater Pittsburgh Community Food Bank to involve volunteers and money to grow food for agencies that run feeding services for the poor.
- General Mills donated trainloads of food products to food banks.
- Sara Lee provided early funding for HOME (Housing Opportunities and Maintenance for the Elderly) which is "devoted to funding alternative housing for low-income elderly at no cost."
- General Motors matched employees' food and cash donations and together they raised about $5 million for the hungry.
- The Minnesota Gas Company and the Salvation Army joined forces in "Heat Share" to pay the heating bills of the unemployed. Company customers were offered this opportunity to contribute to the program and the funds were used by the Salvation Army to help some 10,000 families.
- In Massachusetts, State Mutual Life Assurance Company joined with the Worcester affiliate of Habitat for Humanity to secure decayed inner-city property for tenant/owners with whom they worked to restore the houses.
- Pacific Mutual Insurance took the lead to raise $1 million for the YWCA Hotel for Homeless Women.

These examples of corporate charity in times of hardship have their precedents. During the Depression, Whelan Drug Stores filled "without charge all prescriptions for sick and ailing unemployed." Also during the Depression, the William Lowenstein Memorial Fund of the New York Community Trust was established "to set up at least one eating place in New York City where people without means could get a good hot meal for virtually nothing." According to the Trust, Lowenstein's will asked that a sign be displayed at the entrance saying: "If you are hungry and without means, come in and have a meal as my guest."

Relief of human misery has always been synonymous with charity. Many contributions of the earliest philanthropists, particularly before the development of governmental programs, were inspired by religious thoughts such as those expressed in Matthew 25:31–46: "Truly I say to you, as you did it to one of the least of these my brethren, you did it to me." Many contributions were made in connection with religious organizations and institutions. This connection between philanthropy and religion was especially strong in seventeenth- to nineteenth-century America although it continues to be an important factor today.

Many important gifts were inspired by a desire to help children. The January 13, 1912 issue of *Outlook* reported:

> Some years ago, as the *Sun* tells the story, a shabby old man visited nearly every hospital and charitable institution in New York, examined the kitchens, and inquired into the details of management and accommodation. Forgetful of the possibility of angels travelling in disguise, he is reported to have been roughly treated in many places, but the Presbyterian and Hahnemann hospitals showed him the greatest courtesy . . . and when he died it was found that he had left his estate of $2,559,514.55 to four institutions, the Hahnemann and Presbyterian Hospitals getting $1,146,826.13 each. This is a very eloquent sermon on the advisability of treating human beings as human beings and not as the wearers of clothes.

The early orphanages were run by the churches or by nonprofit organizations established and sustained by people of means and conscience. Religion was the driving motivation for gifts that created Girard's College for Orphans and Hershey's Industrial School for Boys, for example. Charles Loring Brace started out to assist boys selling newspapers on the streets, and gradually his philanthropy broadened to become one of New York's most important agencies, the Children's Aid Society.

Samuel and Emily Graves Williston had five children, all of whom died in childhood. They adopted five children who lived to carry on the Willistons' philanthropic example. The Willistons gave away a large part of their annual income to all sorts of philanthropies in northwest Massachusetts, including asylums, schools, and colleges. The Reverend Seymour Tyler, President of Amherst, said of the two, "Mr. Williston overcame the obstacles of poor eyesight, ill health and poverty and became a blessing to tens of thousands. His wife was equally a giver with him."

George Eastman of Eastman Kodak established a free dental care clinic in Rochester for needy children and later extended that example to many other cities in this country and in Brussels, London, Paris, and Rome. According to Merle Curti in *Philanthropy Abroad,* Julius Rosenwald followed Eastman's example and "gave a million dollars to Berlin for the establishment of a similar dental clinic."

More recently, the Robert Wood Johnson Foundation provided grants to train dentists to take care of handicapped children and adults. The foundation's former president, David Rogers reports: "We discovered the handicapped were usually given terrible dental care or none at all because dentists were afraid of them. Thanks to our earlier efforts, programs to train dentists in the care of the handicapped are now a part of the required curriculum in every dental school in the country." Rogers also indicates that the foundation provided important support for "the work of Henry Kempe on child abuse and the whole medicalization of this problem which used to be viewed as simply a social horror, and is now being dealt with by the courts and police."

James Couzens, who served as vice president of the Ford Motor Company, mayor of Detroit, and U.S. Senator, gave $12 million to establish the Children's Fund of Michigan "to promote the health, welfare, happiness and development of the children of the state of Michigan primarily, and elsewhere in the world." During the 25 years this "time-limited" foundation was chartered to exist, it became a model for direct service and advocacy. William C. Richards and William J. Norton told the Couzens story in *Biography of a Foundation*. They note that at the end of the quarter century, a Detroit editorialist wrote:

> . . . a masterful accomplishment which has made countless children sturdier, parents happier, the nation sturdier. If he, the Senator, were here, he would have the right to be jubilant.

> A second said, "probably the most ambitious and successful attempt by one man to help his own generation."

> A third summed up the work in these words: "Couzens endowed his good work with something more than millions. He endowed it with self sufficiency. The Children's Fund blazed a trail; then left to posterity the dignity of following that trail on its own feet, on its own strength. Each local community in its own way has carried on the activities the Fund launched."

The Metropolitan Life Foundation has already given more than a million dollars to "The Chemical People," a program that, according to Sybil Jacobson, President of the foundation, is "an amalgam of public television programming and grassroots community efforts designed to curb drug and alcohol abuse among the nation's young." An anonymous donor put Eden House in Minneapolis on its feet, and according to James Shannon, Executive Director of the General Mills Foundation: "The rest is history. Eden House purchased its building, matured in management and today is thriving. The program is one of the leaders in the nation in tackling the perplexing problems of chemical dependency."

Working with the Enterprise Foundation, local corporations, and city government, the Lyndhurst Foundation has undertaken a plan "to upgrade all of Chattanooga, Tennessee's housing for the poor so that no individual living in that city will occupy housing that is not decent, fit and livable. The goal is to accomplish this task in ten years, beginning January 1, 1987."

Many philanthropists are motivated by a desire to reach out to people who are faced with the same barriers they faced or who share the same culture. The Baron de Hirsch Fund was established to assist Jewish immigrants in the United States. The baron was born in Bavaria and lived all his life in various cities of Europe where he concentrated most of his philanthropy. However, he established his fund in this country as a part of his concern for the plight of Jews everywhere. The story of the impact of his charity in America is told by Samuel Joseph in *History of the Baron de Hirsch Fund: The Americanization of the Jewish Immigrant*. Joseph reports:

> The trustees of the Fund attacked the problem of the adjustment and the assimilation of the immigrant Jewish population from many angles: relief, temporary aid, the promotion of suburban industrial enterprises, removal from urban centers, land settlement, agricultural training, trade and general education, and the aid and protection of the immigrants through port work and legislative and legal channels. Hardly a phase of Jewish immigrant life in the United States remained untouched.

A lesser but still interesting gift to help one's own was a bequest by William McClary of Philadelphia who, according to F. Emerson Andrews in *Foundation Watcher*, left "$20,000 for the support of the Home for Aged Masons in Lancaster." Perhaps the extreme example of watching out for one's own was the gift Marcus L. Ward made to establish Ward House in New Jersey, a home for men who had lost their fortunes in the depression whom Ward felt should be allowed the letdown of "genteel poverty."

At least Ward House was established with more readily attainable goals than those associated with Philadelphia's Magdalen Society often credited with being the first formal foundation in the country. The Society was created in 1800 "to ameliorate the distressed conditions of those unhappy females who have been seduced from the paths of virtue and are desirous of returning to a life of rectitude." In *The Future of Foundations*, Thomas Parrish writes that "after more than a century of patient attempts to keep going in the face of the chronic insufficiency of unhappy females desirous of rectitude and of the frequent intractability of those who did present themselves, the trustees voted in 1918 to broaden the work of the Foundation." The organization is now the White-Williams Foundation devoted to the special needs of young people.

Seeking Causes and Cures

In an article, "Compassion and Protection: Dual Motivations in Social Welfare," which appeared in the March, 1959 *Social Service Review*, Ralph E. Pumphrey of the Graduate School of Public Administration and

Social Service at New York University observes that the "motivations for philanthropic effort . . . are divided into compassion and protection." He defines compassion as "the effort to alleviate present suffering, deprivation or other undesirable conditions . . . ." This is direct intervention and assistance. "Protection," he writes, "is activity in which the promoters not only on their own behalf, but on behalf of their group or of the whole community, endeavor to prevent unwanted developments." We might refer to this as prevention.

One of the stock expressions that is used to delineate compassion from protection says: "Give a man a fish and he is fed for a day. Teach him to fish and he is fed for life." Using a similar metaphor, many discussions of philanthropy emphasize such terms as "seed corn" and "seed money."

A. R. Hands, who wrote *Charities and Social Aid in Greece and Rome*, suggests that charity is direct intervention and philanthropy is protection or prevention. In modern times, the role of direct intervention and assistance falls primarily to government while the more modest resources of private philanthropy are more often focused on helping find the root causes and the means of preventing human misery. This is certainly not an exclusive role for philanthropy. Indeed, one of the responsibilities of philanthropy is to encourage other basic institutions, including government, to develop ongoing activities in research, prevention, and assistance. As Pumphrey expresses it: "It seems probable that historical examination would show that, when they have endured, institutions originating in compassion have changed their programs usually to reflect a protective urge to forestall the need for the sort of service which they had been providing."

Many of the philanthropic efforts to give people the power and skills to help themselves described in the preceding chapter could as easily be described as efforts to relieve misery through prevention. Providing opportunity to people, encouraging ability, and discouraging disability have helped to prevent or ease much misery. The desire to prevent or alleviate misery has also motivated philanthropists to support research, teaching, and service programs addressing a range of human problems.

The project that more people mentioned to me than any other by far was "The Green Revolution," which covered a number of related programs funded initially by the Rockefeller Foundation and then jointly by Rockefeller and the Ford Foundation, and finally by foundations and governments throughout the world. "The Green Revolution" has become the prototype of efforts to relieve human misery through a combination of assistance, research, and prevention. In *Philanthropy Abroad*, Merle Curti describes the program's beginnings as follows:

> In 1943 the Rockefeller Foundation in cooperation with the
> Mexican Ministry of Agriculture initiated a program to improve the

maize yield. Controlled experiments tested the productiveness, disease resistance, and other characteristics of the many varieties of maize grown all over the country. Out of this developed the famous bank of corn germ plasm. An expanding program, in which much emphasis was put on participation of Mexican scientists, included similar genetic and cytological investigations of beans, wheat, and forage crops. The improved varieties of these basic staples, together with progress in controlling pests and blights, enabled Mexican agriculture to shift, in one category or another, from a food-importing to a self-sufficient or even a food-exporting economy. Similar programs in Colombia and Chile produced measurable results in increased production of high quality, rust-resistant varieties of corn, beans, wheat, and other food-crops.

Warren Weaver picks up the story in U.S. *Philanthropic Foundations:*

> Roughly two-thirds of the people in the world derive 80–90 percent of the calories of their diet from carbohydrates, chiefly grain . . . . It has in fact been estimated that for about 60 percent of the world's population, something like 80 percent of the calorie intake comes from rice.
>
> In 1952 the Rockefeller Foundation began considering the possibility of setting up an institute for the study of rice. After a series of exploratory studies, and extensive trips throughout the Orient by experienced agricultural scientists, the project was inaugurated in 1959. The government of the Philippines furnished the necessary land and cooperated in other ways. The Ford Foundation appropriated over $7 million for the capital plant, and the Rockefeller Foundation undertook the scientific and financial responsibility for operation.

That overall effort was expanded to include wheat and other food products. By the 1960s, Weaver was able to record that "research, education and extension projects to increase crop production have been undertaken in nearly every food-deficit country." He indicated that in the interim other foundations had begun to participate in the project, most notably Kellogg and Milbank.

In his 1977 "President's Review," then Ford Foundation president McGeorge Bundy began:

> This year I want to tell an unfinished success story which begins in private foundations and ends on the world scene, engaging most of the major democratic governments of the industrial world and a number of major international donor agencies. The story deals with

the dramatic expansion of scientific research on the food crops that are the staples for the vast majority of the world's people— everything from rice and wheat to corn and cassavas.

Bundy underscores the subsequent development of eleven regional agricultural research institutions and of the Consultative Group on International Agricultural Research, which he said had recently been "the instrument by which 28 international donors reached decisions that will provide support in 1978 to a set of international institutes and centers concerned with research on food production in the developing world."

Robert F. Goheen, former president of Princeton University, Ambassador to India, foundation official, and now Director of Mellon Fellowships in the Humanities, gave this advice for my project:

> One I would focus on is the Rockefeller Foundation's establishment of the International Center for Research on Rice in Mexico. Not only has that led . . . to Norman Borlaug's Nobel Prize—but to a now sizable number of international agricultural research centers devoted to different crops and/or different growing conditions, under joint public and private funding, and spread across the world. It's a story that illustrates the value of going after causes rather than symptoms, the importance of choosing or creating effective agents, the virtue of persistence, and the possibilities of trail-blazing out ahead of public agencies and of private–public collaboration.

At a different level, but for the same purpose, the Syntex Corporation provided pioneering help to an organization called Ecology Action. Frank Koch of Syntex describes it this way:

> In 1972 we were asked to loan four acres of our company site in the Stanford Industrial Park to an environmental, educational and research organization called Ecology Action. The objective was to develop and test bio-intensive food raising methods.
>
> It involved some risk because it would tie up our land for a minimum of three years [and] it would bring outsiders onto our property each day. . . . We balanced these risks against the fact that we had some successful involvement previously with Ecology Action, and that a successful project could provide important agricultural data that might prove valuable to developing nations.
>
> We decided to go ahead and Ecology Action spent eight productive years at Syntex. The results were remarkable. It has been demonstrated that the Biodynamic/Frech Intensive method of horticulture can provide on a given plot of soil up to 30 times the

amount of vegetables and up to 5 times the amount of grain or beans than was heretofore thought possible.

In their efforts to alleviate human misery, foundations have often supported research into the causes and cures for disease and other threats to human health. The Carnegie Corporation provided the primary support for a research project at the University of Toronto and as a result, as early as the late 1920s, insulin has been available for the treatment of diabetes.

The Rockefeller Foundation shows up again as a pioneering and persevering grantor in its steadfast support of Howard W. Florey, the principal researcher in the discovery of penicillin, for which he, Alexander Fleming, and Ernest Chain received the Nobel Prize. To read the full story is inspiring and demonstrates the successful collaboration of scientists and funders. Beyond the glorious outcome, achieved in time to markedly reduce deaths toward the end of World War II, the story provides a glimpse into the influence of the Rockefeller Foundation's Fellowships in the Sciences. They deserve a chapter or a full book.

In a March, 1956 *New York Times* series on health research, Howard Rusk, himself preeminent in research on rehabilitation, cites many successful partnerships between foundations and researchers and traces the development of and changes in foundation interest in health. For example, in referring to the writings of F. Emerson Andrews, Rusk says:

> In both publications, Dr. Andrews points out that when many of the large foundations were established in the first two decades of the century, education was a primary interest with medicine a close second. Support of medical research increased later because of many striking medical discoveries and such highly successful projects as the hook worm and yellow fever programs of the Rockefeller Foundation. In recent years with increased medical research funds available from the government and such voluntary agencies as the National Foundation for Infantile Paralysis, the American Heart Association and the American Cancer Society, foundation interests have veered toward increased support of medical education.

Rusk also gave several examples of how foundation grants made an enormous difference in medical research, for instance:

> It was the Sarah Mellon Scaife Foundation which provided Dr. Jonas Salk with $15,000 in 1948 to establish and equip his virus laboratory at the University of Pittsburgh and start his work which led to the anti-poliomyelitis vaccine. . . . The National Foundation

for Infantile Paralysis invested wisely and well in Dr. Salk's work, but it was the Sarah Mellon Scaife Foundation that put up the original "risk capital."

The New York Foundation and Lasker Foundation. . . teamed up in 1945 to support Dr. Selman A. Waksman in his studies in the use of streptomycin in tuberculosis.

In 1941 . . . when a grandchild of James Edgar Pew was born blinded as a result of retrolental fibrophasia, the Pew Memorial Foundation organized the Foundation for Vision to support the research of the late Theodore L. Terry, Professor of Ophthalmology at Harvard. Dr. Terry did the basic work in recognition that this condition resulted from premature infants in incubators receiving too much oxygen. Today the solution of this problem means sight for more than 1,000 infants each year who would otherwise be blind.

Dr. Arlington C. Krause of the University of Chicago Medical School also contributed to the solution of this problem with research funded by the Chicago Community Trust.

The Edna McConnell Clark Foundation has persistently devoted more than a decade of funding to both basic and applied research on the little known but devastating disease called schistosomiasis. According to a special report the November/December, 1985 *Foundation News*, written by Judith Reusberger:

> When the Edna McConnell Clark Foundation began funding major medical research 12 years ago, it chose to attack schistosomiasis, one of the developing world's most debilitating diseases.
>
> Determined to get the most for its money in an area where needs vastly outstripped resources, Clark borrowed a management tool from the corporate world—strategic planning.
>
> The result was the first edition, in 1974, of "The Strategic Plan: Schistosomiasis Research." That plan set forth a targeted program of made-to-order medical research—thereby making it instantly controversial, since scientists can hardly be expected to "plan" a discovery.
>
> Its purpose was to "develop the means to control" schistosomiasis. For the next decade, all grantmaking in the foundation's new tropical disease program would be guided by this plan and directed to this goal.
>
> To date, this commitment has absorbed over $30 million, but it has not brought schistosomiasis under control. A major objective— the development of a safe and effective vaccine by 1984—has not been achieved.

Despite this, the Clark program is widely regarded as successful. It has been praised by scientists, including some who do not endorse Clark's view that strategic planning is the way to fund medical research.

Very recently the Howard Hughes Medical Institute announced a $1 billion program in biomedicine. According to a story by Kathleen Teltsch in the February 3, 1986 *New York Times:*

> Most of the research undertakings will be in four areas of specialization: genetics, immunology, metabolic control and neuroscience. . . .
> . . . Under the institute's billion-dollar program, more than 900 scientists and researchers will be employed. . . .
> Dr. Donald Fredrickson, the Institute's President said "The important element is that we will create a new capacity for interaction between those engaged in fundamental research in molecular genetics and those engaged in the sophisticated application of this research to clinical problems. . . .

The path to cures of specific diseases is not always straight or even intentional. In *U.S. Philanthropic Foundations,* edited by Warren Weaver, there is an insightful chapter titled "Foundations and the Development of Modern Biology," written by George W. Beadle. Beadle includes many good examples of breakthroughs. He also provides an interesting glimpse of the problems of trying to target research to specific diseases. A young biochemist was being supported by "a local benefactor of science" to study the cause of cancer by working with a particular strain of mice. As Beadle tells it: "In the course of his work, he had occasion to make use of bacterial viruses. Working with Delbruck, he became so interested in these amazing organisms that he all but abandoned the mice." While the funder became wary because for the life of him he "could not see what these viruses had to do with cancer," the two researchers "worked out quite quantitative methods for investigating the phage life cycle and soon designed a technique for studying the growth of viruses that has since become famous and is widely used for other viruses [and] phage genetics was born." Weaver indicates that this was a basic step in the development of DNA. Beadle doesn't say whether the funder ever realized what he had made possible by his contribution. If targeted research sometimes yields findings with unexpected applications, so too does basic research some-times produce advances in treating specific diseases. Bringing it full cycle, basic research on DNA has already led to better understanding and treat-ment of cancer.

The Commonwealth Fund has had a long record of tenacity in the health field, including the area of child guidance largely labeled and developed by the Fund, studies of midwifery, support of longitudinal studies on arthritis, and, more recently, the obstacles to delivering quality health services to the poor. In *American Medical Research Past and Present,* published by the Commonwealth Fund in 1947, Richard Shryock indicates that:

> . . . some of the funds granted for studies of particular diseases were quite substantial. The Crocker Research Fund, for example, established at Columbia University in 1911 and devoted primarily to cancer studies amounted to about $1,444,000, by 1920, providing an income of more than $70,000 in that year. Harvard alone had some 28 medical research funds by that time. Indeed the catalogues of all outstanding schools showed numerous special research endowments and organizations.

Kate Macy Ladd, according to Keele and Kiger, "established the Josiah Macy, Jr. Foundation as a memorial to her father." They write that "Kate Ladd's letter of gift is remarkable for the clarity of its mandate and the freedom it provides for adapting the foundation's programs to meet changing needs." It reads, in part:

> It is my desire that the foundation . . . should primarily devote its interest to the fundamental aspects of health, of sickness, and of methods for the relief of suffering . . . to such special problems in medical sciences, medical arts, and medical education as required for their solution, studies and efforts in correlated fields . . . such as biology and the social sciences. . . . I hope, therefore, that the foundation will take more interest in the architecture of ideas than in the architecture of buildings and laboratories.

In the chapter, "Private Foundations and Modern Medicine," in Weaver's *U.S. Philanthropic Foundations,* Joseph C. Hinsey says "The Macy Foundation, led by Doctors Willard Rappleye and Frank Fremont-Smith, made available funds that had real influence in advancing teaching, research, and care in the field of obstetrics and gynecology. . . ."

Few people know the name of another woman who had an even greater impact on social services and philanthropy. Margaret Slocum Sage was married to Russell Sage, who was reputed to have been "acquisitive and ungenerous." According to Joseph C. Goulden in the *Money Givers,* "contemporaries called him 'the embodiment of the Yankee skinflint.' Even at 86, when he was worth $100 million, Sage rode the trolley to business meetings, grumping that he couldn't afford a hack. When an office boy brought him a 15-cent sandwich for lunch rather than the preferred nickel variety, Sage deducted a dime from the lad's pay." Another writer, Horace Coon, in *Money to Burn: What the Great American Philanthropic Foundations Do With Their Money,* has a chapter titled "Creating A Profession" that tells much of the story of how Mrs. Sage "compensated for a usurer's greediness after her husband's death." In addition to giving large amounts directly to charitable activities, predominantly human service activities, she also established the Russell Sage Foundation to "seek out the underlying causes of poverty chiefly through research and to make the facts behind conditions known to those in a position to further reform." Coon adds:

> . . . it is obvious that by its research, its publications, its grants to schools of social work, its functions as a clearinghouse for information for social workers and agencies throughout the country, its aid in finding jobs for professional workers, its publicity and promotion for the idea of bigger and better social work through public and private agencies, no other institution has even had a comparable influence in the creation of a new profession.
>
> . . . as we watch the effect and the influence of professional social workers in American government and politics, as their number and their power grows, we can have no doubt about the "affirmative" impression or the part that this relatively small foundation has played in creating a new and extremely vocal profession.

Another grantor with its eye focused on prevention is the Harris Foundation, established by Irving B. Harris, which has recently devoted funds and provided other leadership in the field of teenage pregnancy. The Harris Foundation is the principal funder of an organization called "The Ounce of Prevention Fund," a "Public/Private Partnership . . . [including] the Illinois and Family Services, to reduce the incidence of serious family problems." Among their current priorities is "school dropouts and the poverty cycle."

The George Gund Foundation is one of several funders that are devoting special attention to the problems of battered women and children.

Another approach was taken by the Community Service Society of New York which set out in 1970 to study the "maintenance (or survival) needs of the chronically mentally disabled living in the community." This quickly led to a larger concentration "on the entire homeless population." At that point, this not very popular topic was embraced by the Ittleson and Van Ameringen Foundations, both served by William Beaty as staff director. The Society's initial report was "Private/Public Spaces: Homeless Adults on the Streets of New York City." Based on these findings, the two foundations expanded funding in this field. A subsequent 1982 report, "The Homeless Poor in New York City," is probably the most comprehensive study of and blueprint for the problem released to date.

Armed with these early but encouraging findings, the Society expanded its work to eight other cities. Its 1984 report, "Hardship in the Heartland:

Homelessness in Eight U.S. Cities," includes among its recommendations: "preventive measures both to preserve (and even expand) the affordable housing stock that still exists [and] antidisplacement legislation, inclusionary zoning provisions, a moratorium on conversions of low-cost housing, and job training and placement programs that offer those who are able to work the wherewithal to avoid the dole or the streets." These projects had particular influence on the development of the Task Force on Homeless of the National Governors Association.

A different effort spanning service, research, prevention, and advocacy is the Amherst H. Wilder Foundation, a large operating foundation that provides a range of human services in St. Paul, Minnesota. The foundation is one of the largest providers of services and uses its hands-on experience to explore the causes of social problems and advocates appropriate public and private remedies for those problems.

Public education, with emphasis on health education, has been an important tool for prevention of illness and protection of health. For example:

- The Metropolitan Life Foundation voted $4 million to promote health education among school age children. Its "Healthy Me" program has five points:

    Awards for excellent programs in health education;

    matching seed grants to form community health coalitions;

    orientation sessions for school superintendents;

    high-quality materials to enhance school health programs; and

    a promotional campaign to heighten awareness of the importance of comprehensive school education on health matters.

- The Union Mutual Foundation undertook a five year health promotion effort aimed at:

    Smoking cessation

    Stress control

    Reducing abuse of alcohol and drugs

    Improved nutrition

    Exercise and fitness

- The Aid Association for Lutherans provided its several million members with a "Well Now" kit as part of the organization's "Wellness Program" designed to show members how to improve their health.

- The Pittsburgh Foundation provided support for a health educator for the staff of the Family Health Council of Western Pennsylvania.

Prevention may also require education about social choices and their implications. For example, the Gulf Corporation supported Notre Dame's studies of violence and the Pittsburgh Foundation helped to start that city's Holocaust Center. Fr. Theodore Hesburgh, president of Notre Dame responded to my inquiry about "great gifts" by writing that one of the most important he knew about had come unexpectedly: "During the days of student violence and revolutions in universities across the land . . . Gulf Oil Company, out of the blue, gave me $100,000 so that we could activate a course on nonviolence. . . ."

A different type of community education is illustrated by the Holocaust Center in Pittsburgh, an educational program of the United Jewish Federation, "committed to increasing awareness and knowledge of the Holocaust under the Nazi regime and its impact on society."

Support of Basic Institutions for Ongoing
Research, Prevention, and Assistance

> The activities of Rockefeller and Carnegie reflected an interest shared by other wealthy men. This was a period when medicine, offering new hope, captivated the imagination of wealthy benefactors somewhat as religion had once done in a less secular age. Instead of building churches and monasteries, philanthropists now endow hospitals and laboratories or set up foundations to do this for them. Some acted only when, as Hans Zinsser put it, "ambition was satiated and the blood pressure had passed 180."

This is the delightful way that Richard Shyrock begins his description of the massive wave of privately endowed hospitals that began to sweep across many American communities about 100 years ago. He goes on to write, "Some (philanthropists) hoped for recognition in this world or the next, yet as Zinsser added: 'sincere benevolence surely played a part. At any rate it brought the desired results.'" So began the deliberate development of basic human service institutions for ongoing assistance, research, and prevention.

In his chapter, "Philanthropy in the Hospitals," from *Philanthropy's Role in Civilization*, Arnaud Marts writes:

> The oldest general hospital in Boston, Massachusetts General Hospital was also founded by private initiative, but with the added help of legislative appropriations. In 1804, a bequest of $5,000 was received from William Phillips for the founding of the hospital. After other gifts were made and a substantial fund accumulated, the state legislature offered property for the institution—if $100,000 should be obtained by private subscription for the cost of

construction, this challenge was hopefully met, and the institution was opened in 1818. . . . In 1827 it received a gift of $100,000 from John McLean and a few years later John Redman gave another $100,000. This scale of giving was most unusual a hundred years ago. An institution which was able to attract such gifts in those days must have early proved itself indispensable.

A more recent example of hospital development involves the generous support of the Charles A. Dana Foundation for the Sidney Farber Cancer Institute, also in Boston, which is now known as the Dana-Farber Cancer Institute. Similarly, the William Randolph Hearst Foundation established the Hearst Laboratory of Radiation Biology at the Memorial Sloan-Kettering Cancer Center in New York.

In the nineteenth and early twentieth centuries, the emphasis was on private institutions, but gradually there developed dual systems of public and private facilities that have provided Americans with options. This dual system has persisted even during the period of increased emphasis on government's role in providing basic human services. The pattern for the transition from private to public/private facilities and service was established by the Rockefeller Foundation. Once the Foundation understood the causes of hookworm, they established the Commission for the Eradication of Hookworm, which deliberately included involvement of the states with both funding and the basic field work. In their implementation of initial agricultural research, the Rockefeller and Ford foundations set up mechanisms by which people from other regions and countries were involved in the establishment of their own agricultural research centers.

Closer to home, the March 29, 1913 issue of *The Survey,* published by the New York Association for Improving the Condition of the Poor, reported that Elizabeth Milbank Anderson gave a million dollars to the Association to establish "a new department for preventive and constructive social work. It is to be known as the Department of Social Welfare. . . . The Association has also accepted the sum of $150,000 which Mrs. Anderson has stipulated to cover initial or capital charges in the cost of certain experimental and research work." In announcing acceptance of the gift by the board of managers, John A. Kingsbury, general agent of the association, wrote:

> Mrs. Anderson's gift makes it possible for the Association to bring its work nearer to the original purpose as expressed in the Constitution; namely the elevation of the moral and physical condition of the indigent and, so far as compatible with these objects, the relief of their necessities.

Almost everyone has heard of Jane Addams and her pioneering work in social work and settlement houses, but few know the name of Helen

Culver who contributed Addams' famous Hull House. Kathleen McCarthy notes in *Noblesse Oblige: Charity and Cultural Philanthropy in Chicago 1849–1929*, that in addition to contributing Hull House:

> [Culver] donated one million dollars for scientific research laboratories in 1895. Undoubtedly influenced by her war-time experiences as a Sanitary Commission nurse, she stipulated that part of the money would be set aside for west-side university extension lectures on science, sanitation and hygiene, to make "lives more sound and wholesome."

A great many other grants have been given to pursue prevention of disease and promotion of health, for example:

- The Metropolitan Life Foundation provided support to the American College of Physicians for development of their national health promotion company.

- Equitable Life Assurance provided about $5 million in grants and loans to develop the rural health programs of such groups as the Local Initiatives Support Corporation (LISC).

- The J. M. (Milbank) Foundation started the National Medical School Scholarship Program in Alcohol Abuse and Alcoholism of the American Medical Student Association to develop awareness of and training about alcoholism in the practice of medicine.

- The Prudential Insurance Company contributed $2.5 million for the construction of a "state of the art" child-care center for children of the workers of the Hacienda Business Park in Pleasanton, California, south of San Francisco. According to Alex Plinio, President of the Prudential Foundation,

  > "[we] look for opportunities to contribute to projects that provide assistance to an ever-growing segment of society—namely female heads of households. We believe by donating the cost of building and equipping this child care center we are helping in a very direct way those parents in this area who wish to enter the work force and need to find a way to provide for their pre-school children."

- The McKnight Foundation announced recently a grant of $150,000 to the Boise Forte Reservation Business Committee "to establish a comprehensive health care complex on Indian reservations."

- A recent grant to one of the best known service organizations in this country and abroad came from the Lilly Endowment to the Salvation Army to establish a Salvation Army World Service Office (SAWSO). Ernest A. Miller of the Army writes: "The real story is the degree to which the work of SAWSO is leveraging the resources available to the Salvation Army in those poor countries, stimulating and upgrading the management techniques and appropriate technologies in the projects funded by SAWSO and motivating an expansion in growth in programs to meet the needs of people in many less developed parts of the world. . . . I think it is one of the outstanding examples of the leverage of a grant. . . ."

Earlier in this chapter, I cited Ralph Pumphrey's definitions of "compassion and protection" from an article published in the March, 1959 *Social Service Review*. Pumphrey's conclusion to that article provides a fitting close to this chapter as well:

Finally, might not historical examination of compassion and protection give some further clue to philanthropists and professional workers regarding the nature of the components of a successful institution? A hypothesis that might well be tested is that no matter what their auspices or sources of support, those social welfare institutions which have proved enduringly useful to society as a whole have embodied in a balanced relationship both compassion, that is, a desire to do something for the benefit of unfortunate people in the present, and protection, a concern for the well-being of the donor's group both now and in the future.

5

To Preserve and Enhance Democratic Government and Institutions

I. CLARIFYING THE ROLES OF GOVERNMENT AND THE
MEANS OF EFFECTIVE GOVERNANCE
II. STRENGTHENING SUCH PRIMARY PUBLIC SYSTEMS AS
LAW AND EDUCATION
III. STRENGTHENING THE OTHER STRUCTURES AND
SYSTEMS OF OUR DEMOCRATIC SOCIETY
IV. BUILDING AND STRENGTHENING INTERCONNECTIONS
SO THAT SYSTEMS WORK FOR PEOPLE

Clarifying the Roles of Government and the Means of Effective Governance

The Citizens' Union was created in 1897 and the New York Bureau of Municipal Research followed in 1904. Their establishment stemmed from concerns about corrupt and inefficient city government. In the case of the New York Bureau, a few courageous individuals had finally decided to confront the corruption and power of Tammany Hall. Their objectives were simply stated, but almost impossible to fulfill. They wanted to create citizen interest, involvement, and control in the exercise of democratic government, to attract able people into government service and to study how to achieve effective and responsible governance. The bosses and clubs that exercised iron-fisted control of municipal government in almost all major cities were bound to resist such goals. The story of the organizations that first fought for reform and of the thousands of civic associations and societies for good government that followed in their wake has dramatically demonstrated how important it is that private philanthropy and voluntary action remain independent of government and how substantial their impact can be as a result of that independence.

The New York story is told by Luther Gulick in the *National Institute of Public Administration: A Progress Report* and by Jane S. Dahlberg in the *New York Bureau of Municipal Research: Pioneer in Government Administration.* The two give appropriate credit to many, but clearly assign primary credit to three people: a civic leader, a professional administrator, and a generous and steadfast donor. The civic leader was R. Fulton Cutting, the founding chairman of the Bureau, who also headed the Citizens' Union where the Bureau started. The professional was Dr. William H. Allan, author of *Efficient Democracy*, and the philanthropist was Mary (Mrs. E. H.) Harriman.

R. Fulton Cutting was the first of the funders, and of him Dr. Dahlberg writes: "Mr. Cutting offered $1,000 a month for twelve months for demonstration of what could be done, and the Bureau of City Betterment was established as part of Mr. Cutting's Citizens' Union." Later, when the decision was made to have the Bureau concentrate on research, Cutting came forward again. According to Dahlberg, at the end of 1906, Mr. Cutting decided to support the proposed institute and asked Rockefeller and Carnegie to help finance it. In this way he set in motion the machinery for organizing the Bureau as an independent organization—independent of politics as well as of the Citizens' Union. Dahlberg indicates that there were many other citizens, professionals, and supporters who provided support, but the funder who remained steadfast was Mrs. Harriman.

Much later, when the Bureau sought to establish a training school for public service, Mrs. Harriman donated the necessary money. Dahlberg writes:

> Mrs. Harriman whose husband had been one of the early supporters of the New York Bureau, maintained contact with the Bureau after her husband's death in 1910. She returned from a visit late in 1910, enthusiastic about the caliber of men in the British Government's Career Service. She thought that more young men from families of influence in this country should enter public life. She offered to contribute money to Harvard, Yale or Columbia for training of such men for government service, but was scornfully turned down as politics was considered dirty at worst and non-academic at best.

Mrs. Harriman instead gave the money to establish what became the New York Training School for Public Service, the prototype for schools of public service that thereafter began to spring up across the country. The New York School's training activities were later taken on by another philanthropist, Mr. George H. Maxwell, who, according to Dahlberg, "wished to donate money for citizenship training." The Maxwell School of Citizenship and Public Affairs, providing for graduate education and preparation for government service, was established at Syracuse University and is still one of the most respected institutions in this field.

By 1925, just 40 years after the formal beginnings of organized reform, 20 years after the establishment of the Bureau, and only 15 years after the establishment of the Training School, the discipline of public administration was safely launched. It was to become one of the major factors in the country's new commitment to effective governance.

Special credit for early and steadfast support to development of the field of public administration should also be given to The Spelman Fund for its help to many of the early players, including the Institute for Public Administration and the Public Administration Clearing House.

This story has a later ironic twist. As with many fields, disciplines, and professions, public administration has now become so professionalized that some of its leaders are worried that it is leaving behind responsiveness to the notions of citizen participation and responsibility that were its initial inspiration. Encouraged by the Kettering and Exxon Education foundations, the Maxwell School has begun to address these issues through its new Center for the Study of Citizenship. In a longer term effort, the heirs of Lincoln Filene have provided funding to establish and help maintain, at Tufts University, the Lincoln Filene Center for Citizenship.

A time-limited foundation that devoted most of its substantial funds and influence to the encouragement of active citizenship was the Emil Schwarzhaupt Foundation. Its work is summarized in an important book, *Education For Citizenship* by Carl Tjerandsen, who served as executive secretary of the foundation.

———————

The Brookings Institution was established in 1916, the outgrowth of the Institute for Government Research (IGR) which had been formed for "1) knowledge of the best methods of administrative organization to be obtained by means of thorough scientific study, so that it may be possible to conduct governmental activities with maximum effectiveness and minimum waste, and 2) the development of active public interest in administrative efficiency."

Robert S. Brookings was a successful St. Louis businessman who, though largely self-educated, became Chancellor of Washington University. He was a strong believer in the need for more effective government. At Washington University, he established the Institute for Economics and the Brookings Graduate School (for public administration). Because these two schools were related to the IGR, Brookings became involved with it and supported its work. Later, IGR was renamed the Brookings Institution, in acknowledgment of Brookings generosity. The Institution has made many contributions to better government, among them the modern federal budget system.

Brookings, Hoover Institution, American Enterprise Institute, Heritage Foundation, Urban Institute, CATO Institute, SRI (formerly the Stanford Research Institute), Freedom Foundation, Joint Center for Political Studies, National Bureau of Economic Research, and Institute for Contemporary Studies are just some of the better known research and policy "think tanks"—organizations of public policy analysts and publishers who help think through and advise on the appropriate roles of government and the means of effective governance. Many of these groups have very different views of the roles and functions of government, some of which are even antithetical and antagonistic toward one another, but they share an interest in active citizenship, and they are mutually dependent on foundations and corporate support.

The CATO Institute is producing studies that support the notion of privatization, that is, the transfer to private organizations of every possible function of government. The National Conference on Social Welfare's project on "The Federal Social Role" has begun to produce documents that suggest that transfer of authority from the public to the private sector has already gone too far and that there is now a need for more centralized government.

Such diversity and debates not only stir peoples' souls but also spark their interchanges. In the end though, exposure to all this diversity of opinion helps people learn and grow, and that is a major object of citizenship education. Some funders encourage debate for its own sake, but the majority, like most of us, tend to donate money to support the perspective they espouse and are aghast at the work on which others seem to squander their resources.

Private funders have also supported a number of other programs which examine the role of government in our society. For example, the Aetna Foundation funds a chair in "public policy and corporate management at the Kennedy School of Government at Harvard; a grant from the Woods Charitable Fund, Inc. will enable the University of Chicago to establish a center for urban research and policy analysis; and Philip Morris Companies has funded a program at Baruch College of the City University of New York to examine, among other issues, the roles of business and government in education, job training, and social policy.

In his publication *Private Philanthropy in the Making of Public Policy*, James A. Joseph, president of the Council on Foundations wrote:

> It is in the debate about whether foundations should seek to transform government—clarifying policy options or advocating policy positions—that we find opinions most firmly fixed and

emotions most easily stirred. Advocates of private foundation's involvement in the formulation of public policy come from both the left and the right of the political spectrum. They argue that private foundations can and should seek to affect public policy because laws, regulations and appropriations powerfully affect the environment which they are seeking to stimulate progress. . . .

. . . The affects of private foundation engagement with public policy are engraved widely and deeply—in legislation, in court decisions, in public attitudes, and in social changes across a wide front.

. . . The Villers Foundation included in its first round of grants support for Blue-Ribbon board of inquiry into health care coverage. . . . The new Ameritech Corporate Foundation is supporting studies on reducing government regulations. Earlier this year, the John D. and Catherine T. MacArthur Foundation announced plans to spend $25 million on a broad program of national security research.

Philanthropy's role all along has been to support the search for a better way and to test different kinds of solutions. Then it tackles the often more difficult assignment of convincing the public about these solutions. The Rockefeller Foundation funded the research that helped to discover that hookworm was causing many serious health problems in the South and then supported the establishment of the Sanitation Commission to convince states to participate in treatment and prevention of hookworm. Even then the job was not done. For years the foundation has persevered in the effort to convince people and governments that basic public health programs are a responsibility of the public sector. The Field Foundation funded major studies on hunger and then undertook to prove that hunger existed in the United States and that food stamps were one way to help.

This pattern of identifying the problem, testing solutions, and finally winning public acceptance has also characterized philanthropy in the field of human rights. One of the largest program divisions of the Ford Foundation is called "Human Rights and Governance" and within this program are at least a dozen major spheres of activity involving research and field testing on such subjects as civil rights and social justice, Hispanic concerns, international human rights, legal services and womens rights.

The New York Community Trust set up an emergency fund to help the city and the citizens of New York during a budget crisis. The Trust described the effort as follows:

In the summer of 1976, when the city of New York was in the throes of a major fiscal crisis, the groundwork was laid to create the Corporate Special Projects Fund. It was established with

contributions of $25,000 from each of several participating
corporations. Collaboratively, executives from each corporation—
along with administrative staff from the New York Community
Trust—identify, review, and recommend grants that can have a
sizable, long-term effect on the city's institutions and spirit. In its
first year, the Corporate Special Projects Fund supported ten
projects in the areas of family services, community affairs and
economic development, health, and parks improvement. In that
same year, the trust published the first in a series of reports that
ascertained the depth of need for technical assistance in the areas
of art and culture, housing, health care, youth services, and
programs for girls and women. The reports examined the extent and
types of agency assistance serving those areas and suggested roles
that the Trust should play in providing further support.

The Gund Foundation is just one of hundreds that now support neighborhood organizations in their efforts to achieve empowerment at the
most local level. Some donors emphasize giving people enough power to
get their share of government programs while others stress maximum self
help without recourse to government. The examples are not limited to
philanthropy's role in dealing with human misery and rights. The Mellons,
with their support of the National Gallery of Art, have done more than
anyone else to demonstrate and assist government's role and participation
in the arts, and the Ford Foundation and many others have led the way in
funding and encouraging government participation in noncommercial
public broadcasting.

Strengthening Such Primary Public Systems as Law and Education

Louis Schweitzer believed passionately in the ability and obligation
of ordinary men to make the Constitution work. He thought that
the Constitution and the Bill of Rights should mean what they said.
    He thought it was morally wrong to let men rot in jail before
they were tried, their families left without support, their jobs
forfeited. Law professors and reformers for decades had talked
about the injustices of automatic high bail based on a man's charge
alone; how he ought to be released on his word if he checked out
as a resident with firm ties to the community. Louis Schweitzer was
the first person willing to stick his neck out and try the new way
that others talked about, to invest his time and his money and his
reputation in developing a fairer system.
    Louis Schweitzer founded the Vera Institute of Justice, named for
his mother. Vera means truth, literally, but what Louis Schweitzer

stood for was commitment—personal, persevering, undaunted by "experts." That is what the criminal justice system in America needs more than anything today—citizens who care enough to put themselves on the line, to go into prisons and see what is happening to men, to devote energy, money, but most of all themselves to translating grandiose words like "rehabilitation" into something real that can make a difference to a man.

Louis Schweitzer . . . was a modest man who, in his giving, always stayed in the background. There are no Lectures or Awards or Chairs or Buildings named for Louis Schweitzer. The legacy left is the thousands of human beings who have their liberty because he cared, as well as the administration of criminal justice which is more humane and has a more hopeful horizon, because he cared.

> From a eulogy delivered by
> Nicholas de B. Katzenbach
> September 23, 1971

Schweitzer's quiet outrage led to the creation of the Manhattan Bail Bond Project and the Vera Institute for Justice, which was to become one of the largest research, demonstration, and service programs in the fields of criminal justice and equity-related issues. His full-time partner in the effort was Herbert J. Sturz, and his largest funding partner was the Ford Foundation. Years later, Sturz was able to say the following to the National Commission on the Causes and Prevention of Violence:

> . . . Many irritants in the system arise from the lack of coordination among agencies. The principle mechanisms for dealing with a problem which cuts across agency lines—the interdepartmental committee and the task force—have been largely unsuccessful. A neutral private agency such as Vera can successfully bring together several agencies in a joint innovative program or experiment. . . . Vera can intercede with a city's power structure; we are not bound by chains of command.

The Institute sets forth its mission as follows: "Vera works with government to introduce innovations in policy and practice that reduce crime, raise the quality of justice, conserve scarce resources, and will remove obstacles to productive lives for those who have become dependent on the public purse." In a *Foundation News* article written in Vera's 20th year, John LaHoud wrote: "Vera has applied these considerable talents to dozens of programs designed to provide better treatment for those caught up in the criminal justice system, and to make the system itself more efficient. Many of its programs have been duplicated in cities throughout the country. . . ."

Louis Schweitzer's type of influence on public policy is seen in many other fields of human endeavor. Katherine Ordway was concerned that neither the federal government nor the midwestern states were doing much to protect and preserve the remaining prairie lands. She developed a plan to conserve this part of our natural heritage that has come to involve many jurisdictions and individuals. The program continues to grow in participation and significance. Patrick Noonan, former president of the Nature Conservancy, says that Ordway initially gave $10 million of her own money, but when she realized that the plan was working she established "a $50 million foundation which was instructed to give away all of its assets within five years. Importantly, this was recently completed and her legacy will continue forever."

A more recent example of related influence occurred when the Charles Stewart Mott Foundation "awarded the Corporation for Public/Private Ventures $30,000 for partial support for a three-year evaluation of the California Conservation Corps."

Educational policy has long been a concern of private philanthropy. A July/August, 1985 *Foundation News* story reports: "Another example of the increasing involvement of grantmakers in forming public policy occurred this August when William S. Woodside, energetic chairman and CEO of the American Can Company, told a Congressional panel that business can help fight illiteracy if it is willing to get into political debate over the quality of public schools. Woodside and American Can had previously announced programs to direct more of its resources into programs for the K–6 levels, where illiteracy can best be prevented.

There have been a great many efforts to help strengthen public schools. For example:

- The Amoco Foundation has provided almost $200,000 for "Designs for Change," a program that "will provide courses for parents and community leaders on what makes a school effective and how to become active in local school reform efforts."
- The Upjohn Company provided $2 million to Kalamazoo County to establish an Advancement Math and Science Center to assist and encourage top high school students and teachers.
- The Washington Post Company has a strong interest and record for support of public education through programs that honor and reward teachers, provide grants for creative classroom projects, improve reading and math skills, help students find jobs, and promote cross-cultural understanding.

- BankAmerica has provided close to a million dollars to its "California Educational Initiatives Fund" which provides grants to public elementary and secondary schools in California that propose the best plans to improve their teaching.
- Shell Companies Foundation, through its Shell Teachers Training Program, worked with the Houston Independent School District to design a pilot program to upgrade student performance in Algebra I and Physical Science through innovative teacher training. Only 38 percent of the district's students made a "C" or better in these subjects. The program is based on the theory that student success in the classroom is directly related to the teacher's ability to present subject material to his or her students. Through 1986, the foundation has contributed $750,000.
- AMD (Advanced Micro Devices) provided an initial grant of $7,500 for in-service training of teachers in grades 4–6 and then expanded the program to K–3 for teachers of math and other sciences. As a result, San Jose State University has adopted the program for its local school district.
- Chevron provided $275,000 to the University of Santa Clara to train teachers to teach math and science. Most of those involved had not been trained in those subjects and needed "retooling" in order to direct their teaching skills to these areas of teacher shortage.
- The Aetna Foundation provided $150,000 for a "three-year study to see how computers might be used effectively in hard-core urban public schools."
- The Lyndhurst Foundation played a leading role in encouraging the city school board to create a new inner-city magnet school, the Chattanooga School of the Arts and Sciences, a public school that will emphasize the liberal arts and sciences for all students. What sets this school apart are its aggressive efforts to have a student body that is economically, geographically, racially, and intellectually diverse. No more than 70 percent of the students can be above average on reading scores and no more than 70 percent can be below average in reading. All parents have pledged to perform two hours of volunteer service each month.
- Both the J. Paul Getty Trust and the Rockefeller Brothers Fund have participated in studies of art education in the schools. The Trust's study, "Beyond Creating: A Place For Art in America's Schools," concluded that "a more substantive and rigorous approach to teaching the visual arts is consistent with the ambitious challenge of educational reform and that it is incumbent upon all of

us—parents, teachers, and educators—to explore how we can work together within the American system of education to achieve academic excellence that is all encompassing."

- John Hancock Companies created a $1 million endowment for Boston's public schools.
- The Grand Rapids Foundation provided a challenge grant to keep that community's special education program in operation.
- Ralston/Purina provides classrooms and equipment for a business education program for high school seniors in St. Louis.

In school health, the Robert Wood Johnson Foundation developed a National School Health Services Program at a cost of $6.5 million. The program's objective is to learn how to include comprehensive health services in schools. One of its findings was that "nurse practitioners, supported by community physicians, can improve children's access to health care by expanding services available in schools. . . . For example, these nurses can be remarkably successful in identifying previously undiagnosed medical problems in children."

On a broader level, the National Academy of Sciences and the National Academy of Engineering—which were set up to "advise the Federal government on public policy issues"—were given a $20 million grant from the Arnold and Mabel Beckman Foundation "to build a new research and administrative center in southern California."

Strengthening the Other Structures and Systems of Our Democratic Society (Media, Free Enterprise, Labor, and the Voluntary/Philanthropic Sector)

In mid-1984 Gannett announced another action that confirmed its evolution toward entrepreneurial grants. With an initial $15 million, five-year commitment, it brought into being the country's first center for advanced studies in journalism and communications. The new Gannett Center will be located at Columbia University but will be operated directly by the foundation. In addition to continuing education seminars for professionals, it will accommodate advanced research fellows in residence and will maintain a laboratory to demonstrate new technologies in the media. With this commitment the Gannett Foundation carried its established interest in journalism education a long step further and helped fill an area neglected by most other major foundations, namely journalism and issues related to the media.

The quote is taken from Waldemar Nielsen's *The Golden Donors* in which he describes the media interests of the Gannett, Hearst, and Knight Foundations. He notes: "It's not altogether surprising that foundations established by Frank Gannett, William Randolph Hearst and James Knight should wish to reflect their benefactors' interest and would want to preserve and strengthen that part of society." Among its journalism activities the Hearst Foundation has a journalism awards program that assists journalism students in nearly 100 schools. The Knight Foundation was founded by James Knight and after his recent passing is likely to become a very large entity, devoted in significant part to journalism and a free press.

The Markle Foundation's recent grants provide many examples of how private philanthropy is working to improve the media and to define the role of the press in a democratic society. Among its 1983–84 grants were the following:

- *Television Audience Assessment, Inc.:* "To develop and test a practically viable system of television audience measurement based on viewers' attitudes and responses to programs as an alternative form of program ratings to supplement the standard Nielsen and Arbitron ratings."
- *Harvard University:* "To conduct a two-year interdisciplinary research project on how new communications technologies may affect democratic values and governance in our society."
- *British Film Institute:* "To continue the Broadcasting Research Unit to stimulate research on broadcasting and communications policy."
- *Media Commentary Council, Inc.:* "To continue publication of *Channels* magazine, enlarge circulation, increase advertising, and expand its editorial coverage."
- *Dalhousie University:* "To demonstrate the effectiveness of "computer conferencing" as an interactive system which enables large numbers of people to communicate with each other."
- *The Hastings Center:* "To examine the relationship between legislative ethics and media ethics as a means for considering the adversarial relation between legislature and press and implications for the democratic process."
- *University of California, Los Angeles:* "To study and evaluate the introduction of a computer-based electronic news editing system at the *Los Angeles Times.*"
- *National Public Radio:* "To increase quantity, diversity, and quality in public radio news and information programming in order to enhance NPR's potential for financial independence."

The Kiplinger Foundation has provided more than $2 million to establish the Washington Journalism Center to train journalists in public affairs reporting. The Benton Foundation took the initiative in developing the film "We Don't Fund Media," now distributed by the Council on Foundations. The film was designed to catch the attention of donors who have generally stayed away from funding films, but who, according to the film, are failing to take advantage of mass communications to further their program interests. The Film Fund "makes grants to filmmakers addressing social change issues around which there are few or no films."

Private funders have supported a variety of efforts to strengthen the nation's free enterprise system. The Anne Burnett and Charles D. Tandy Foundation gave $6 million to endow the new Charles Tandy American Enterprise Center at Texas Christian University. The Edwin H. and Helen Land Foundation concentrates its grants on projects to strengthen industrial management. The Land Foundation's dual purposes are to improve productivity and equality of opportunity and recognition.

The Joint Council on Economic Education has received more than $300,000 from the Kellogg Foundation "to help Michigan students in grades K–12 to improve their understanding of the United States economic system." The John M. Olin Foundation also focuses on free enterprise, and especially favors projects that increase public understanding—particularly among young people—of the importance of free enterprise to our way of life. The foundation's Chairman, William Simon, believes that too many philanthropic and voluntary organizations have not helped build our system of free enterprise and that many have in fact undermined it. David Packard of Hewlett Packard and the David and Lucille Packard Foundation holds many of the same views. He is quoted in the August 20, 1981 *Industry Age:* "In the future, let's focus our money and our energy on those schools and departments which are strong and which also contribute in some specific way to our individual companies or to the general welfare of our free enterprise system."

The Sarah Mellon Scaife Foundation and the Scaife and Mellon Funds operate under the assumption that foundation assets should be directed to institutions that build the business side of America from which their assets are derived. Those donors have provided important support to groups that examine policies that promote free enterprise, such as the Foundation for Research in Economics and Education, the International Center for Economic Policy Studies, the Heritage Foundation, and the Institute for Contemporary Studies.

In his seminal work, "Major Challenges To Philanthropy," commissioned by INDEPENDENT SECTOR, Robert Payton, commented "there are few fields of such vast magnitude that have stimulated such little curiosity among scholars." He concluded the work with: ". . . the new *Britannica* overlooks philanthropy . . . although its predecessors dealt with it quite adequately. That's the way it goes: one day you take it for granted, and the next day it's gone."

I have often supported and applauded policies that allow trustees discretion in interpreting legal testaments that might grow out of date and miss the original intent of the donor. However, there is one case where I very much wish the philanthropist's word had been taken more literally. Shortly after the turn of the century, John Stewart Kennedy left more than $1 million for the "development of a school for philanthropy." This charge could have been interpreted as an injunction to study and encourage the giving of money or to promote the application of charity to indigent populations. Had the powers that be decided for the former we would be almost 100 years ahead of where we are now in trying to make philanthropy a legitimate and attractive field of study. As it was, the needs of the time and the frequent use of the word philanthropy to describe the emerging profession of social work caused the decision to be made the other way, and out of that determination has grown the important New York School of Social Work. Despite my admiration for that profession and that school, I would have much preferred that there be one less school of social work, so that the nation could have had its only school for philanthropy.

Nonetheless, I am happy to report that philanthropy is seen increasingly as an important aspect of our society and therefore a subject worthy of scholarly activity and professional training. In the 1960s, the Commission on Foundations and Private Philanthropy (The Peterson Commission) and in the 1970s, the Commission on Private Philanthropy and Public Needs (The Filer Commission) laid important groundwork for the increased research currently being conducted. The Yale Program on Non-Profit Organizations, initiated by John D. Rockefeller, 3rd and headed by John Simon, has been at work for a decade. During that time it has developed the first sustained comprehensive research effort on the sector.

One of the principal reasons the organization INDEPENDENT SECTOR was formed was to develop "an identifiable and growing research effort that is producing the body of knowledge necessary to accurately define, describe, chart and otherwise understand the sector and the ways it can be of greater service to society." With the initial support of 39 funders, IS works with academic institutions and disciplines and with researchers and other organizations to encourage research in and on the sector. Recently, IS worked with the Mandel Family of Cleveland and their Premier Industrial Corporation, which took the lead in establishing the Mandel Center for Nonprofit Management at Case Western Reserve University, now also funded by the Cleveland and Gund foundations and by SOHIO.

The Hubert Humphrey Institute at the University of Minnesota has received a challenge grant from the Oakleaf Foundation, established by Kenneth N. Dayton, to establish a Chair on Nonprofit Activity, so that there will be an intellectual presence helping faculty and students to understand the roles of philanthropy and nonprofit activity and the different ways this country does its public business. The National Association of Schools of Public Administration and Affairs is helping their member schools to broaden their definition of "public" so that graduates recognize the philanthropic and voluntary sector as a career possibility and have a clearer grasp of the role of these organizations in developing and carrying out public policy and service. The Duke Endowment and Duke University have established a Center for Philanthropy. The Endowment provided the initial challenge grant.

The National Center for Charitable Statistics, which seeks to develop and maintain reliable statistics about giving, volunteering, and philanthropic and voluntary organizations, was formed originally by the National Charities Information Bureau, later joined by the Council on Foundations, United Way, and INDEPENDENT SECTOR. Substantial initial funding was provided by the Ford, Mott, and Rockefeller Brothers foundations, the Equitable, Atlantic Richfield, and Exxon corporations, and the Lilly Endowment. In 1985, the Center was incorporated as part of IS.

Over the past decade there has been a burgeoning of nonprofit management assistance groups. One of the earliest of these was the International Executive Service Corps, founded by David Rockefeller and Frank Pace and designed to involve retired executives in assistance to organizations and governments in developing countries. More recently but still more than a decade old, is Pace's companion National Executive Service Corps which benefited from a $300,000 seed grant from the Edna McConnell Clark Foundation. Yet another long-term participant is Jonathan Cook's Support Center (now the Support Centers of America) which had early support from the Meyer, Strong, and Cafritz foundations in its home base of Washington, D.C., and from the Norman, New York, and J.D.B. foundations for its national activities. Brooke Mahoney's Volunteer Consulting Group had the initial good idea to assist organizations which needed good board members by working with business groups that could supply them. Her efforts have now branched out to many other aspects of assistance to nonprofits. Early funding was provided by the New York Community Trust, the Fund for the City of New York, and the United Way. Many consultants and consulting groups are now part of an organization called the Nonprofit Management Association.

The Donner Foundation developed a program, "Administration in the Arts," to provide assistance to cultural institutions, including management development. The Dayton Hudson Foundation provided support to the Minnesota Nonprofit Assistance Fund of the Minneapolis Foundation for a "cash reserve for the arts program—designed to promote financial stability and continued operating support to small and mid-sized arts groups."

Examples of funding programs designed to improve the management of nonprofits abound. For example:

- The New Hampshire Charitable Trust channels corporate grants to nonprofits in need of management assistance.

- The San Francisco Foundation has a large "Technical Assistance Grants" program "in support of the development of healthy, well-managed nonprofit organizations."

- Morgan Guaranty Trust Company has provided management consultants to nonprofit associations, including performing arts groups.

- The Weyerhaeuser Company produced annotated bibliographies on nonprofit management topics and fundraising.

- Terry McAdam, while at the New York Community Trust, established an organization with the fascinating acronym NOPEC (Non-Profit Energy Conservation Program) to provide assistance to voluntary organizations suddenly faced with a massive increase in costs of heating their churches, hospitals, recreation centers, and the like.

- The John Ben Snow Foundation developed a large energy-saving program for institutions in upper New York state.

- Amoco organized a "community services program to make energy-efficient 150 buildings owned by nonprofits in Chicago." These experiences have led to savings of 30–50 percent on energy bills.

- The Commonwealth Fund has a long and continuing record of assistance to voluntary hospitals. For example, it was the Fund's interest in New York City health services that led it to support a major recent study "The Financial Condition of New York City Voluntary Hospitals," which was conducted by New York City's Graduate School of Public Administration.

- VOLUNTEER: The National Center was begun with substantial support from W. Clement Stone. Through the years its programs to encourage and strengthen volunteering in our society have received significant support from a wide variety of individuals and philanthropic organizations, notably the Charles Stewart Mott and Kellogg foundations.

- The Morris Goldseker Foundation "awarded the Community Investment Institute $6,000 for a Training of Trainers Program. The project helps volunteer trainers share their community development skills and experiences with other nonprofit community organizations."
- The Gannett Foundation gave more than $300,000 to INDEPENDENT SECTOR to develop the film "To Care: America's Voluntary Spirit," the first such effort to help acquaint Americans with the magnitude and variety of voluntary effort in the country.

There are scores of ways that funders help build the other basic systems of our society. Aetna helped create a "public/private funding partnership focusing on revitalization of an historic market district in Wheeling, West Virginia. The New York Community Trust funded a study of camps serving its area and helped establish a subsequent joint purchasing program. The George Gund Foundation provided emergency funding to keep open Ohio's shelters for battered women and children during a state funding crisis. The Rosenberg Foundation has funded many projects to study and improve California and federal immigration policies, and the Cleveland Foundation provided more than $1 million "to transform the landmark Ohio, Palace, and State Theatres in Cleveland into one of America's largest arts and entertainment centers."

Building and Strengthening Interconnections so that Systems Work for People

It's happened to everyone driving a car at night. The lights of oncoming cars suddenly blind you. You look away, toward the right, over the edge of the paving. A white stripe gives you a bearing and you steer the car out of danger.

That strip of white paint was the direct result of a foundation initiative. To persuade the Connecticut Highway Department to try it, the Dorr Foundation, a small family foundation, financed the experiment. Marginal stripes were applied to a busy stretch of highway and, as the late foundation historian F. Emerson Andrews told the story, traffic accidents dropped about 65 percent on that section of roadway, amazing John Dorr, whose foundation financed the project, as well as the highway officials.

We are grateful to Saul Richman for that fascinating tale from his article, "Down the Highways and Byways with American Philanthropy," in the January/February, 1980 *Foundation News*.

A similar and equally innovative example of how philanthropy has helped to make systems work was described by Professor Barry Karl in his 1983 testimony before the Ways and Means Committee: "My favorite one is the Guggenheim Foundation that offered to help paint direction signs on roof tops and in open fields to aid early airplanes in finding their way from one city to another." I have never been sure whether Karl intended it as a play on words but he followed immediately with: "Foundations were there to help find the way. . . ."

The problem of stolen art reached such proportions that the International Foundation for Art Research believed that something had to be done to alert police, auctioneers, dealers, and buyers to be on the lookout for stolen property. The Jerome Foundation provided the initial grant for what is now a major international project under the heading "Stolen Art Alert." This includes the publication ten times a year of a full-size periodical called *Stolen Art Alert* with pictures and detailed descriptions of missing objects. The magazine also includes an encouraging section called "Recoveries," and regular features telling fascinating stories about how the program has helped capture thieves and break criminal rings. The project has received ongoing support from the J. Paul Getty Trust.

One system that has not been working very well relates to escalating costs of all kinds of insurance and the clogging of the courts with claims for damages. The Walter E. Meyer Research Institute of Law funded early work by Robert E. Keaton and Jeffrey O'Connell, designed to figure out how to deal with court backlogs and rising insurance fees. This work led them to recommend "no fault" automobile insurance, and later resulted in Professor O'Connell's proposals and plans to apply the "no fault" principle to product liability, medical malpractice, and other personal injury cases.

The founding of TIAA (Teachers Insurance and Annuity Association) by the Carnegie Foundation for the Advancement of Teaching provides a striking example of how philanthropy can find dramatic innovations that make a system work better. The problem they were trying to address involved the paucity of retirement plans for college teachers and the inability of insurance plans that did exist to "travel" with an educator when he or she went to a different institution. The solution they developed was TIAA. In his book, *The Big Foundations,* Waldemar Nielsen says "one outgrowth of the foundation's work was the establishment in 1918 of the Teachers Insurance and Annuity Association which has been invaluable to American higher education by providing teachers with greater financial security." Alan Pifer, President Emeritus of the Carnegie Corporation of New York, wrote to me that "TIAA is one of the great accomplishments of foundations."

The interest and influence on city planning of the Russell Sage Foundation is another example of how philanthropy has helped build connections between the various sectors and structures of American society. In *Foundation Watcher*, Andrews wrote:

> . . . a sound plan for New York would necessarily involve its environs, and these included territory in three states, New York, New Jersey and Connecticut. It would be useless for New York planners to start a trans-Hudson bridge on Washington Heights unless New Jersey planners agreed on its termination in Fort Lee. In the absence of interstate compacts, it seemed necessary that a private agency formulate the needed regional plan.
>
> . . . Looking back at it now, more than forty years after its formal presentation (the report of the Committee on Regional Plan) one finds most of the proposals sound, and many realized . . . [that] perhaps the greatest contribution was the popularization of planning itself.

The Babcock Foundation has had a major influence on regional planning in North Carolina and the South generally. The Duke Endowment has also had major influence in that region on health and hospital planning.

This whole section, and indeed the whole chapter and book, could be taken up with examples of the influence of the Commonwealth Fund and the Robert Wood Johnson Foundation on health planning and use of health services. The two organizations have been especially effective in generating new approaches to cost containment, reduced hospital stays, utilization of professional aides, and on and on. Waldemar Nielsen often cites these two foundations for their unflagging efforts to make the health systems work through a combination of research, prevention, and service. Two examples are as follows:

> In his testimony before the House Ways and Means Committee in 1983, Dr. August G. Swanson, director of academic affairs of the Association of Medical Colleges, said:
>
> > "In 1970, a $900,000 grant from the Commonwealth Fund permitted the faculty of the University of Wisconsin to initiate the WAMI (Washington–Alaska–Montana–Idaho) Program. The successful educational experiment built upon the strengths of the University of Washington to provide medical education opportunities throughout that four state region could not have been started without the support of the Commonwealth Fund . . . now the program is totally supported by the four states."

The Robert Wood Johnson Foundation has established a "program for hospital initiatives in long term care," which provides $16 million to 23 organizations in 19 states to establish "model projects to help hospitals better meet the health needs of the elderly."

The Kellogg Foundation recently provided close to $1 million to Dartmouth College "to organize and deliver a nation-wide health promotion program for older Americans." The Lucille P. Markey Charitable Trust has given close to half a million dollars to Columbia University for a commission that will "help chart the future of basic medical research in America," while the John A. Hartford Foundation has given more than a half million dollars to the University of Rochester "to develop a national model for containing health care costs."

One of the most frequently mentioned foundation projects that has influenced American society involves earlier support of Abraham Flexner's work on medical education. The Carnegie and Rockefeller foundations combined to fund Flexner's seminal work on the state of medical schools and medical education. The study resulted in the establishment of high standards and a rigorous accreditation process that purged the country of below-standard institutions. Books on philanthropy often refer to support of this project as one of the most vivid and important impacts on health care and on our expectations of institutions that serve the public.

There are thousands of examples of partnerships between philanthropic institutions and innovative nonprofit organizations aimed at every conceivable aspect of the human condition. The Otto Bremer Foundation gave $75,000 to the Mental Health Association of North Dakota "to support the work of the Governor's Commission on Services to Children and Adolescents at Risk." The New York Community Trust has established a new Center of Aging Policy to "serve as a neutral forum where experts and organizations in the field of aging can exchange information, analyze problems, and work together to access current and future problems affecting the elderly." Aetna supported the "Youth Practitioners Network" at Brandeis University "to get agencies and organizations working on youth employment programs to work together more effectively." The Metropolitan Life Foundation has established an awards program to help community colleges evaluate services to their populations.

An increasing number of corporations are taking interest in how they can help the communities in which they do business and they are supporting activities that range across the spectrum of human needs and aspirations. Patrick Noonan, now of Conservation Resources Group, wrote:

Concerning corporate gifts, I think of the major gift in 1973 by Union Camp Corporation of 50,000 acres which really began the corporate movement in this country in support of land conservation endeavors. Heretofore, conservationists and industry had been at odds with one another but it was through the leadership of a unique individual, Alexander Calder, Chairman of Union Camp, that this creative gift was made to the Nature Conservancy. . . . Moreover, since the initial gift in 1973 Union Camp has made ten additional gifts of land and, most importantly, over 50 other corporations have since followed their leadership. It is truly a precedent setting gift, valued in excess of $12.6 million which in addition to its value, led the way for a whole new era of philanthropy which heretofore had not been considered.

William Norris and the Control Data Corporation have long believed that many public services will be more effective if performed under contract to private companies. In an op-ed piece in the *New York Times*, September 13, 1981, Norris writes: "This sad state of affairs [the problems of our cities] exists because we have not utilized the country's major source of technical, managerial, professional and financial resources: namely the business community." Norris calls for "business to take the initiative to address the major unmet needs of our society as profitable business opportunities and to do so in partnership with government and other sectors." Control Data has experimented with the ideas Norris describes.

The 1983 report, "Corporate Community Involvement" from President Reagan's Task Force on Private Sector Initiatives, "provides an overview of the range of strategies utilized by for-profit corporations to respond to community needs. It demonstrates the way companies and their associations—large and small—seek to establish relationships with community groups and government."

One increasingly important aspect of creating systems that are responsive to public needs is to seek greater consumer involvement in planning, supervision, and evaluation of services. This is a central thrust of many of the "change-oriented" funders and associations. It is also very much part of the thinking and activity of many other groups. The Foundation for Child Development, for example, provided close to $100,000 to the Mental Health Law Project "for an advocacy program for mentally handicapped children," and the Commonwealth Fund provided a quarter of a million dollars to Louis Harris Associates to "survey 3,600 New York City residents to determine their views about health and health care delivery."

Many of philanthropy's efforts to make government and society work more effectively have met with bitter opposition. Yet many of these controversial efforts, particularly those assiduously addressed by daring crusaders, have eventually been accepted as "common wisdom." For example, who could imagine today that the idea of kindergartens was at one time terribly divisive? Elizabeth Peabody, a sister of Horace Mann, donated her own funds and raised money from other well-to-do men and women to establish in Boston the first American kindergarten. Arnaud Marts tells part of the story in *Philanthropy's Role in Civilization:*

> In 1859, another specialized field of education . . . the kindergarten was opened up by private initiative. It was first organized as a charity kindergarten for poor and uncared for waifs but was soon discovered to be an excellent form of preschool training for normal children. Though some German-speaking preschool programs for children had been organized earlier, Mrs. Peabody's was the first English speaking one. It took more than 30 years for the idea to begin to catch on and some states enacted laws which prevented the use of public school funds for the education of children of kindergarten age.

There were fierce arguments about whether kindergartens wasted money on children too young to learn, took children out of the home too soon, created bloated government, encouraged family dependence on government, and on and on. It took almost 50 years for the idea to gain general public acceptance. A hundred years after Mrs. Peabody's first kindergarten, Head Start took the idea a step further with a preschool program for disadvantaged children. Thirty years later the fur is still flying. Will day care be next?

6

To Make Communities a Better Place to Live

I. PAYING BACK
II. GIVING FUTURE GENERATIONS
THE SAME OPPORTUNITIES
III. BUILDING LOCAL PRIDE AND MAKING
OUR COMMUNITY SPECIAL
IV. THE CAUSE OF COMMUNITIES AND NEIGHBORHOODS

Paying Back

Ithaca, New York, is large enough to have a "Spare Room" and caring enough to want it used. Its "Spare Room" is a community emergency shelter "for individuals and families in need of temporary shelter . . . victims of fire, flood or other emergencies; stranded travelers; transients and newcomers; deinstitutionalized or ex-offenders; or homeless due to domestic situations." Salem, Oregon is a community with SHINE, which stands for Self Help in Neighborhoods Everywhere. SHINE provides seed money to neighborhood groups for self improvement projects. Springfield, Missouri, has a "Crime Stopper," a program designed to involve residents in neighborhood watches and other education programs to reduce crime in the community.

These and more than 140 other projects are supported by the Gannett Foundation's Community Priorities Program (CPP). The foundation has already committed close to $10 million in a program designed to:

> Identify crucial community problems through an ascertainment process which involves local leaders from all parts of the nonprofit and business community. Proposals addressing these problems are then solicited from local community organizations and submitted under the CPP Competitive Selection Process . . . and are judged on the basis of thoroughness of the ascertainment process used to

identify the community problems and the creativity and feasibility of the solutions proposed to address them.

The program, started in 1981, involves communities in which the Gannett Company has newspapers, television or radio stations, and other local media properties. Gannett sees the program as a way of paying back to communities where the corporation has a responsibility to be part of the civic process. The local subsidiary must be fully involved in the process of planning and grantmaking, which brings other major advantages to the cause at hand, including publicity for it.

Other ways that CPP grants pay back and build communities are:

- The Geriatric Health Service of Senior Friendship Centers in Ft. Myers, Florida received $75,000 to provide "free medical check-ups and advice to residents aged 60 and older who could not otherwise afford them. Services are provided by retired volunteer physicians and nurses . . . . The fund is now operating with funds from other sources."

- The Family Daycare Satellite Program of the Eastside Community Center in Rochester, New York received $40,000 "to expand the daycare opportunities available on a neighborhood basis in the city of Rochester. . . . The program is now totally self sufficient . . . ."

- The Housing Maintenence/Home Repair Project of the Vermillion County Citizen's Action Committee for Economic Opportunity in Danville, Illinois received $97,000 to assist the elderly "who are unable to maintain their homes and to keep them from deteriorating due to needed repairs."

- The Kare-4 Project of the Girls' Club of Sioux Falls, South Dakota received $40,000 to help "provide after-school daycare and enrichment programs for children age 6 through 12 years who otherwise would go home to an unsupervised environment. The Kare-4 (Kids After School Recreation and Enrichment) program includes buses "enabling up to 500 children to participate in Boys Clubs, Girls Clubs, YWCA and YMCA activities by providing transportation from 26 elementary schools."

The IBM Company, like Gannett, believes in paying back to communities in which it has a substantial presence. One of the ways it has done so is through its "Community Service Fund," described in Frank Koch's *Corporate Giving: Policy and Practices:* "In 1972, IBM started a program that enables employees to obtain company support for volunteer service programs in local communities across the country. IBM's aim is to stimulate more voluntary community action by its employees." Koch also describes

Levi Strauss' program to involve employees in local voluntary efforts in its nearly 50 plants and distribution centers across the country, as well as Xerox Corporation's Social Service Leave Program "which makes talent available for work on social problems, recognizing that people are often a greater resource than our dollars."

A story in the November 25, 1985 *New York Times* reports that many Hartford companies are playing "a major and growing role in housing, educating and employing the poor." Leonard Lund, a senior research associate at The Conference Board, is quoted as saying: "Still Hartford is in many ways unusual. I can't think of another city that size where the corporations are so involved in urban affairs." The story notes that: "Recent examples abound. Led by several major insurance companies based here, including Ætna, the Travelers Companies, the Cigna Companies and the Hartford Insurance Group, the city's corporations have been committing huge amounts to help cure municipal problems."

For hundreds of years, some of the most important gifts to communities have been motivated by a desire to pay back to communities that have been good to the donor.

Anna Ottendorfer came to America in 1837 at age 22 and settled in New York City where she married another Jewish immigrant, Jacob Uhel. In *Famous Givers and Their Gifts*, Sarah Knowles Bolton tells their story:

> [of buying] a small weekly paper called the *New Yorker Staats–Zeitung* . . . which finally became a daily. . . . Her husband died leaving her with six children and a daily paper on her hands. She was equal to the task. She declined to sell the paper and managed it well for seven years. Then she married Mr. Oswald Ottendorfer who was on the staff of the paper. . . . Both worked indefatigably and made the paper more successful than ever. Along the way, she gave generously to many causes to indicate her gratitude to her adopted country and community and her belief that fortunate individuals had an obligation to assist those who came after them.

Bolton refers to a piece in an 1844 issue of *Harper's Bazaar* which said of Ottendorfer: "Her callers were many . . . there was advice for the one, assistance for the other; an open heart and an open purse for the deserving; a large charity widely used." She funded the Women's Pavilion of the German Hospital of New York City and the German Dispensary also in New York City. According to Bolton, Ottendorfer "built the Isabella Home for Aged in Astoria New York . . . in memory of her deceased daughter, Isabella."

Almost every corporation and foundation report indicates some commitment to local civic responsibility. Even the huge MacArthur Foundation, which appropriately is focusing its resources on national and international problems, has established a "Special Grants Program for Chicago-area cultural and community development in recognition of John D. MacArthur and Catherine T. MacArthur's residence in Chicago for many years and the presence of the foundation staff in Chicago. Grants have been made in support of theater groups, art museums, dance groups, symphonies, opera, and groups dedicated to urban and minority group problems and community revitalization."

The Altman Foundation, Benjamin Altman's "legacy to the people of New York," was established "for the purpose of receiving and maintaining a fund or funds . . . to promote the social, physical or economic welfare and efficiency of employees of B. Altman and Company . . . and for the use and benefit of charitable, benevolent or educational institutions within the State of New York. . . ."

In 1985, the Vincent Astor Foundation issued a report, "Twenty-Five Years of Giving in New York City," which describes almost $150 million in gifts. It, too, is a story of paying back by investing in the future. A September, 1985 *New York Times* editorial put it this way:

> When John Jacob Astor arrived in New York City in 1783, he had two suits, enough money for a few meals and seven flutes to sell. When he died 65 years later he was the richest man in America.
>
> Since money when carefully bred begets money, Astor's fortune has endured well into the 20th century, and seeing how much of it has been handed around the city in which it was earned is a great pleasure. Brooke Astor, the widow of Astor's great great grandson, Vincent, is responsible for a lot of the pleasure.
>
> . . . Where that money has gone is where New Yorkers of good will would like to see it go—most of it helped young people, education, museums, and libraries; a lot of it to zoos, parks, health and housing.

The editorial ends with this interesting twist: "'I don't like the thought of it lying in great piles, useless, motionless, in the bank,' said Dolly Levi, the heroine of Thornton Wilder's *The Matchmaker*. 'Money should circulate like rainwater . . . setting up a little business here, and furnishing a good time there.' Mrs. Astor's rainwater has made New York flower."

Over the years, the Chase Manhattan Bank has, like many other New York institutions, supported important services to its city. A recent list of its grants includes money for distress alarm devices for firefighters, cold water rescue suits for police officers, horses for urban park rangers, the revolving emergency loan fund for police officers and firefighters, an executive development program for high school principals, and an emergency intervention to help keep the New York Public Library open on Thursday evenings. That latter challenge grant alone involved $375,000.

Samuel J. Silberman and his Louis and Samuel Silberman Fund have been devoted literally and figuratively to their city of New York. Silberman's $4 million gift to the City of New York in 1964 was targeted "for social work, education and research through the massive expansion and rebuilding of the city's School of Social Work at Hunter College." The fund has continued to "bring together public and private resources for the common purpose of strengthening New York and our attention to human services generally."

In almost every city in the country there are encouraging and heartwarming examples of ways that individuals, groups, foundations, and corporations have made deliberate efforts to pay back, do their share, and leave the community a better place for those who follow. I happened to start with New York, but, with other communities, the examples are also rich and tend to flow. Kathleen McCarthy has written a full book on Chicago's philanthropists, and to make it manageable, she had to limit it to one relatively brief period. The book is titled *Noblesse Oblige: Charity and Cultural Philanthropy in Chicago, 1849–1929.*

One part of my search for examples of grants that had made a difference involved a sampling of state and local historical societies, but it yielded so much material that I had to decide not to pursue that source or be inundated by it. One could do a series of books on the philanthropy that has made an impact in many different communities, states, and regions. I hope someone will pick up on it. The stories are rich, inspiring, and instructive for all who care about the quality of life where they live.

George Robert White left most of his money to charities in Boston and to the city itself. The neighborhood health centers established with his funds had tremendous influence on hundreds of thousands, if not millions of immigrants and set a model for the country. Morris Goldseker, a poor immigrant from Poland, made a great deal of money in Baltimore real estate and left his money to establish the Goldseker Foundation, which is concerned primarily with inner-city problems, beginning with housing.

In a very resourceful book, *The Very Rich Book: American Supermillionaires and Their Money—Where They Got It, How They Spend It,* Jacqueline Thompson describes the largess of E. Claiborne Robins who has already given more than $100 million to his hometown of Richmond, Virginia, including more than $50 million to the University of Richmond. Thompson also describes Edith Rosenwald Stern's generosity to the city of New Orleans:

> Mrs. Stern's philanthropic interests are hereditary. Her father,
> Julius Rosenwald, was one of the founders of Sears Roebuck Co.,
> the world's largest retailer; and gave away about $63 million before

his death in 1932. Black and civil rights causes got the major portion of his gifts. Mrs. Stern and her husband continued the family tradition of supporting black causes, but in the Southern city of New Orleans, that can be dangerous. Through the years, the couple received threats and hate mail for their trouble, but the growth and prestige of Dillard University, which prospered with their largess, is one of their rewards . . . . Mrs. Stern has expressed her philanthropic nonconformity in other ways as well. In the not so distant past, New Orleans had such a sloppy voter registration system that elections could easily be rigged by shady politicians. It was so bad that Mrs. Stern recalls, "you could register a dog, an old cat and all your dead relatives and then cast a vote for them if you wanted." Mrs. Stern became the co-founder and chief financial supporter of the Volunteer Voter Registration League, which has since been incorporated into the city government.

Doctor D. K. Pearsons believed that he had a responsibility to pay back to the country as a whole, and in his case he gave away almost everything he had. The May 11, 1912 edition of *Literary Digest* quotes the *New York Tribune:* "Many millionaires have given away larger sums than any of his —but none more fully attained the ambition to spend all his money for the advancement of good causes and to die poor." The *Digest* also quotes the *Chicago Evening Post:* "This man, instead of making the acquisition of his wealth the excuse for putting every ounce of his strength into increasing it, turned deliberately to the task of putting it back into the future of his country." The article concludes with an indication that Doctor Pearsons also gave with good humor. When he sent $50,000 to the Montpelier Seminary, he added this note:

> Fifty-thousand dollars, farewell! You have been in my keeping for many years, and you have been a faithful servant. Your earnings have helped to educate many young men and women who have helped to make the world better. You came to me from the grand old white pine forest of Michigan, and now you are going into the hands of other stewards in the state of Vermont. There you will become part of a perpetual endowment fund of $150,000 for Montpelier Seminary, $100,000 of which sum has been given by the people of Vermont. When you arrive in Montpelier you will go into the keeping of good businessmen and you will be safe: as I expect that every dollar of this perpetual-endowment fund will be kept intact and actively doing good for 500 years . . . go into the keeping of young men and God's blessings go with you! Do your duty, and give the poor boys and girls of Vermont a fair chance.

Paying back is a core rationale for tithing which began in ancient Greece and Rome as a consent of what one owed to a community. Many of the gifts described in this book began with the donors' conviction that they should give back ten percent of their income. Charles Page went several steps beyond. He readily admitted that his tithing started as a "deal with the Lord" that, if his wife survived a serious illness, he would become a strict tither. Although Page first gave his money out of strict obligation, gradually he began to realize that this side of his life gave him far more satisfaction than his success in making money. Harry A. Stewart told the story in the July, 1925 issue of *American Magazine* in an article entitled "I Believe in Shooting Square with Man and God." Stewart recounts "the remarkable story of Charles Page, one of the biggest businessmen in the West, who has made millions only to give them away. First he contributed 10 percent of his income, then 25 percent, then 50 percent and, quoting Page, 'finally I decided to pass along everything I didn't need for living expenses, and I have been happier than I ever was before.'"

Giving Future Generations the Same Opportunities

Another book that profiles philanthropists and community service is Edward Pessen's *Riches, Class and Power Before the Civil War*. He writes largely of committed leaders in major American cities and provides examples of their "charities and other good works." Pessen also makes an additional contribution to our understanding of the history of philanthropy in the U.S. He portrays a growing gulf between society's elite and "the era of the common man" and suggests that many of the most sensitive and forward-looking philanthropists wanted to accelerate the transition rather than retard it.

The transition has indeed accelerated, with even greater changes in recent years. Much of the money is now seen as an investment to empower citizens to speak and act for themselves. Some recent random examples follow:

- The Cooperative Assistant Fund has existed since 1969 to improve the economic health of disadvantaged and low-income communities, particularly those communities in the urban North and rural South where large numbers of poor blacks and other minorities live. This Fund was begun by the Taconic Foundation and now involves twelve foundations and two church groups which pool program-related investment funds for loans to community based groups, including government-related bodies, to help develop minority-controlled businesses.

- The Dayton Hudson Foundation is involved in neighborhood revitalization offering, for example, substantial support over five years to restore the Whittier neighborhood in Minneapolis. The Whittier Alliance is composed of local residents who want a larger role in tackling their own community's problems and development, including housing and small business development.

- The Pfizer Company seeks partnerships with local groups in communities with special needs. For example, it supports units of ASPIRA of America serving Hispanics through educational programs and vocational counseling, leadership development, school placement and remedial tutoring.

- The Mellon Bank established the Mellon Community Fund to expand the bank's charitable support of local nonprofit initiatives that address economic development in the Pittsburgh area. For example, the bank supported a project to foster business and job growth in neighborhoods and communities in a six-county region of western Pennsylvania.

- Mellon Bank has also joined with the Howard Heinz Endowment, the Ford Foundation, and the City of Pittsburgh to fund the Pittsburgh Partnership for Neighborhood Development which works, "to provide multi-year operating support for community development organizations in five Pittsburgh neighborhoods."

- In 1984, Amoco awarded more than $1 million to 60 community development and neighborhood rehabilitation organizations in the Chicago area, including a $150,000 grant to Bethel New Life Inc., "To add staff for the nonprofit organization's housing rehabilitation efforts."

- The American Can Company launched "America Can!" a public service program designed to spotlight the diverse ways Americans and American business are solving "complex economic and social problems, addressing quality of life issues and making significant contributions to their communities." The company's employees are encouraged to apply for funds to help strengthen projects in their own communities.

- Andrew Sigler and his Champion International Corporation accept a major responsibility for strengthening communities in which they do business, including their headquarters community of Stamford, Connecticut. Sigler has served as Chairman of the Stamford Economic Assistance Corporation.

- General Mills undertook a program to rehabilitate the Stevens Court inner-city neighborhood in Minneapolis. As part of the program, more than $8 million of corporate assets were invested in renovating 17 residential units in 26 buildings.

- Ogilvy and Mather established a program called "block builders" to help rebuild selected blocks in New York City.

- Federated Department Stores, headquartered in Cincinnati, trains their employees and others to identify and address neighborhood needs in Cincinnati and other cities where the company has stores.

- The Sun Company has made a major commitment to fund community development organizations, including a $1 million investment in a run-down riverport in Chester, Pennsylvania.

- Battelle Memorial Institute in Columbus, Ohio made a major commitment for "inner-city service," which included investing $21 million in rehabilitating 330 residential structures and 114 vacant lots in a specific neighborhood.

- Ætna established FOCUS, a major program to target the efforts of the company and its managers and employees in 18 cities, to marshall the company's funds, talents, and other assets to address specific needs in distressed communities.

- The Riley Foundation adopted a major program priority called "Community Development and Neighborhood Democracy," which involves a major investment in Boston's Dudley Street neighborhood, a multi-racial and economically depressed community.

- The Phil Hardin Foundation in Meridian, Mississippi joined with the National Conference of Black Mayors and the Robert F. Kennedy Memorial to develop a training program for black public officials in poor regions of Mississippi.

- The Enterprise Foundation is dedicated to developing housing for the poorest of the poor. Its Jubilee Housing Projects began in Washington, D.C. and are now located in inner-city neighborhoods of many cities.

- The Headwaters Fund in the Twin Cities launched "Change Not Charity" to help develop local leadership in neighborhoods that have not been able to get adequate attention paid to their urgent priorities.

- The Hunt Alternatives Fund targets its work in Dallas, Denver, and New York, the three communities where the founders have strongest ties. The fund has given priority to neighborhood development and community-wide activities that relate to vulnerable people and populations.

Building Local Pride and Making Our Community Special

I am not sure that one can make a very clear distinction between civic duty and pride, but there are some philanthropic activities that, while responding to real needs, nevertheless focus on the amenities, spirit, and joy of a place. The closest I can come to a distinction is fixing streets and planting flowers.

Mary Lasker plants flowers. Like many generous people, she is active on many fronts including health research, but she also plants flowers, and flowers help make her community special. A *New Yorker* story called "Lady Philanthropist" began: "We just had a talk with Mrs. Mary Lasker, who gave the city all those tulips and daffodils that came up this spring in the middle of Park Avenue between 50th and 72nd streets." The story quotes Lasker,

> In the Fall of 1955, I persuaded the parks department to let me contribute tulip bulbs for planting in front of the Public Library and the Metropolitan Museum and on 4 blocks of Park Avenue . . . and grow tulips, roses, and lilacs. . . . I think there should be a three-season festival of flowers in New York, with tulips and daffodils in the Spring, begonias and salvia in the Summer, and chrysanthemums in the Fall. My three stepchildren and I gave 300 Japanese cherry trees to the United Nations, in memory of my husband, and I wish someone would give 10,000 lilac trees to Central Park. New York should be full of flowers and flowering trees, our buildings should be lighted at night, and all the fountains in town should *play.* Washington Square and the borders of the Westside Highway should be alive with flowers. This sort of thing makes the city gay and pleasant, and is good commercially. We should make joy and pleasure for ourselves, *and* attract new business to New York.

When Syntex loaned some of its land to the organization Ecology Action for agricultural testing it made sure that some of the land was devoted to flowers to make that common ground beautiful as well as productive. The organization, Gardens for All, is dedicated to making certain that urban areas are dotted with flowers, shrubs, and trees that lift the spirit. James Rouse and his Enterprise Foundation want to be certain that every neighborhood includes a community park, gardens, and playground not unlike the original New England "common green."

"Public Spirit in St. Louis" was the title of an article in the 1890 *Review of Reviews,* which observed:

> The most conspicuous philanthropist of St. Louis was the late Henry Shaw who, twenty years before his death, gave to the city the beautiful Tower Grove Park, which he himself laid out and cared

for. He founded the world-famed Shaw's Garden—undoubtedly the finest botanical garden in America—which upon his death at the age of 86 two years ago, he left to the city, together with his fortune of $2 or $3 million for its maintenance.

In *Philanthropic Foundations,* Andrews records: "The estate of Henry C. Trexler provides that one-fourth of the net income 'shall be paid annually and perpetually into the treasury of the City of Allentown, to be used by the City for the improvements, extension and maintenance of all its parks.'" Andrews also says: "The Sarah Mellon Scaife Foundation built a Children's Zoo in Pittsburgh, supports a recreation program for Pittsburgh teenagers, and financed a three-year planning program enabling the city to plant some 700 trees a year along its streets and establish a tree and shrub nursery."

In a 1961 article, "Tradition and Innovation in American Philanthropy," prepared for the American Philosophical Society, historian Merle Curti wrote:

Closely related on the one level to the effort to encourage the role of esthetic values in American life has been the more comprehensive growth of the civic spirit, as expressed in support for parks, buildings and civic improvement in general. In a sense, a legacy of the Greek and Roman emphasis on the community in contradistinction to the Judaeo-Christian concern with the individual, the civic spirit has developed in America largely without direct government initiative and support, with such notable exceptions as the building of the nation's capital and the creation and maintenance of state and national parks. In the history of every American city the town fathers and solid citizens who made or enlarged their fortunes while contributing to the industrial and commercial growth of the city were spearheads of civic benevolence . . . .

. . . In later decades of the 19th and in the early 20th century, the wives of these urban leaders began to play a similar role which greatly impressed many foreign visitors. These men and women took pride in the reputation of their city for benevolence, public spirit, and civic duty.

For example, Stephen Girard's bequest of $500,000 to the city of Philadelphia to improve the Delaware River waterfront . . . the gift of a group of New Yorkers, including Harriman and Morgan, which made possible the preservation of the natural beauty of the Palisades and of Bear Mountain . . . the gifts of William Kemp to salvage and preserve the giant redwoods north of San Francisco . . . and the fund established by George Robert White to create in greater Boston works of public beauty and utility not to be expected from the city treasury.

Kathleen McCarthy's *Noblesse Oblige* also describes ways in which philanthropic arts changed the face of cities. For example: "Travel reinforced benevolent impulses, registering vivid models for new undertakings. When Chicago lumberman Benjamin Ferguson visited Europe for the first time, he was dazzled by the civic statuary which he beheld at every turn. On his return, he drew up a will bequeathing $1 million for the commissioning of municipal monuments." McCarthy quotes Ferguson: "'I would that at every turn were statue or monument or building, rich in artistic design, which would set forth ideas of beauty, grace or power, or speak of some noble soul whose life was far above that of his fellows.'" McCarthy notes later that this effort to uplift Chicago served two purposes: "By celebrating Chicago, they celebrated themselves."

Some of that effort was, according to McCarthy, prompted by a sense that Chicago was somehow a second-class city and that its leaders were therefore less prominent than those in New York and Boston. McCarthy notes, "In addition to serving as lasting monuments to their creators, cultural amenities help to mitigate the city's decidedly unsavory reputation as the home of pig stickers . . . and the notorious Scar-Face Al Capone." She concludes,

> Donors touted their gifts in quantitative terms, emphasizing that each was the first, biggest, or best. The Adler Planetarium was the first in the Western Hemisphere; the Shedd Aquarium, the largest in the world; the Museum of Science and Industry, the first in the nation. Suitably embellished by museums and universities, patrons hoped to make Chicago once again, the Athens of the West.

New York's civic leaders were not without similar motivations. In *Bankers, Bones & Beetles: The First Century of the American Museum of Natural History,* Geoffrey Hellman presents this excerpt from the minutes of the 1890 trustees meeting, marking the death of Mr. Hugh Auchincloss:

> In associating himself with us, Mr. Auchincloss was not prompted by any peculiar interest in any special branch of science, but by the larger view of affording support and encouragement to an enterprise embracing a wide field designed to aid in freeing his native city from something like scientific aridity . . . .

As a total aside and only for the fun of it, Hellman goes on a bit about the fact that years after it was built, no one could recall where the cornerstone was. "The cornerstone itself, containing a copper box stuffed with

Museum and Parks Department reports, a manual of the State's legislature, a Congressional Directory, copies of 12 New York newspapers, three magazines, a paper dollar, a silver dollar, and some small change also disappeared, or was lost, probably forever." No one at the museum today knows where it is, and no one knew on September 17, 1941 when Mr. Wayne M. Faunce, vice-director and executive secretary of the Temple of Nature, wrote the late Edward Ringwood Hewitt:

> I recall that at one of the annual meetings of the Anglers Club held in the American Museum of Natural History, you referred to the fact that you had been present at the laying of the cornerstone of the museum. It is a source of chagrin that no one now connected with the museum knows the location of this cornerstone. . . . Can you throw any light on the matter?

Mr. Hewitt responded,

> My Dear Mr. Faunce,
>
> I was only a small boy when the cornerstone of the museum was laid and the whole place was covered with a cloth except the stone. There would be no way in which a small boy could tell where it was as there was a wooden stand erected all over the place. Besides, I can't see the location of the cornerstone as a matter of any importance at all.
>
> Yours truly,

Mr. Hewitt concluded, "There the matter rests; the museum is in good company, since no one at the Smithsonian knows where *its* cornerstone, laid in 1847, is either."

Returning momentarily to Chicago: the Consolidated Foods Foundation continues the effort to build pride in the city through its annual "Chicago Spirits Awards." The awards are given annually in recognition and support of nonprofit organizations that demonstrate leadership in improving the quality of life in Chicago."

Atlanta was blessed with the interest of Robert W. Woodruff and his Coca-Cola Company. In the *Big Foundations*, Waldemar Nielsen writes:

> The major program interest of the foundation has been capital projects in the Atlanta area, particularly those serving a regional purpose. Woodruff wanted to help make Atlanta into an absolutely first class city, offering its city and people throughout the South an opportunity for the best health care, best art, and best education. Much of this he attempted to do through his enormous gifts to Emory University, including the major gifts to its medical school and the famous gift of $100 million.

Nielsen adds, "Another major project initiated by Woodruff is the Atlanta Arts Alliance, which has received some $8 million from the foundation and an additional $6 million from Woodruff friends and other foundations." In his biography of Woodruff titled *Mr. Anonymous*, Charles Elliot says: "His largess has transformed the face of his hometown of Atlanta and enriched its cultural institutions." Woodruff and his longtime associate, Boisfeuillet Jones, also exercised sustained influence over the desegregation of Atlanta institutions.

Many philanthropic efforts that have focused on building community pride and making a community special have focused on the arts. For example, the New Canaan Community Foundation launched the New Canaan Society for the Arts in the old carriage barn of an estate that the town purchased, and the San Francisco Foundation, in addition to its support of major arts organizations, developed a program to fund "emerging arts groups which reflect the heritages of the area's Latino, African, Asian, and American Indian populations." Cleveland has been home to many generous philanthropists including Frederick Goff, who added to his accomplishments by establishing the Cleveland Foundation, thereby giving inspiration to the community foundation movement. Cleveland philanthropists and philanthropies have a remarkable record of providing service and stimulating civic pride even during the city's most difficult times. Two recent projects suggest that civic pride in Cleveland is still very much alive. The first example goes by the title, "Cleveland Tomorrow." The story is told by the group's President, William R. Seelbach, in 1983 testimony before the Ways and Means Committee:

> Cleveland Tomorrow's ability to clearly articulate the key problems facing the region, to investigate and screen the best programs of other communities and to understand the detailed organizational dynamics of the Cleveland community rests largely on the fact that we have the resources to study and learn these things, unburdened by the constraints of an insufficient budget to complete a particular investigation . . . . Over an 18-month period, the Gund Foundation contributed over $800,000 to support the committee . . . without that funding, I am confident that we would not have been able to achieve the kind of program we're experiencing today . . . . In my mind, the Cleveland Tomorrow project, funded by the Gund Foundation, represents a particularly good example of the benefits resulting from private, nongovernmental initiatives which can produce important and broad public benefits.

The second Cleveland project involves a peculiar partnership between the Cleveland Foundation and the German Marshall Fund. Even in this age of collaboration, it is curious to see a foundation focused on one community working so closely with a foundation established to improve international understanding. What brought them together was their mutual interest in a lakefront. The Marshall Fund's interest and involvement stem from its efforts to help European and American communities learn from one another, and the Cleveland Foundation wanted to learn how European cities were able to make their waterfronts accessible and attractive. Cleveland, like many American cities, had allowed its waterfront properties to be taken over for industrial use and they gradually became unsafe eyesores.

With the small sum of just $15,000 the Cleveland Foundation was able to take advantage of the Marshall Fund's offer of help, and out of that has grown one of the most massive projects in the histories of both Cleveland and Ohio. In the beginning, however, the idea that foundation money would be used to support an inspection tour of European cities and their waterfronts was greeted with cynicism and suspicion. Critics called it a terrible boondoggle, a waste of public officials' time and a waste of foundation funds. Imagine the furor over a trip to Europe to look at parks for people who worked in such offices as the city planning department, state house of representatives, and department of natural resources.

Patricia Jansen Doyle of the Cleveland Foundation was part of the study team and has written an account of the team's trip and its outcome. Her account is provided under the good heading, "People on the Waterfronts of Europe: The Preview for Cleveland Lakefront State Park."

> As Cleveland stands on the threshold of developing its long-neglected asset, its lakefront, it could well take cues from European port cities. Places like Hamburg and Rotterdam, Helsinki and Stockholm reveal a potential for welcoming people to the water's edge and provide insights into changing lifestyles in an increasingly energy-troubled yet leisure-oriented society.
>
> This was evident to a Cleveland study group which this summer (1979) visited European parks and met with park and town planners on a tour funded by the German Marshall Fund in cooperation with the Cleveland Foundation. . . .
>
> The urban parks draw hundreds, sometime thousands of visitors on a sunny day or summer evening—a testimony to the skillful management of space which caters to many recreational tastes. And the urban parks overlooking coastlines, rivers, and bays show sophisticated development of beaches, fishing piers, rowing courses and marinas, marinas and more marinas. The stroller, long

welcomed at the shoreline, is now being joined by the physical
fitness enthusiasts. . . .

Furthermore, European cities are willing to accept mixed uses of
their harbors; parks, children's playgrounds, bird sanctuaries and
even houses are accepted among shipping docks, industrial plants
and warehouses while the most central stretches of shoreline often
are reserved for promenades and important public buildings,
including museums, theaters and convention centers.

After six long years of controversy and struggle, the city and state are
committed to a $71.1 million construction program along the lake-area
shore stretching from Cleveland to Toledo. The area around Cleveland
will include a stadium, parks, promenades, shops, and aquarium, and lots
of running room. At this point, there are still many obstacles to overcome
to make the dream a total reality, but the plan is at hand, and the work has
begun. Incidentally, Jansen has also told this story under another attractive heading, "Urban Parks: From Europe with Love."

A similar "junket" funded by the German Marshall Fund for Washington D.C. and Northern Virginia officials was criticized initially by the
press but has turned out to be an important stimulus to the almost miracu-
lous restoration of the Potomac River waterfront. The Mayor of Alexandria, Virginia has described how the assistance made a difference to his
community:

Alexandria's waterfront objectives call for public access, mixed use,
a continuous promenade along the water's edge and plenty of public
green space and recreational land along the Potomac river, as well
as the recycling of obsolete industrial structures on the waterfront.
All of these objectives have been accomplished in various ways in
the European locales visited by the Alexandria team and some of
the European solutions are being put into effect along the
Alexandria waterfront. . . . European city planners who led us
through their plans and thought processes, through their finished
products of green spaces, bricks and mortar, will have a tangible
effect on Alexandria's mile and a half long waterfront and its
contiguous two square mile hinterland.

A smaller scale but still impressive project, and one that is closer to real-
ization, was funded by a gift of $1 million from the Procter and Gamble
Fund to the City of Cincinnati in 1976, coinciding with the bicentennial,
to permit the development of the riverfront. This planning and development grant has also multiplied thousands of times in terms of investment
by others and results for everyone in Cincinnati.

The city of Chattanooga, Tennessee has benefited by the money and effort of the Lyndhurst Foundation, which sparked the creation of a visionary twenty-year plan for Chattanooga's 20-mile riverfront. Lyndhurst also joined with the city, surrounding county, and other publicly appointed citizens in a planning process that covered four years and involved more than 60 public meetings in all parts of town. The collaboration led to the creation of a $750 million long-term economic development plan that embraces the city's history and natural environment, as well as its industrial and economic base. Lyndhurst further played a role in creating, designing, and funding a public–private partnership to lead the development, drawing upon the participation of elected officials, top corporate chairmen, and representatives of the black and labor communities. It is estimated that all of the major Chattanooga foundations will jointly capitalize this nonprofit development corporation at about $12 million.

In many communities, philanthropy, in partnership with enterprising nonprofit organizations, has taken the lead in restoring buildings, blocks and neighborhoods. Speaking of some of the efforts in Dallas-Fort Worth, Texas, David Rockefeller said:

> If I were fortunate enough to live in your community, I am sure I would feel similar pride and satisfaction if I could be involved in such projects as Wilson Block, which was spearheaded by the Meadows Foundation, or the keystone project, which was spearheaded by the Richardson Foundation. Both are splendidly deserving projects that have demanded not only money, but substantial vision, time and personal involvement. The Pyramid Project, also sponsored by the Richardson Foundation, is an excellent example of the very real benefits of *long-term* commitment to the careful development of concept.

The Cause of Communities and Neighborhoods

The value of building a sense of pride in and paying back to one's community have become so obvious that many of the larger national foundations have begun to seed the development of community foundations which in turn provide a vehicle for local participation. Eugene Struckoff, former President of the Council on Foundations and specialist on community foundations, was the first to call formal attention to this development in an article in the January/February, 1985 *Foundation News.* His theme was that "a growing number of private foundations are helping to start community foundations." Among the examples cited are the following:

- The Bush Foundation has given $750,000 to help form the Duluth-Area Community Foundation in Minnesota.

- The Kresge Foundation has given $5 million to help establish the Community Foundation of Southeastern Michigan.
- The Hewlett Foundation has given $500,000 to create several new community foundations in northern California.
- The Charles Stewart Mott Foundation has "initiated a nation-wide program to encourage the formation and growth of community foundations . . . and has committed $750,000 to community endowments in six areas from the District of Columbia to North Dakota."
- The Levi Strauss Foundation and Aetna Life and Casualty Foundation "have instituted grant programs to start and revitalize community foundations in areas where their related business corporations have facilities and interest."
- The Gannett Foundation has already committed more than three quarters of a million dollars for "start-up or revitalization grants to nearly two dozen community foundations."
- The Bremer, Northwest Area, and Bush foundations have provided grants to develop a statewide community foundation in North Dakota.
- The Jessie B. Cox Charitable Trust has given the New Hampshire Charitable Fund a $200,000 grant to "energize community foundations in Maine and Vermont."
- The Irvine Foundation has given $150,000 "to start a community foundation for California's capital area of Sacramento."

In all, Struckoff lists 45 communities that have been helped by these and other national foundations to develop community foundations. He summarizes:

> These are the directions in which the community foundation field is headed: a community foundation to be put in place in every significant population center, revitalization of community foundations whose growth is slowed, purposefully accelerated growth to its takeoff point for every community foundation with assets under $10 million, and an increase in permanent unrestricted endowment to give each community foundation a greater capacity to respond to changing needs in its area.
>
> These are the objectives of the community foundation field and of the growing number of private foundations and corporations that see community foundations as the prime device for the formation of flexible, private charitable capital for our nation's communities.

Struckoff concluded his article on community foundations by saying, "Their ultimate goal is the long-term strength of each community's capacity to respond to its own needs with private resources raised from local donors."

To test his expectation against grants actually being made by community foundations already in operation, I sampled some community foundation reports. The exercise made clear that a good community foundation does facilitate local investment in a wide variety of community endeavors. For example, at its June 11, 1985 meeting, one of five grant-making sessions for the year, the Greater Boston Foundation voted approximately $1.25 million to 71 projects of which the following are illustrative:

> **Allston-Brighton Community Development Corporation,** $15,000 for the Community Parks Improvement Project.
>
> **Anchorage, Inc.,** $50,000, one-time grant to establish a group home for adolescent girls in Beverly.
>
> **Boston Committee, Inc./Partnership, Inc.,** $200,000, for initial operating expenses of the Partnership, Inc., a newly merged entity focusing efforts to address problems of racism in Boston.
>
> **Boston University School of Social Work,** $50,000, a conditional challenge grant to establish an education center for human service professionals to work with Southeast Asian refugees.
>
> **Bridge Fund, Inc.,** $25,000, a conditional grant toward start-up costs of the preschool day care program.
>
> **Cardinal Cushing Center for the Spanish Speaking,** $31,000, to support the community women and education components of Project AMOR.
>
> **Coping with the Overall Pregnancy Experience, Inc.,** $25,000, to increase the services of the child abuse prevention project at Boston City Hospital.
>
> **Cotting School for Handicapped Children,** $62,700, a two-year grant to establish a special-education service program.
>
> **Don Orione Nursing Home,** $70,000, for modification of the heating system.
>
> **Greater Boston Legal Services, Inc.,** $40,000, for the cost of staff salaries for the new High Volume Eviction Defense Program.
>
> **Help for Abused Women and Their Children, Inc.,** $20,000, toward renovations of its temporary shelter for battered women and their children.
>
> **Hospice Care, Inc.** $50,000, a conditional grant for the costs of merging with the Hospice of Middlesex East.

Judge Baker Guidance Center, $27,000, for the Divorce
Mediation Service.

Massachusetts Committee Arts for the Handicapped, $20,000, a
two-year grant toward the cost of developing a model, in-school
arts program for children in separate special-needs classes at five
Boston Public Schools.

Massachusetts Law Reform Institute, Inc., $59,000 to establish
a pilot program for indigent, disabled, and mentally disabled
clients at Cambridge/Somerville Legal Services.

North End Union/North Bennet Street School, $120,000, a
three-year grant to the North End Union to assist with the
merger of the social service programs with the North Bennet
Street School.

Public/Private Ventures Program, up to $50,000 for a six-month
grant to support the continued administrative operation of the
Fund for the Homeless satellite office.

Regional Family YMCA, $100,000, a conditional grant for
construction of an addition to the main building in Framingham.

Salvation Army, $25,000, for a second-year support for the
salaries of the program director and bilingual social worker at
the Chelsea Community Center.

South Cove Community Health Center, $40,000 to establish
Family Focus, a mental health and social service project for
Indochinese refugee families.

South Cove Nursing Facilities Foundation, Inc., $100,000, a
challenge grant for construction and initial operating costs of
South Cove Manor.

Span, Inc., $20,000 to expand the Boston counseling and
assistance program for ex-prisoners.

Suffolk University, $100,000, a challenge grant for expansion of
its endowment for support of the Learning Center.

Trustees of Health and Hospitals/City of Boston, $25,000, grant
for the Boston Growth Survey Project to support completion of
a study of malnutrition in children who attend Boston City
Hospital's walk-in and primary care clinics.

Tufts University, Dept. of Urban & Environmental Policy,
$31,000 to support completion of the Boston Primary Health
Care Project.

United South End Settlements, $120,000, a conditional, two-
year grant for development of programs in housing/
neighborhood development, and employment education and
training.

Just as community foundations are increasingly committed to community and neighborhood development, so too a growing number of private foundations and business corporations have chosen as their primary focus the support of the vitality of communities.

San Francisco's Rosenberg Foundation has a 50-year history of service to the Bay Area and to California. Its recent emphasis has been on early childhood development, older youth, neighborhood development, and immigration policy.

From its earliest years the Gund Foundation has concentrated its resources on community-based solutions to problems in the Greater Cleveland area. A recent evaluation report of the Gund Foundation said:

> Perhaps one of the most lasting contributions by the foundation to its community is the organized neighborhood movement. Beginning in late 1977, the foundation supported the efforts of the Catholic Commission on Community Action to systematically organize several core neighborhoods. Professional organizers were hired to work with neighborhood block clubs to create coalitions to advocate for the residents' interest with city government and private institutions such as banks. . . . The thesis underlining the organizing strategy was that the empowerment of lower-income residents to enable them to confront the problems in their neighborhoods was essential to achieving progress in Cleveland. The organizing effort had several purposes. First it was hoped that community institutions would become more responsive to the concerns of neighborhoods. Second, it was believed that organized neighborhoods would begin to play a more active role in undertaking self-help initiatives. Third, it was believed that the active involvement of residents would give them more of a sense of hope in face of the difficult circumstances they confronted . . . . The final element in the foundation's neighborhood strategy is the Neighborhood Self-Help Development Program which, beginning in 1981, made nearly $750,000 available for projects. The intent of this program was to provide the necessary "seed" to encourage neighborhood initiatives to provide lower cost food, energy, and housing to low-income residents. Innovative projects including housing rehabilitation, food cooperatives and weatherization were initiated. Several of these projects have mushroomed into community-wide, and even state-wide programs, thus leveraging significant public and private resources into low-income areas.

The Piton Foundation in Denver has been a leader in that community and increasingly a model for the country in its approach to community and neighborhood development. The foundation's name is symbolic. A piton is a "metal spike fitted at one end with an eye or ring through which to pass a rope, used in mountain climbing as a hold." The foundation's mission statement is "to foster community processes and development resources which enable citizens to come together to solve community problems." Current priorities are affordable housing, community economic development, family violence, families and adults in transition, strengthening neighborhoods, and local leadership development.

In the July/August, 1984 issue of *Foundation News*, Henry Lansford describes a project that was funded jointly by the Piton and Gates foundations, in an article titled "Resurrecting Denver's Lost Neighborhoods." He begins with a question:

> Can a large piece of valuable real estate—contiguous to a rapidly growing downtown business district—be redeveloped on a comprehensive "city building basis" rather than through a random series of individual private ventures?
>
> The boards of two Denver grantmaking institutions, the Piton and Gates foundations, have answered "yes" to this question by approving grants to support the work of the Platte Valley Development Committee . . . to "develop a plan that will include all the necessary zoning changes, public transportation, activity and recreational centers and general asthetic considerations." The chairman of the committee concluded "My vision of what will come out of our work is a concensus that the developers, the neighbors, downtown business people and all of the interests can live with and support for the next 30 years. The only way this plan will work is to represent a real consensus."

Another foundation that has long displayed leadership and vision in supporting neighborhood-based problem solving is the Charles Stewart Mott Foundation. From its organized interest in community education projects, the foundation has expanded into many related areas. It was instrumental in establishing a "C-grant program aimed at strengthening citizen initiative at the local level . . . . We've funded six Intermediary Support Organizations—ISOs (the United States was divided into six regions, each covered by one of the six ISOs)—which in turn provided seed grants and technical assistance to neighborhood-based groups working to solve critical neighborhood issues." These intermediary organizations included the Center for Community Change, the National Council of LaRaza, and the Youth Project. The Mott Foundation has also been a major force in a public/private venture known as "Flint Revitalization," which attempts "to turn around a distressed city which had the highest unemployment rate in the country at the depths of the recession."

The Winston-Salem Foundation has formed a nonprofit housing corporation which, according to a Council on Foundation's *Newsletter*, will "act primarily as a loan facilitator in conjunction with the housing programs of the city of Winston-Salem to deal with inter-city housing needs."

The Evelyn and Walter Haas Fund, the Bothin Helping Fund, and the San Francisco Foundation were the initial funders of Reality House West, a project to help rehabilitate one of the most dilapidated hotels in one of San Francisco's worst neighborhoods. The project was part of "a linch-pin effort" to improve the "tenderloin" district of San Francisco. It's a good story, told here by a Reality House report:

> In the mid-seventies, Reality House West was a ten-year-old social service agency, created by ex-convicts and other concerned people, that had developed a variety of rehabilitation, criminal justice, drug abuse, training and economic development projects under government grants and contracts. The agency, frustrated with government regulations and anticipating the tax payers revolt, decided to develop assets and an independent funding base by buying a residential hotel and providing housing, social services and economic development with the building.
>
> Located at the heart of San Francisco's seedy tenderloin district, the Cadillac Hotel was a seventy-year-old building that had been neglected for decades and was only one-third habitable when Reality House West convinced the owner to sell the building with no down payment in 1977. Reality House West then struggled to convince the community that not only did it own a major piece of downtown real estate, but that it also had the vision and capacity to be a leader in the preservation of an important central city neighborhood, to improve the Cadillac Hotel, and to develop a model for other central cities.
>
> The first financial support came from private foundations, and Reality House West hired senior citizens, ex-offenders and other low-income people to work together to rehabilitate and operate the hotel. With the hotel as a base, the staff and tenants worked to organize the 20,000 people that live within a four-block radius.
>
> Seven years later the Cadillac Hotel provides 157 units of low-income, non-subsidized housing and cultural activities. A franchise restaurant is being developed which will complete the complex and make the building and the reorganization self-supporting. The combination of entrepreneurial vision of Reality House West with

the trust and support of the foundation community created an important model, helped seniors and ex-offenders work together to improve their lives, and significantly strengthened a threatened low-income neighborhood.

Since that was written, the restaurant, against almost everybody's best bet, has come into being. Major help for that part of the effort and additional general support came from the Cowell, Irvine, and Wells Fargo foundations. Along the way, other major donors have been the Hewlett Foundation, Franciscan Charities, and Chevron U.S.A.

It is a natural transition from this role, "To Make Communities a Better Place to Live," and the next role, "To Nourish the Spirit," to cite the establishment of Paley Park, a "vest pocket" park and sanctuary from the urban bustle that surrounds it. The tale is best told by the funder William S. Paley, founder of CBS:

> Like many other cities, New York has become increasingly congested as new and larger buildings have risen to take care of our growing commercial and residential needs. As a New Yorker, I have long been convinced that, in the midst of all this building, we ought to set aside occasional spots of open space where our residents and visitors can sit and enjoy themselves as they pause in their days' activities.
>
> When I was casting about for an appropriate way to create a memorial to my father, Samuel Paley, who died in 1963 after a long and productive life largely spent in two great American cities, it occurred to me that to provide one such area in the very center of our greatest city would be the kind of memorial that would have pleased him most. And so, through the William S. Paley Foundation, Paley Park was established at 35 East 53rd Street, between Fifth and Madison avenues.
>
> The location, just east of Fifth Avenue, is in the midst of a heavily concentrated area of stores, hotels, offices, and museums. It is between two of the world's most favored avenues for strollers and shoppers. It is close to the bus and subway travelers. It is at the center of that part of the city most frequented by visitors. Altogether, it seemed an ideal place to try a new experiment for the enjoyment of the out-of-doors in the heart of the city.
>
> Consisting only of 4200 square feet on the north side of the street, the property has a frontage of 42 feet. The size of the plot is central to my concept that small areas in urban communities can be used for park purposes and that this can be done attractively and invitingly. A talented landscape architect and site planner, Robert

L. Zion, of Zion and Breen Associates, was commissioned to prepare plans and drawings. A detailed model was built from these drawings. Construction and plantings took nearly a year, and the Park was opened on May 23, 1967.

The basic plantings in the Park are 17 full-grown locust trees, placed at 12-foot intervals, the tops of which form a natural foliage canopy over the entire site. The side walls are covered with ivy, and geraniums are planted in the seating wall gardens. At the rear, there is a high "waterwall" which provides an effective visual background, softens traffic noises, and gives a pleasant and relaxing sound. The flooring of the Park is mahogany granite squares and the steps, walk and seating walls are blocks of Laurentian pink granite. The sidewalks and steps are heated to melt snow.

It is an integral part of the idea of the Park that it provide a comfortable and relaxing place for people to refresh themselves. Instead of the traditional benches, there are individual chairs and tables. Coffee, soft drinks, and sandwiches are available. The Park is suitably lighted to make its use possible during the evening.

While the primary purpose of the Park is to provide an attractive outdoor resting place in the midst of a huge city, I hope that it will have equal importance as an experiment in a new kind of small urban park. It is still possible, of course, to acquire large tracts of land for traditional parks in some of the outlying areas of our major cities. But there is a need also to have more parks of this kind in central urban locations where the population of residents, commercial employees, and visitors is most concentrated. In order to make the most of such relatively little areas, new approaches, new designs, and new techniques seem necessary. Paley Park is but one example of how a small site can be treated. But one of its promises would be fulfilled if it served as a pilot project that inspired others to undertake similar ventures and proved that small parks can be made inviting and add greatly to the variety and delight of city life.

The Park contains a small plaque with the following inscription:

This Park Is Set Aside
In Memory of Samuel Paley, 1875–1963,
For the Enjoyment of the Public

In his book, *To Dwell in Unity,* Philip Bernstein reminds us that through their basic religious and educational texts, headed "Ethics of the Fathers," Jews are taught, "Separate not thyself from the community" and that Jeremiah added, "Seek the welfare of the community in which you live, and pray for it, for in its welfare will be your peace."

7

To Nourish the Spirit

I. PRESERVING SPACES AND PLACES
II. ENCOURAGING CREATIVITY AND CREATIVE PEOPLE
III. BRINGING THE ARTS TO PEOPLE

Preserving Spaces and Places

The following testimony was prepared for delivery at hearings on "Tax Rules Governing Private Foundations" conducted by the Oversight Subcommittee of the Ways and Means Committee of the U.S. House of Representatives held in Washington, D.C., on June 27–30, 1983:

Mr. Chairman,

In its 31 years of non-profit, privately funded operations, The Nature Conservancy has brought under protection more than 2 million acres of carefully chosen wetlands, barrier islands, virgin forests and unploughed prairie remnants, and other examples of rapidly disappearing natural communities. These unique examples of our natural systems harbor numerous threatened species of plants and animals and constitute a priceless genetic and economic resource as well as an aesthetic and spiritual one for present and future generations of Americans.

The Conservancy is almost entirely dependent on contributions received from the private sector—some 350 private foundations, 165,000 individuals and more than 500 corporations which share our belief in the necessity of protecting our rich and diverse natural heritage. Such support has resulted in the preservation of irreplaceable natural land and water systems in all 50 States. It also permits us to own and manage the largest private sanctuary system in the United States, if not the world. And, at this time, The Nature Conservancy is probably acquiring more land for preservation of rare and endangered natural systems and species than any other agency, public or private.

In recent years, over one-half of our total revenue has been contributed by private foundations. Each year we are the recipient of private foundation grants ranging in size from less than $1,000 to, in a very few cases, as much as $10–25 million. . . .

The newest of these initiatives is our recently announced five-year, $50 million private/public effort—The National Wetlands Conservation Project—to protect outstanding examples of our country's most threatened aquatic and water-related ecosystems. The program was initiated with the largest grant ever made by a private foundation for conservation purposes; a $25 million 1:1 challenge grant from the Richard King Mellon Foundation.

. . . The Conservancy's Katharine Ordway Endangered Species Conservation Program was launched early this year with a $5 million, 1:2 challenge grant from the Goodhill Foundation of New York. The program . . . is designed to protect some of the vanishing habitats of plant and animal species in greatest danger of early extinction.

. . . Foundation support has also enabled the Conservancy to work cooperatively with state governments in establishing innovative state Natural Heritage (Inventory) Programs. These comprehensive inventory efforts, now established in more than 30 states, provide the Conservancy and other private and public agencies with sound ecological data on the natural areas and flora and fauna most in need of protection. This results in the effective and efficient use of scarce private and public conservation dollars. The Andrew W. Mellon Foundation has made a number of major grants to these programs, most recently a $1 million grant which will help extend the heritage process all across the country. Other foundations have supported individual state heritage programs, and a generous grant from the J. N. Pew, Jr. Charitable Trust led to the establishment of a New England Regional Heritage Program, the first such regional inventory, last year. . . .

William D. Blair, Jr.
President
The Nature Conservancy

If anything nurtures the spirit in this urbanized society, it is access to open, undeveloped space of the kind preserved so effectively by The Nature Conservatory and many other such groups. The extraordinary list of foundations and corporations involved in these efforts—not only to improve the quality of human life, but also to protect endangered animal and plant life—is testimony to the impact philanthropy has had in preserving our country's resources for future generations.

The Nature Conservancy's projects have also produced some philanthropists who may not have known what "philanthropist" means or that they had the money to qualify. In the January/February, 1985 issue of *Foundation News*, Craig Smith tells the story of one of these unintentional philanthropists:

> Old Willie Brown was in a bind. The "river rat"—that's what his rural Florida neighbors called him—had to come up with some quick cash. He'd never had to worry much about money before. After all, he and his brother built this home with bare hands and just a few dollars. And his suit of clothes he bought 50 years ago, and it was still just fine.
>
> All the income he'd needed before was just a few hundred bucks a year. He got that by selling alligator skins, enough of them to thin out the over-supply that dozed like dead logs around his nearly 400 acres of untouched swamplands.
>
> But now, as the Jacksonville suburbs closed in on him, Willie was thrust unhappily into the cash economy. Land taxes were skyrocketing.
>
> The prospect that he might have to sell his property to developers disgusted Willie. After all, to his mind it wasn't really his land at all. He was just its protector. His father gave him the title in 1905 on his 16th birthday. "Dad said 'Now you look after it. Don't let the hunters in here.' And I never have," says Willie.
>
> Word of Willie's dilemma found its way to the Florida field office of a non-profit organization called The Nature Conservancy, which offered a solution. In return for donating all his property to the Conservancy, Willie would get everything he wanted: the right to live there until he died, a small salary to continue as caretaker and, most importantly, the assurance that the swampland would remain forever in its natural state.
>
> The Conservancy, for its part, acquired one of the few remaining natural wetlands in the Jacksonville area, the home of endangered bald eagles and precious yellow crowned night herons. On the open market, the property would have cost well over $1 million. But to conservationists, the land was priceless. . . . Willie Brown's solution was business as usual for The Nature Conservancy.

William Gladstone Steel faced a different kind of dilemma, one that led him to become a very deliberate philanthropist. John Ise was commissioned by Resources for the Future, to produce *Our National Park Policy,* in which he tells the story of Steel's lifelong effort to preserve Crater Lake in California:

> He was probably still in his teens when he stood on the rim and saw the unearthly, unbelievable blue of the lake, lovelier than ever he could have pictured it and he resolved that he would make it a national park; and he devoted the rest of his life to this great purpose, and to the care of the park after it was established. Many years later, he was to summarize the experience at a 1911 National Parks conference. "Aside from the United States government itself, every penny that was ever spent in the creation of Crater Lake National Park came out of my pocket, and besides that, it required many years of hard labor that was freely given. When that was accomplished, I felt that my long labor was finished, and was so green, so simple-minded, that I felt that the United States government would go ahead and develop the proposition. In this, I found that I was mistaken, so I had to go to work again. All the money I have is in the park, and if I had more, it would go there too. This is my last work, and I propose to see it through."

Ise also provides glimpses into the beginnings of the Muir Woods National Monument in California, which saved the giant trees for people to marvel at for what we hope will be endless generations. Ise writes: "These giant redwoods had been saved from the lumbermen by former Congressman William Kent and his wife, who offered the grove to the government, asking that it be named not after themselves, but after the famous naturalist John Muir."

When I asked Paul Pritchard, president of the National Parks and Conservation Association, for ideas about "great gifts" he sent three books that have proved fascinating reading and have yielded many more stories than space permits me to recount here. It was particularly instructive to learn of the pioneering effort of Steven Mather from the book *Steven Mather of the National Parks* by Robert Shankland, who writes:

> Many hands have joined in the common effort to build up our unparalleled National Parks system. But the untrammeled vision, steady purpose, and indefatigable labor of one man stand out above all else. To Steven Tyng Mather, father of our National Park Service, the people of the United States owe a lasting debt of deep gratitude.
>
> In 1914 Mr. Mather, an influential and wealthy Chicago industrial leader, visited some of our National Parks in the West. He was dissatisfied with the manner in which they were conducted, and he

wrote a letter of protest to Washington. Soon he received a reply
from Franklin K. Lane, Secretary of the Interior, and an old college
chum at the University of California, urging him to come to the
Capital, take charge of the parks, and "run them yourself." . . . Two
years later the National Park Service was founded, with Mr. Mather
as its director. . . .

Congress lagged far behind the new director's plans in
appropriating funds to carry out his progressive ideas. So Mr.
Mather dipped into his own pocket to advance the National Parks.

Scenic Tioga Road, for example, was the only entrance across the
Sierra Nevada into Yosemite National Park. It was a toll road
owned by a mining company. Aided by some California friends, but
contributing most of the money himself, Mr. Mather bought the
road and gave it to the government. Today tens of thousands of
visitors to Yosemite enjoy this spectacular approach.

Mr. Mather gathered many groups of men and women—
journalists, businessmen, and those prominent in public life—often
giving dinner parties in Washington and in the different states, at
his own expense, for four or five hundred people, to arouse interest
in the National Park program.

His guests heard addresses and saw amusing skits based on the
preservation of our scenic wonderlands. By his genius for friendship
and his astonishing energy and enthusiasm he fired their interest in
the movement and put the parks on the solid ground they occupy
today. He took a leading part in adding many new National Parks—
Grand Canyon, Bryce, Zion, Acadia, Lassen, Hawaii, and Mount
McKinley—and through enabling legislation made certain the
future creation of Great Smoky Mountains, Shenandoah, and
Mammoth Cave.

The National Parks system that Mather brought about is an
American innovation. No other country, not even Switzerland,
despite its world-renowned scenic splendor, had attempted to
develop areas for public use along such lines. Many other countries
have in recent years copied the American plan for National Park
preservations.

Mather was succeeded by Horace M. Albright, himself the subject of a
book, *Wilderness Defender: Horace M. Albright and Conservation,* by
Donald C. Swain. Albright, in addition to being a brilliant administrator
who carried forward many of the ideas of Mather and other conservationists, was the individual who cultivated the interest of John D. Rockefeller,
Jr. and his sons, particularly Laurance, in land conservation. Swain's book
describes Rockefeller's growing interest in the park system:

. . . John D. Rockefeller, Jr. visited Yellowstone and went away
wondering how he might assist the superintendent in enhancing and
preserving the park's natural beauty. He had previously purchased
several parcels of land for Acadia National Park in Maine, but this
trip marked his full entry into national park philanthropy. In tow
with Rockefeller were sons John, Nelson and Laurance, who though
only 14, obviously caught a spirit that was to influence him and his
philanthropy all his life.

For every example of a major contribution to the National Parks and
Forests there are scores of local efforts to preserve and beautify land that
is closer to home. One typical but still inspiring example is Gardens in the
Woods in Framingham, Massachusetts. The Gardens is one of hundreds of
official botanic gardens nurtured by individuals or organizations for preservation of space and beauty. Now 50 years old, The Gardens was established by Will C. Curtis with his own funds and labor. He was joined later
by a partner Howard O. "Dick" Stiler. The story is told by Margaret
Hensel in the May, 1981 issue of *Horticulture:*

The setting for this springtime spectacular is a dramatic landscape
of sharp, glacier-made ridges spilling into narrow valleys. At each
turn, exciting vistas and uncommon flowers entice visitors exploring
the three miles of trails. While 30 acres of the sanctuary have been
left as natural woodland, the remaining 15 acres are landscaped in
a naturalistic manner with over 1,500 species and varieties of native
wildflowers and plants, making the Garden in the Woods the largest
landscaped collection of native plants in the Northeast.

The Gardens is now maintained through the voluntary labor and management of the New England Wild Flower Society.
    One very early morning, with my internal clock still on Eastern time, I
was wandering through San Francisco's Golden Gate Park and came
across a small but elegant garden that has this inscription at its entrance:

The Garden of Shakespeare's Flowers
Established By
The California Spring Blossoms and Wild Flower Association
1928

As I strolled the garden which I gather is changed regularly to reflect
Shakespeare's references to blossoms of the season, I found these familiar
quotes:

Daffodils
That come before the swallow dares and take
The winds of March with beauty.

The Winters Tale IV, 4

I know a bank whereon the wild thyme blows,
Where oxlips and the nodding violet grows.
Quite overcanopied with luscious woodbine,
With sweet musk-roses and eglantine.
There sleeps Titania, some time of the night,
Lulled in these flowers with dances and delight.

A Midsummer Nights Dream II, 2

Whenever I think about gifts that nourish the spirit and warm the heart, I think of the California Spring Blossoms and Wild Flower Association.

On an even smaller scale, there is a spot in Central Park in New York City that is known as the "secret garden." The story was told by Susan Heller Anderson in the April 26, 1986 *New York Times* under the heading "In Central Park's Secret Garden, a Burst of Spring":

> The heady scent of lilacs, seductive and mysterious, wafts onto Fifth Avenue, luring pedestrians through an ornate wrought-iron gate at 105th Street. Inside is a six-acre explosion of color and smell and verdure that might be more at home in the English countryside than in upper Manhattan.
>
> This is New York's secret garden, the Conservatory Garden in Central Park. The garden, the triumph of the optimism of one woman, combined with the generous gift of a second, is in its full flower of lilacs, tulips, daffodils, crabapple and magnolia blossoms, azaleas and hyacinths—a fragrant breath of springtime that will last about 10 days.
>
> As she does most days, the director, Lynden B. Miller, was grubbing about in the dirt yesterday, marveling at tiny shoots whose progress only she could measure. In four years, she, more than anyone, has restored the garden to its original glory. . . . The flowering shrubs and bulbs are the gift of a Glen Vietor, who makes a yearly monetary contribution to the Conservatory Garden in memory of her daughter, Barbara Foster Vietor, who died in 1966 when she was 9. "My child died on May 17, which is when things burst into bloom" Mrs. Vietor said. "The flowering of spring seemed a nice thing in her memory."

The Hasbro Childrens' Foundation and the Center for Human Environment of the City University of New York collaborated to create "The
Playground for Ill Children" to serve as a model for play environments
across the country. These playgrounds will "1) provide play opportunities
for each type of disability and 2) encourage social interaction between disabled and non-disabled children."

In her article on community foundations in the March/April, 1982
Foundation News, Lois Roisman reports on two projects that are also preserving green spaces:

> The community foundation in Elizabeth City, North Carolina,
> worried about the deterioration of beautiful landscape along the
> causeway, acquired through donation 14,000 feet of land along the
> Pasquotank River, and has since made grants to a local beautification
> organization to turn the land into a causeway park. . . .
> In celebration of its 50th anniversary, the Watertown Foundation
> allocated $50,000 from its pool of unrestricted funds to the
> residents of the City of Watertown, New York. The funds will be
> used to build a Victorian garden in downtown Watertown, designed
> by the director of the office of horticulture at the Smithsonian
> Institution.

Even small special vistas are important to preserve. The Report of the
Commission on Foundations and Private Philanthropy mentioned that "[a]
foundation created by Mrs. Frances P. Bolton, former Congresswoman
from Ohio, saved the view from Mt. Vernon when it was threatened in
recent years." The Mt. Vernon estate itself had been restored and is
maintained by a voluntary organization, assisted by foundations and corporations—most recently as part of a major campaign spearheaded by
American Express.

Not only does philanthropy help preserve green spaces, it also works to
preserve our cultural and social heritage. For example, the Pittsburgh
Foundation awarded two grants to projects to preserve log cabins:

> The foundation awarded a $15,000 grant to the West Allegheny
> School District to restore the McAdow-McAdams log house owned
> by the school district and located in Findlay Township. Restoration
> will allow Wilson Elementary School to use the facility as part of its
> history and social sciences curricula. . . .
> The foundation also awarded a grant of $9,300 to the Ben Avon
> Area Historical Association to help restore the 1797 Dickson family
> log house, the oldest authenticated house in Ben Avon and one of
> the oldest in the north boroughs of the county. When restored, the
> Dickson family log house will be open for public tours, for school

field trips, and for interpreted exhibitions of local history. The grant will also be used to help develop an educational history-in-the-schools program.

Like the Nature Conservancy, the National Trust for Historic Preservation raises many millions of dollars each year from foundations, corporations, and individuals, and garners even more assets through the gifts of property. It works with more than 1,000 locally designated historic districts and has registered 250,000 buildings in its National Register of Historic Places. Its funding sources are fascinatingly varied. In 1984, seventy-six foundations, corporations, and individuals provided major general support gifts and many companies invested in the trust's Mortgage Fund. For example, the Travelers Companies provided $1 million in support of mortgages for rehabilitated urban housing. Yankee Publishing, Inc. gave $300,000 to support trust interns in New England, Margaret Douglas Hall bequeathed Brucecore, her family's estate in Cedar Rapids, Iowa, which is now used as an arts and conference center; Marion duPont Scott bequeathed Montpelier, President James Madison's home in Virginia; the Rockefellers placed their estate in Pocantico Hills, New York in the trust's stewardship; and 140,000 individuals and 800 organizations became members of the Trust.

Another project too well known to describe in detail, but too important to skip altogether, involves the contributions of John D. Rockefeller, Jr. for the restoration of Williamsburg. In response to my request, William Bennett, then chairman of the National Endowment for the Humanities, wrote:

> My list of great grants would have to include John D. Rockefeller, Jr.'s support for the restoration and operation of Williamsburg, Virginia, which has helped millions of young and old Americans get some sense of our Colonial life and of the ideas and principles which produced the Declaration of Independence and the Constitution.

During a conversation with John Gardner, he urged me to present the story of Williamsburg less in terms of preservation of a place than in terms of the living reminder of our history, an essential part of our elementary understanding of ourselves as a nation. Gardner commented that the founders of the effort to restore Williamsburg had foremost in mind the purpose of "out-of-school education." He described the results as "one of the best examples of an effective way to educate future generations to the basic roots and tenets of our democracy." Rockefeller himself described Williamsburg as "a place where the future may learn from the past."

Other massive philanthropic efforts to preserve a clear glimpse of our

early history for future generations include Henry Ford's support for
Greenfield Village in Michigan and George Wells and his family's support
for Sturbridge Village in Massachusetts.

In his paper, "The Philanthropic Impulse and the Democratization of
Traditions in America," commissioned by INDEPENDENT SECTOR as
the keynote for its 1986 Research Forum, Pulitzer Prize-winning historian Michael Kammen spoke of these gifts that preserve our past:

> What seems so intriguing from the perspective of a cultural
> historian is the process by which philanthropists have played such a
> crucial role in literally giving the American heritage back to the
> American people. Philanthropic individuals do many different sorts
> of things with their resources, obviously, and we have been tracing
> only one option. In my view it is a particularly noble choice; yet
> clearly it could not happen until the "climate of opinion" was right.
> You cannot give a people their heritage unless they believe they
> have one worth keeping and knowing. Most Americans did not come
> around to that position until about sixty years ago.
>
> Nevertheless, Ford and Rockefeller did have antecedents. The
> pair may have been the most lavish, but they were not the first.
> Consequently it is worth noting both their predecessors and some
> of their contemporaries, because doing so conveys a feel for the
> momentum that gradually accumulated, as well as a clearer sense of
> the particular moment when philanthropic folks decided to present
> America with the gift of its own culture. In 1887 a prominent
> lawyer in Buffalo, New York, James Frazer Cluck, left his large
> collection of manuscripts and letters, mostly written by prominent
> American writers and statesmen, to the Buffalo City Library. In
> 1901 George Rea Curwen gave all of his household effects to the
> Essex Institute in Salem, Massachusetts. That bequest largely
> furnished the period rooms and exhibition cases of the Institute's
> new museum, which opened in 1907—a turning point in the history
> of museum displays in the United States. In 1904 the first major
> collection of high style American furniture given to a public
> institution was bequested to the Museum of Art at the Rhode Island
> School of Design. Charles Pendleton made this gift with the
> provision that a Georgian-style structure be built to house it.
>
> The trend gained momentum in 1909 when James Ten Eyck gave
> his collection of fine china (more than 5,000 pieces) to the Albany
> Institute of History and Art. A year later Judge Alphonso Clearwater
> of Kingston, New York, began to place a superb 550 piece
> collection of American silver on loan to the Metropolitan Museum
> of Art. (In 1919 that ensemble became the most important

collection of native craftwork yet given to an American museum.)
In 1911 the Aldis American literature collection was presented to
Yale University. In 1923 William L. Clements gave the University
of Michigan his great compendium of materials pertaining to Britain
and her colonies during the American Revolution. Just one year
later the Clements library was opened to researchers.

Two years after that, J. P. Morgan, Jr. donated to the Wadsworth
Athenaeum in Hartford, the "Pilgrim Century" furniture and
related decorative arts that had been assembled by Wallace Nutting.
In 1926 Arthur A. Schomburg donated his remarkable collection of
Afro-Americana to the New York Public Library. Four years later
Issac Newton Phelps Stokes gave that same institution his unique
collection of Americana—much of it rare iconography pertaining to
the growth of Manhattan—as a memorial to his parents. Also in
1930 Francis P. Garvan, who had begun to collect objects of
American material culture in 1912, presented his accumulation of
some 100,000 pieces to Yale University. Two years later John M.
Phillips, curator of the Garvan Collection, offered the first course
in our collegiate history concerning the decorative and fine arts in
America. The course was affectionately called "Pots and Pans."
Mahogany and silver might have been more accurate.

What these gifts really meant in historical terms could be called
the institutionalization of Americana. Objects that people had vied
for and purchased for their own gratification and self-esteem
gradually became accessible to the American people, particularly
during the 1940s, when, for example, John S. Williams of East
Chatham, New York, opened his Shaker collection as a private
museum (1940), and Henry Francis du Pont decided that his home
in Winterthur, Delaware, would also become a museum (1947).
That was just phase one in the process of institutionalization. In
1951 the Henry Ford Museum launched a variety of new outreach
programs and four years later it initiated its own television series,
"Window to the Past." The Winterthur Museum soon established a
graduate program in conjunction with the University of Delaware.
These kinds of educational endeavors marked an important new step
in the democratization of American traditions.

Yet another aspect of this larger phenomenon ought to be
specifically noted, even though we have touched upon it implicitly.
Quite a number of these patriotic benefactors wanted to make a
contribution in the field of historic preservation. One thinks, for
example, of Lila Acheson Wallace (1890–1984), the co-founder of
Reader's Digest, who contributed more than $8,000,000 for the
restoration of Boscobel, an eighteenth-century mansion located on

the Hudson near Garrison, New York. She became personally involved in every detail of the restoration, especially the gardens. One also thinks of Henry Hornblower 2d (1917–85), a Boston stockbroker and history buff who conceived and made possible the creation of "Plimouth Plantation" as a living history museum. The idea first occurred to him as a child during the 1920s, when he spent summers at Plymouth. One thinks of Louise Steinman Von Hess (1899–1980), co-owner of Lancaster Newspapers, Inc., who felt a strong sense of responsibility to restore landmark homes in the area of Lancaster, Pennsylvania. In 1973 she established a foundation for the preservation of outstanding examples of American architecture. The foundation also provided funds for a Lancaster County Museum for the Decorative Arts. And one thinks of John L. Loeb, Jr., the New York financier who made possible (in memory of his grandmother) an expansion of the Fraunces Tavern Museum. The inaugural exhibition in this gallery (1979) was devoted to "The Jewish Community in Early New York: 1654–1800."

Needless to say, the process of institution building that took place during the decades following World War II meant that fewer decisions about *which* historical activities to support would be personally made by collectors, and more would be made by foundation executives. It is impossible to overstate the significance of a $2,000,000 grant made by the Ford Foundation in 1964, for instance, to support the National Historical Publications Commission and editorial work on the papers of five of the so-called founding fathers. Similarly, seventeen miles from midtown Manhattan you will find the Queens County Farm Museum, located on Little Neck Parkway. The weathered colonial farmhouse there, built in 1772, needed a lot of repairs in 1982 when the Vincent Astor Foundation made $50,000 available to get the restoration process going. That gift permitted access to federal funds, and as a result an eighteenth-century farm will survive in an improbable place. Its educational value for urban schoolchildren alone is incalculable.

Williamsburg, Greenfield, and Sturbridge and so many current preservation and restoration projects in hundreds if not thousands of communities also preserve examples of early architecture and help us understand the processes by which communities evolved. J. Irwin Miller and the Cummins Engine Company have focused on an infusion of new architectural design that enriches their hometown of Columbus, Indiana. Frank

Koch, in his chapter, "Support of the Arts," in *The New Corporate Philanthropy*, summarized:

> In a 1964 *Saturday Evening Post* article, this quiet country town of 30,000 in the southeastern corner of the state, was called the "Athens of the Prairie"—and with good reason. Columbus is the location of more than two dozen outstanding buildings by some of the world's leading architects.
>
> The man responsible for what the *New York Times* in 1971 called "the finest architecture per capita of any city in the United States" is J. Irwin Miller, an extraordinary person. He has degrees from Yale and Oxford; is a Republican who helped lead the March on Washington for Jobs and Freedom in 1963; is a former Sunday school teacher who relaxes by playing the violin. Mr. Miller is a fourth-generation member of a family that made its fortune in Columbus in real estate, banking, electric railroads, corn-starch refining, and diesel engines.
>
> In 1941, the Miller family arranged for Eliel Saarinen to design the new First Christian Church, whose most striking feature was a rectangular tower the height of an 18-story building. It was also the first contemporary church building done by Saarinen.
>
> In the early 1950s, Miller selected the late Eero Saarinen—Eliel's son and a former classmate—to design new quarters for Irwin Union Bank & Trust Co., which his family controls.
>
> About the time the bank was being built, Columbus completed a new high school, and Miller decided, according to the *New York Times*, that better things could be done. He implemented his idea by establishing the Cummins Engine Foundation in 1954. The foundation offered to pay the architect's fee for any new school building if the board of education would select the architect from a list compiled by experts in the field. The result has been the construction of 11 new schools of innovative design by well-known architects since 1965.
>
> Columbus has averaged two architectural masterpieces a year, according to an eight-page review in *The Architectural Forum*, and the *New York Times* has called the result a stunning potpourri of creation.

Encouraging Creativity and Creative People

In *Ladies Bountiful*, William G. Rogers, speaking of patrons of artists, comments on assistance given to James Joyce by the "eminent and self-sacrificing angel, Lady Gregory, for whom Joyce coined this limerick:

> There was a kind lady called Gregory
> Said, "Come to me, poets in beggary,"
> But found her imprudence
> When thousands of students
> Cried, "all, we are in that category."

Almost a hundred years later, support of artists has hardly become pervasive, but at least it is a bit more organized.

One early and sustained approach has been the MacDowell Colony, a refuge for artists founded in the early 1900s. In the introduction to Margaret Widdemer's "Summers at the Colony," Frank Piscor describes the background of the Colony:

> Composer Edward MacDowell spent his last productive summers on a farmstead at Peterbough, New Hampshire. With his wife, he dreamed of capitalizing on the natural beauty and the seclusion of the surrounding woodlands by developing it into a place where creative people might spend nourishing and imaginative summers. The purpose of the MacDowell colony, as it has come to be called, was to provide working conditions most favorable to the creation of enduring works of music, painting, sculpture, drama and literature. Edward Arlington Robinson called the Colony the "worst loafing place in the world." It invited sustained effort and hard work.

"Summers at the Colony" became a chapter in Pulitzer prize winner Widdemer's *Golden Friends I Had.* In it she writes, "Nothing will ever be as wonderful to me again as that first time at the Colony." She then goes on to elaborate how much that retreat and the artists she met there meant to her personally and professionally.

The Colony has now grown to 600 acres, with at least 25 secluded studios. Among the writers who have found quiet and inspiration there are Stephen Vincent Benet, Willa Cather, Sara Teasdale, Lewis Untermeyer, Thornton Wilder, James Baldwin, Louis Bogan, DuBose Heyward, Stanley Kunitz, W. D. Snodgrass and Amy Lowell. The Colony has had a major influence on arts and artists across the nation. Though founded with the personal gifts of the MacDowells and their friends, a great many philanthropies have helped to develop and sustain it.

Yaddo is a slightly younger retreat for artists located in Saratoga Springs, New York. On its 50th birthday Yaddo received the kind of practical grant that organizations don't like to ask for and most foundations don't want to consider. Despite all its assets of space, serenity, and reputation, Yaddo's future was threatened because its underground water supply was running sparse and sour. Everything that Yaddo had going for it was about to be lost when the Gannett Foundation made one of those unusual gifts to the arts, $75,000 to hitch Yaddo to the city water supply. That may seem undramatic, but it has had dramatic results for an institution and its cause.

During the early 1920s, Mrs. Edward W. Bok formed the Curtis Institute of Music in Philadelphia. In "Scope of American Philanthropy," an article appearing in the February 1931 issue of *Current History,* Edwin L. Shuman reported that the Institute "is giving free musical education to about 290 students with proved talents in that line, its express purpose being 'to hand down through contemporary masters the great traditions of the past' and 'to teach students to build on this heritage for the future.'"

The Juilliard School of Music, funded by the Juilliard Music Foundation, was another early effort to create an institution that was specifically designed to develop extraordinary young talent.

Donald L. Engle's chapter, "Foundations and Serious Music," in Warren Weaver's *U.S. Philanthropic Foundations,* indicates that the Avalon Foundation supported the Brevard Music Foundation and the Manhattan School of Music. Engle adds: "Others have shown interest in summer music camps and festivals, as has particularly the Kresge Foundation, in the expansion of facilities at the National Music Camp and in the founding of the Meadowbrook Musical Festival at Michigan's new Oakland University."

That same resourceful chapter on music and similar ones dealing with visual arts, dance, and theater provide helpful reminders of philanthropy's encouragement of individuals and groups of artists. Just in the area of music, for example:

> The Martha Baird Rockefeller Fund for Music averages about 100 grants annually in a continuing program of assistance to young artists. . . . The John Simon Guggenheim Memorial Foundation grants . . . are awarded to about 10 to 15 composers annually and also to 2 or 3 musical scholars or theorists. . . . The Fromm Foundation has acquired a distinctive position in its support of contemporary music in various ways, including commissions and a performance laboratory at the Berkshire Music Center. . . . The Koussevitzky Music Foundation and the Elizabeth Sprague Coolidge Foundation have also done much to assist through commissions . . . and a new turn in foundation support was initiated recently when Francis Thorne, a musician and composer himself, established the Thorne Music Fund for aiding composers.

Engle and Weaver give credit to the Rockefeller Foundation for being the first major foundation to begin concentrating on the arts; for example, Engle refers to a 1953 grant to the Louisville Orchestra "for a ten-year project for commissioning, performing and recording new works. . . . This was a bold step in support of contemporary music." The Rockefeller program continues and in many ways has expanded as part of the foundation's general interest in the humanities.

The Dayton-Hudson Foundation has a long record of support for artists and the arts. In one unique public/private venture, the foundation gave the Minnesota State Arts Board a matching grant "to provide fellowship funds for talented people working in cross-disciplinary arts."

An unusual approach to providing help for artists involves the Kaplan Foundation's project for "buying loft buildings in New York for artists who have difficulty in finding living and working space in the city."

The C. Michael Paul Foundation established the Paul Chamber Residencies which, according to Richard J. Margoles in *Foundation News* (November/December 1985), "have made it possible for hundreds of talented musicians to enjoy fulltime careers in chamber music, still an impossible dream for most instrumentalists. . . . More important, perhaps, the Paul Residencies have brought live, classical music to scores of towns that were previously all but tone deaf."

CBS is funding a New Plays Program in cooperation with the Dramatists Guild. John W. Kiermaier of CBS said that the program grew out of discussions with young playwrights who indicated that their greatest frustration is that it's so hard to get their plays produced. The grant created an annual New Plays Competition at five nonprofit professional theaters located throughout the United States. Thomas H. Wyman, former CBS Chairman, commented: "We have long believed that it is our responsibility to nurture creativity whenever possible."

There have been many philanthropic efforts to encourage creative people and institutions:

- The Humana Corporation has helped develop a New Plays Festival at the Actors Theatre of Louisville.
- The Beatrice Company helped develop the New Theatre Company at Chicago's Goodman Theater.
- Reader's Digest gave $3 million to more than 50 theaters and dance companies to create and produce new works.
- AT&T Foundation awarded the National Corporate Theatre Fund (NCTF) almost $100,000 to launch a visiting director's program in each NCTF member's regional theatre.
- The Henry Luce Foundation provided $250,000 to the Asian Cultural Council for a fellowship program for American scholars, curators, and conservators of Asian art. According to a February 10, 1986 *New York Times* story by Kathleen Teltsch: "The joint undertaking will allow Americans to visit museums in China, Hong Kong,

Indonesia, Korea, Malaysa, Singapore, Thailand, Viet Nam and the Philippines."

- Oscar D. Cintas, who served as Cuban Ambassador to the United States in the 1930s, established a foundation in New York "to provide fellowships for young Cuban artists."

- AT&T is a leading supporter of Hispanic art in America. The company is underwriting the largest and most important exhibits of contemporary Hispanic art for tour at many of the country's mainstream museums.

- The Aid Association for Lutherans (AAL) committed more than $200,000 to develop a "full curriculum of high school music instruction to help high school musicians improve their artistry." The program is carried on at a music camp which AAL had also helped to start.

- The Xerox Pianists Program was established through Affiliate Artist Inc. to provide career development for promising American pianists.

- "Jazz Is," a production of North Carolina School of the Arts, toured 20 U.S. cities thanks to a grant from R. J. Reynolds Industries "to call attention to the college's program for the performing arts and to give the young artists tour experience."

- The Metropolitan Life Foundation established a Dance Canada Festival to provide assistance and exposure for five of Canada's major dance companies.

- The Mary Flagler Cary Trust and the Jerome Foundation provided the original funds to start the Commissioning Program of Chamber Music America (CMA). Through the program, funds are awarded to CMA member ensembles for commissioning American composers to write new chamber music works. Commissioning grants also provide funds for the ensemble to present the work. Recent supporters of CMA are the Mabel Pew Myrin Trust of the Pew Charitable Trusts and the Hewlett Foundation.

- The Bagby Music Lovers' Foundation is dedicated to honoring and helping needy and retired musicians.

In an interesting dissertation at Kent State University, Joyce Meeks Anderson reported on "Otto H. Kahn: An Analysis of His Theatrical Philanthropy in the New York City Area from 1909 to 1934." Anderson summarizes Mr. Kahn's loving encouragement of theater in America.

Mr. Kahn was most catholic in his philanthropy. Although no single theatrical criteria seems to be applied to Kahn's financial help, one

thread was common among the groups Kahn assisted: each was
trying to make experimental or classical theater more available to
the general public. A second area which appealed to Kahn was that
of theaters formed as cooperative ventures. A variety of actors and
directors solidifying into one productive collaboration appealed to
his system of management. A third concept which evolved from
analysis of Mr. Kahn's aid was that of freeing an artist to pursue his
creative work. Kahn gave monthly allowances to playwrights for an
extended period of time to release them from the pressures of
earning a living any other way than by writing. . . .

Many established artists have chosen to help younger artists through
their philanthropic efforts. For example, Jerome Robbins established a
foundation to encourage young dancers. Bethsabee de Rothschild established a foundation that "assists individual young choreographers in
bringing their work to the attention of the public." Donald L. Engle's
chapter on "Foundations and Serious Music," referred to earlier, mentions numerous distinguished artists and musicians who have established
foundations with similar goals, including Blanch Thebom, Marian Anderson, Lauritz Melchior, and Leonard Bernstein. Henry Moore left most of
his money to the Henry Moore Foundation for support of young artists.

Recognition has always been an important aspect of the encouragement
of artists. One of the newest efforts that also involves established artists
helping others is the project of the Pollock-Krasner Foundation to provide
"grants to talented artists seeking to continue their artistic endeavor. . . .
Grants will be given to painters, sculptors, graphic and mixed-media artists . . . to recognize not only talent, but the fact that even those who have
reached the level of awards are likely to need financial help also." Meg
Cox described the activities of the foundation in a July 17, 1986 story in
the *Wall Street Journal:*

> Even a small "drip" painting by Jackson Pollock sells for a million
> dollars now. But when the artist died in a car crash in 1956, after
> years of struggle and scathing reviews, he had never sold a work
> for more than $8,000. The paintings of his wife, Lee Krasner, didn't
> fetch big sums until she was in her 70s.
>
> So before she died in 1984 at the age of 75, the childless Ms.
> Krasner decided to devote most of her late-found wealth to helping
> other artists weather rough times.
>
> The Pollock-Krasner Foundation, with assets worth well over $20
> million, has given away nearly $800,000 to 106 artists across the
> country since it was set up in April 1985. It has given artists money
> for rent, food and materials. It has helped an artist dying of AIDS.
> One time, the foundation even sent money by messenger to an artist

who had been brutally mugged and needed neurosurgery. Like many artists, he had no medical insurance.

Most government and foundation grants are based only on merit, not need, and must be spent on such things as paint and canvas. Now several private funds are assisting artists with personal hardships.

For example, the late Adolph Gottlieb, another artist who achieved success late in life, set up a foundation that gives $10,000 each year to 10 needy artists, provided that they have been working for at least 20 years. Artist Robert Rauschenberg started a fund in the 1970s that gives artists $500 emergency grants. And the new foundation of Texas banker Harvey McLean, Jr. is currently aiding seven Texas artists, including an opera singer and a ballerina.

Pollock-Krasner, however, is the biggest and most ambitious organization of its kind.

The up-and-down career of Brooklyn artist Jim Huntington, a long-working, well-regarded sculptor, is typical. "I've had $80,000 years and $10,000 years," says Mr. Huntington, a slender, sinewy man in patched blue jeans. "But before I got the Pollock-Krasner grant, I hadn't had a major commission in two years or a New York gallery show in six years. I was down to my last $2,000."

The $10,000 grant helped immensely, but cash wasn't the only benefit. "It's one thing when you're young and struggling, but when you're 45 and strapped, you start to wonder if you're a crackpot to keep with it," says Mr. Huntington. "The grant gave me a boost of energy. It is someone substantial saying, 'You really are an artist.'"

. . . Over the years, the Pollock-Krasner Foundation will give money to artists whose works may never be critically acclaimed. But it's a chance the foundation wants to take. After all, says Mr. Thaw, the art dealer: "You just don't know who is going to rise above the pack."

The New York Community Trust administers several funds related to the encouragement of artists. Some of these funds are:

- *Eleanor Robson Belmont Fund:* In her lifetime, Mrs. Belmont had been the first woman active in the governance of the Metropolitan Opera. She began the Opera's series, "Student Performances," and underwrote its program of student matinees. The Fund carries forward her interest in music and young musicians.

- *Esther Jean Arnhold Fund:* In her lifetime, the sculptor spent as much time orienting young children to art as she did on her own creations and at her death established the Fund "to benefit needy students, especially those interested in art."

- *Walter W. Naumburg Fund:* His lifetime interest in music, New York and philanthropy led Naumburg to establish the Naumburg Bandshell in Central Park and his Fund is "to continue the Naumburg Orchestral concerts" and other musical endeavors.

- *Oscar Williams and Gene Derwood Fund:* Their lifelong interest in poetry led them to summarize their lives, "We were found by the wayside by poetry and we never looked back," and to leave their money and artists' rights in a fund "to help needy and worthy poets."

One of the great benefactors of poets and poetry, whose story is told by William Roger in *Ladies Bountiful*, was Harriet Monroe of Chicago who used her own funds and help from friends to establish *Poetry: A Magazine of Verse* in 1912. She wanted to broaden the audience for good poetry and to promote an outlet and some financial reward for able poets. She said, "A Milton might be living in Chicago today and be unable to find an outlet for his work."

Monroe gave early publishing opportunities to writers whose names are well known today, among them Edna St. Vincent Millay, Rachel Lindsay, Amy Lowell, Edwin Arlington Robinson, Ezra Pound, T. S. Eliot (including his "The Love Song of J. Alfred Prufrock," the poem that transformed the modern sense of what poetry could do), and many, many more. In *Ladies Bountiful* Roger cites a note from Millay to Monroe that shows how important publication in *Poetry* could be for a struggling writer:

> Edna St. Vincent Millay rejoiced at a sale to Miss Monroe, to whom she wrote: "Spring is here—and I could be very happy, except that I am broke. Would you mind paying me *now*. . . ?" A postscript stressed her plight: "I am *awfully* broke. Would you mind paying me a lot?"

Rogers also tells us that at Monroe's death, Pound said this of her contribution to poetry:

> No one in our time or any time has ever served the cause of art with greater devotion, patience, and unflagging kindness. . . : No other publication has existed in America where any writer of poetry could more honorably place his writings. This was true in 1912. It is true as I write this [in 1936].

Obviously, one of the most direct means of encouraging artists is to buy or help sell their works. On this count, Richard McLanathan in Weaver's book writes, "Though many foundations grant fellowships in other fields, few act to benefit the artist directly except the handfull that, like the Longview Foundation, make possible purchases of works of art. . . ." Earlier, according to *Ladies Bountiful,* at the urgent suggestion of Mary Cassatt, the Chicago Art Institute began "buying contemporary canvasses which insured the painters some income." More recently, the DIA Art Foundation provided major commissions to previously unheralded artists helping launch such current luminaries as Donald Judd, Walter de Maria, Robert Whitman, and La Monte Young. Chase Manhattan is known for consistently being the first purchaser of the works of art of an incredible number of artists who later became world renowned.

The Awards in the Visual Arts Program (AVA), managed by the Southeastern Center for the Contemporary Arts in Winston-Salem, North Carolina, funded by Equitable Life, Rockefeller Foundation, and the National Endowment for the Arts, is designed to recognize artists of substantial achievement whose work is not widely known. Every year, one artist from each of ten regions of the country receives a $15,000 award. Artists' works are presented in an annual exhibition that travels nationally. Each participating regional museum receives a purchase award to acquire works from the show for their permanent collection. For several years, virtually all Equitable art purchases were made from artists nominated for the AVA awards.

The Ford Foundation provides an example of practical help, beginning with its program to provide circulation of well-cataloged, one-person shows of unrecognized artists. Beyond this, the foundation is almost covering the waterfront. In the area of music, the foundation's grants program covers assistance to concert artists, opera singers, conductors, composers, administrators, and even critics. The foundation's assistance to dance includes the support of professional training in both ballet and modern dance and a "Program for Reporters, Editors and Critics." The foundations report on "Assistance to American Drama" describes its support of directors, playwrights, designers, administrators, and critics, and refers to the foundation's efforts to assist experimental theaters. The foundation was also one of the first to support creative efforts relating to radio and television through its "Living-Room Theater" which began in 1951, and its work in developing the "Omnibus" TV series.

The Ford Foundation has also been active in encouraging the development of minority artists. Its report "Minorities in Music" tells this encouraging story of one of the foundation's efforts:

> Part of Elma Lewis' upbringing was exposure through her father to the teachings of the charismatic Black leader Marcus Garvey, who urged that Black people develop their own institutions. In 1950, at the age of twenty-eight, Ms. Lewis opened her apartment in Boston's Roxbury-Dorchester district to twenty-five children, who came for after-school classes in dance, music, drama, and voice. This was the beginning of the Elma Lewis School of Fine Arts.

As Boston's Black community grew, so did the school's enrollment. In 1968, Boston's business community raised funds to purchase a permanent home for the school, a former synagogue and adjacent Hebrew school. Since then, the Elma Lewis School has become the largest ghetto-based arts school in the country.

Bringing the Arts to People

Whenever I think of efforts to make art more widely available to the public, I think first of efforts to support the major museums, but in my research for this section, the grant that riveted my attention was altogether different and was summarized in just a few words: "The Ray and Charles Newman Memorial Foundation voted $125,000 in 1955 for a 'Fragrance-Touch Garden for the Blind' in New York City's Central Park."

Less striking, but still a novel idea for making the arts accessible is the San Francisco Foundation's Arts Loan Fund. It gives businesses and individuals the opportunity to borrow works that they could not otherwise enjoy.

IBM was one of the first companies to provide support for traveling exhibits, which are now a positive part of the cultural life of a growing number of communities. Even earlier, the Spaeth Foundation had sponsored traveling exhibitions that emphasized works of religious art.

I had known that a great many efforts were developing to provide discounts or free admissions for people to enjoy the performing and visual arts, but I was pleasantly surprised to read in Merle Curti's "Tradition and Innovation in American Philanthropy" that the practice goes back at least as far as the turn of the century to "Henry Lee Higinson, father and supporter of the Boston Symphony Orchestra, whose example stimulated many in other cities to make symphonic music possible in their communities." Another act of generosity in making classical music more accessible to the general public dates back to the 1880s in Chicago. The story is well told by Father James O. J. Huntington in "Philanthropy—Its Success and Failure," published as part of *Philanthropy and Social Progress* edited by Professor Henry C. Adams in 1893:

> I would, however, add one incident as illustrating the eagerness the poor will manifest for what is really beautiful. The Apollo Club in Chicago numbers, among its four hundred members, some of the wealthiest people in the city. A few winters ago the leader, Mr. Tomlins, was conducting a rehearsal, and was just in the midst of a chorus that required his unswerving attention, when a messenger-boy came in with a telegram. Mr. Tomlins left him waiting until the chorus was finished; then he stepped down and begged the boy's

pardon as though he had been a young prince, and explained the reason for the delay. As he took the telegram he happened to look in the lad's face; to his surprise he saw that he was deadly pale, his mouth was agape, and the tears were streaming from his eyes. As soon as the boy could get his breath he exclaimed, "Oh, sir, I wish you'd waited two hours, I never heard anything like it in my life."

Mr. Tomlins said nothing at the time but after the rehearsal he remarked to a friend, "If there's that kind of hunger in the people we shall have to feed them."

So some weeks later, before the club broke up for the summer, Mr. Tomlins said to the members, "I want to remind you that you can never rise to the height of Art unless you use it for the highest purposes, unless you use it for the People. You are intending to give four oratorios next winter in the new Auditorium; you will sell season tickets at from five to seven dollars a seat. What I propose to you is that you repeat every performance the next night for wage-workers and sell the tickets at fifteen and twenty-five cents." "They wouldn't care to come," somebody said. "Try them," was Mr. Tomlin's answer.

When the Apollo Club met in the autumn it was decided that the suggestion of the leader should be carried out. The first oratorio to be given was "The Messiah." Arrangements were made to repeat it the next night with exactly the same care, not an instrument less. To make sure that the tickets reached the wage-workers they were sold at the factories. The Auditorium holds forty-five hundred people. There was a demand for twenty thousand tickets. I reached Chicago the following morning. A friend met me at the train. We had hardly greeted each other before he began to tell me about the oratorio. "I have heard the Hallelujah Chorus twenty-five times," he said. "I always knew there was something in it that I had never heard,—but I heard it last night."

In 1915 Adolph Lewinsohn started a series of free summer concerts for New Yorkers. The New York Community Trust says that "when Adolph died in 1938 at the age of 89, it was the day of the last performance of the twenty-first concert season. Audiences by then had swelled to 17,000, and Adolph Lewinsohn had lived to enjoy his dream of making fine music available to people in all walks of life."

Very recently, as reported by the Actors Theater of St. Paul, "the Medtronic Foundation has repeatedly funded a program for senior citizen ticket subsidy, allowing . . . seniors to attend our productions . . . to find theater presentations a significant part of their daily experience." At the other end of the age spectrum, there is even a national organization today

called "Young Audiences, Inc." that attempts to encourage and in some
cases provide opportunities for young people to hear concerts.

The 3M Company has provided close to a half-million dollars to make it
possible for many more people to hear the Minnesota Orchestra. The
money assists students, the elderly, handicapped people, the economically underprivileged, and veterans and supports an outreach program
that includes outdoor concerts in several different communities. Among
the letters of appreciation was the following from a group of youngsters in
a center for the handicapped:

> 3M Foundation Grant
> 3M Plaza
> St. Paul, MN
>
> Dear Friends:
>
> Through your generosity we were able to go to a fantastic concert
> at Orchestra Hall this Friday. For most of us in our organization this
> was the first time we ever went to such an event and heard a live
> musical group and in such a setting! We were overjoyed!
>
> God Bless You.

Shell has supported "Shell Nights" at Houston's Museum of Fine Arts,
keeping the museum open on Thursday evenings "especially for people
who would like to participate in museum activities and visit the galleries
but whose schedules prevent them from visiting the museum during regular hours." Shell has also funded a traveling exhibition of the Louisiana
Museum to help spread awareness and appreciation of the history of the
Louisiana Territory.

An increasing number of foundations and corporations are funding arts
presentations on radio and television in an effort to bring the arts to the
broadest possible number of people. Texaco is credited as the pioneer
with its "Saturday at the Metropolitan" series. Martin Kagan, executive
director of Opera America, responded to my inquiry about important
gifts, "In looking at the field of opera, the most obvious on-going giving
with a tremendous input is Texaco's sponsorship of the Metropolitan
Opera's Saturday afternoon broadcasts. Not only have they sponsored the
radio broadcasts for over 40 years, but they now also sponsor the television telecasts."

The Exxon Corporation spends approximately $3 million a year to
underwrite the program "Great Performances" on public television.
Mobil spent almost as much for "Masterpiece Theatre." In the October,
1980 issue of *Nation's Business,* Thomas Faye of Mobil is quoted: "Mobil
gives generous support to the arts because those individuals, those organizations that are in a position to contribute to the arts, to contribute to the

improvement of the quality of life in this country, have an obligation to do so."

The Revson Foundation funded the development of the television series "Heritage: Civilization and the Jews," which Eli Evans, president of the foundation, describes as "the most ambitious television effort in public broadcasting's history." To make the most of this cultural experience, teaching materials and guides were also contributed. The Getty Center for Education in the Arts and the National Endowment for the Arts developed a television series on the arts "for home broadcast to children between the ages of 8 and 10. Two primary aims of the series were to encourage appreciation and comprehension of the arts and to stimulate individual creative expression."

In his community planning work, the developer James Rouse has sought deliberately to ensure that there is "art in the marketplace." A 1982 article, "Corporate Philanthropy," by Kenneth Bertsch prepared as part of the publication series of the Investor Responsibility Research Center of Washington, D.C., observed that: "Art in the Marketplace, formally started in 1976, is an attempt to enliven Rouse developments, and it has contributed to their success and the wide-spread public attention they and Rouse have received. The program brings to Rouse-connected shopping centers chamber and other music programs, as well as art exhibits in museums in the mall." The Rouse Company also serves as matchmaker between performing and educational arts groups and shopping centers. Rouse vice president Edward A. Daniels, Jr. commented, "If the arts reflect the quality and vitality of the community, and we believe they do, then it is important to us and the people who live in that community, and with whom we do business, to assist those arts organizations and institutions in their attempts to reach broader audiences. . . ."

Champion International, Equitable Life Assurance, and Philip Morris corporations are just three of hundreds of companies that now set aside a large part of their lobbies as auxiliary art museums. These three provide space for branches of the Whitney Museum. The Kress Foundation, in addition to providing major new collections to a number of libraries, developed a program to reproduce the catalogues of museum collections.

The Dow family of Midland, Michigan found a way to combine the preservation of culture, space, and art and pay back a community that had been good to them by sponsoring the Chippewa Nature Center and the Midland Center for the Arts. According to the account in Keele and Kiger's *Foundations*, the center consists of "a symphony orchestra, a concert series, a Hall of Ideas, a variety of theater groups, and other expressions of the arts. . . ."

The Boeing Company found a way to pay back its community, enrich life for many people in Seattle and broaden the country's awareness of the rich heritage of African art when it gave $2 million to the Seattle Art Museum to purchase and exhibit the renowned Katherine White Collection of African Art.

It would be hard to find a city that does not have prominent cultural institutions established with the aid of local people who made good and who wanted to make some return gift to their community. As a Washingtonian, I found the following story particularly meaningful. In *Famous Givers and Their Gifts*, Sara Knowles Bolton says that in 1869 Mr. William Corcoran presented this deed:

> I shall ask you to receive as a nucleus, my own gallery of art, which has been collected at no inconsiderable pains; and I have assurances from friends in other cities, whose tastes and liberality have taken this direction, that they will contribute fine works of art from their respective collections. . . . I venture to hope that with your kind cooperation and judicious management we shall have provided at no distant day, not only a pure and refined pleasure for residents and visitors of the national metropolis, but have accomplished something useful in the development of American genius.

As a "Friend of the Corcoran," I can only say, "Well done and thanks."

For her 80th birthday, Alice Tully went to Alice Tully Hall at Lincoln Center to hear the Chamber Music Society. As Harold Schoenberg recorded it in an October 24, 1982 *New York Times* story, celebrating the occasion there was "only fitting, in view of the fact that it was Miss Tully who provided a good part of the funds for the hall named after her and was also instrumental in the formation of the Chamber Music Society."

A good story about fundraising is associated with another benefactor of Lincoln Center, Vivian Beaumont, for whom the center's theater is named. It may be apocryphal, but several people have sworn to me that it is true that when it was announced that Vivian Beaumont had given the gift to Lincoln Center, people from another theater with which she had been associated approached her and asked why in the world she had not given the money to their theater. Beaumont is reported to have responded with absolute surprise, "because they asked me."

In a different *New York Times* story, this one on July 20, 1984, Schoenberg presents an obituary of Leslie R. Samuels under the headline "Benefactor of Lincoln Center, Dies at 84." In the story he says:

> Mr. Samuels and his wife, Fan Fox, who died in 1981, both ardent music lovers, created the Fan Fox and Leslie R. Samuels Foundation in 1959. The foundation was set up primarily for aid to the arts. Through the years, it has been estimated the foundation gave some $13 million to Lincoln Center alone. . . . Fox and Samuels grants

went to the Metropolitan Opera, the New York City Opera, the New York City Ballet, the Mostly Mozart Festival, the Chamber Music Society and the New York Philharmonic.

The gifts of Andrew Mellon and his children Paul Mellon and Ailsa Mellon Bruce to establish and develop the National Gallery of Art rank as one of the greatest stories of private philanthropy and the arts. Among the other early contributors were Samuel H. Kress, Ruth H. Kress, Joseph E. Widener, Chester Dale, and Lessing J. Rosenwald. Not only did they develop one of the world's most important museums, but showed the way to the federal government for its role in cultural stimulation.

The lists of contributors to the Metropolitan Museum of Art, the Museum of Modern Art, and at museums in every metropolitan area are equally impressive and the sums of money donated have been enormous. Because of my travel schedule, interest in art, and orientation to philanthropy, I often find myself in museums, and I usually end up looking at the list of benefactors, sponsors, contributors, et al. It invariably reads like a who's who of the community's generous individuals, foundations, and corporations.

Increasingly, companies are among the leading donors to museums; witness the gifts of Kodak to the George Eastman collection. Also, Pacific Telesis recently put on a brilliant display of the photographic art of Ansel Adams.

Such impressive records of support are by no means limited to museums. The Wolf Trap Foundation, funded by Catherine F. Shouse, who was a daughter of Lincoln Filene, operates the Wolf Trap Farm for Performing Arts in Washington, D.C., an important cultural addition to the city. Borg-Warner, one of whose founders helped establish the Steppenwolf Theater in Chicago, has provided major grants to help that and other theaters purchase performing space. The corporation, along with others, has also given funds to develop the Victory Gardens Theater, the Organic Theater Company, and the Hubbard Street Dance Company. The Wortham Foundation in Houston made a gift of more than $20 million to the Houston Lyric Theater, now the Wortham Lyric Theater.

The Harkness Foundation, funded by Rebekah Harkness, has been one of the major forces in the field of dance. In a November, 1968 *Atlantic* story titled "The Rise of the House of Harkness," Douglas Turnbaugh writes:

> Another foundation program sponsors the dance festival in Central Park as part of the New York Shakespeare festival season. This remarkable program gives NYC seasoned artists who might otherwise be denied a showing, owing to the expense and difficulty of renting a theater. Selected by the Shakespeare Festival, funded

by the Harkness Foundation, more than 35 groups representing a wide variety of dance have played every summer since 1962 to more than 160,000 people. The audience is composed of sophisticated theater-goers, eager to see work they would otherwise miss, as well as people who have never had the opportunity to see a dance concert before. . . . This is just one of many activities funded and encouraged by the foundation to develop major dance forms, particularly ballet.

Whatever the art form or medium, the intent of all of these gifts is to nurture the spirit. In an address to the Business Committee for the Arts, J. Irwin Miller said it this way:

. . . in this society which is already so rich in things, the single legacy which we might best hand on to our posterity is a legacy of the spirit and mind, a flourishing of all the arts in our time such as would truly give release to the creative potential within us, that would permit us to reach out to each other in expression of our deepest thoughts and needs, and in the release and the expression would help us find a new sense of community such as might make our lives rich and not empty, and might change our view of the future from fear to excitement.

8

To Create Tolerance, Understanding, and Peace Among People

I. PHILANTHROPY IN WORLD AFFAIRS
II. CHARITY AND DUTY FAR BEYOND HOME
III. INTERNATIONAL PEACE AND UNDERSTANDING

Philanthropy in World Affairs

My first exposure to international grantmaking came in 1978 when I was appointed president of the National Council on Philanthropy (NCOP). The organization was about to hold one of its Brookings conferences on international philanthropy, funded by Exxon Education Foundation, General Electric, IBM, and the Agency for International Development. One tangible outcome of those sessions was Richard Eells' book, *International Business Philanthropy,* commissioned with support from General Electric, IBM, and Xerox.

In 1977, Robert G. Chollar, then president of the Kettering Foundation, presented the keynote speech, "Private Leadership and World Affairs: The Challenge to Foundations," to NCOP's International Philanthropy Workshop. The speech provided a strong rationale for international grantmaking and was one of the earliest such explanations I have come across. Chollar referred to a paper, "The Role of Private Organizations in the Foreign Policy Process," written in 1960 by John Sloan Dickey, former president of Dartmouth College, former state department official, and then a member of the Kettering Foundation board. Chollar noted that he and Dickey shared these assumptions:

Assumption 1: Private agencies can play a creative and corrective part in the foreign policy arena. Indeed, they are essential

participants in a democratic republic's policy-making process.
Assumption 2: The health of these organizations cannot be taken for
granted. By nature, voluntary organizations need continual renewal:
new ideas, new leaders, and new money. *Assumption 3:* They are
not as alert and strong as they could be. However alert they are,
world affairs organizations are always weak compared to
organizations working on domestic issues and interests. They
happen to be particularly vulnerable today because money is tight
in the grants economy that keeps most of them alive. *Assumption 4:*
Without the interest and encouragement of key leadership in our
society, including foundations, private agencies in the international
field will not be as alert or as strong as they could be.

Chollar concluded his presentation as follows:

> Several years ago the Kettering Foundation supported an inquiry
> on the Constitution and the conduct of foreign policy sponsored by
> the American Society of International Law. The distinguished study
> panel concluded that the absence of public participation in foreign
> policy decision-making can lead to "ill-considered foreign policy
> and the policy that does not enjoy public support, and breeds on
> healthy conflict between government and citizenry. . . . Foundations
> therefore share in the responsibility for improving the quality of
> this participation by helping these agencies to be both alert and
> strong."

For many years, the Kettering Foundation's Phillips Ruopp, head of its
International Affairs Division, was instrumental in making Kettering a cat-
alyst in international philanthropy. David Mathews, the current president,
has taken this perspective into account in developing the foundation's
interest in and support of citizenship education with an emphasis on
understanding of world issues.

Harlan Cleveland, Dean of the Hubert Humphrey Institute at the University of Minnesota, addressed the question of why donors and voluntary
agencies should be interested in international service, understanding, and
peace when he was still director of the Aspen Institute's Program in International Affairs. His article on "The Internationalization of Domestic
Affairs" appears in the January, 1979 issue of *The Annals of the American
Academy of Political and Social Science* (a special issue devoted to "Human
Dimension of Foreign Policy"). He writes: "Nongovernmental people,
and organizations, have a comparative advantage in penetrating the
porous membranes of national sovereignty." Cleveland gives many examples of how nonprofit agencies and donors have brought about changes for
world understanding. He adds: "Even in political matters, which are sup-

posedly the arena of government, non-official citizens and nongovernmental organizations often presaged the ponderous actions of responsible governments," and he gives as one example: "China's political 'coming out' was accompanied by ping pong matches."

Cleveland concludes with this advice:

> The governance of a world with nobody in charge seems to require this human dimension. Because they are not responsible, nongovernmental people are better able than government (and intergovernmental) people:
>
> • to work, ahead of time, on problems that are important but not yet urgent enough to command political attention;
>
> • to shake loose from conceptual confines and mix up disciplinary methodologies;
>
> • to think hard, write adventurously and speak freely about alternative futures and what they imply for public policy today;
>
> • to generate discussion among people in contending groups, different professional fields and separate sectors of society who might otherwise not be talking to each other; and
>
> • to organize dialogue across national frontiers on issues not yet ripe for more official negotiation.
>
> Perhaps the solution to the reciprocal riddle of our time—the internationalization of domestic affairs and the domestication of international affairs—is not to keep trying to distinguish between them but (in Paul Appleby's durable phrase) to make a mesh of things.

Charity and Duty Far Beyond Home

The Quakers and other pacifists believed that the only way true peace might be achieved is through the practice of brotherly love. A few years ago in studying the "troubles" in Ireland, I learned that much of the aid offered to the devastated Irish people during their awful famine in the mid-1800s came from American Quakers. The Quakers had almost no direct connection with the Irish, but in their concept of the family of man it was understood that they should give. And, as Anna Jeanes would have said: "They didn't go do it to save their souls from hell either." In a world full of violence and injustice in which human beings inflict terrible indignities upon each other, and in a nation more inclined than ever to withdraw into itself, the task of fostering tolerance, understanding, and peace has to begin with a recognition of our inescapable interdependence.

Dr. Robert Hingson invented a pistol that everyone feared; unlike other guns, however, millions of people were willing to let themselves be shot with it. Hingson's friendly gun provided rapid-fire shots that could immunize up to 1,000 people per hour. Suddenly immunization became a swift assembly-line routine. Hingson established the Brother's Brother Foundation (BBF) in 1958 "to help developing countries establish or expand their own immunization programs against such diseases as measles, small pox, polio and tetanus." The foundation estimates that it "helped immunize over twenty million people," and it reports that "in the mid-1960s, the jet injector was adopted for use by Aid for International Development, the World Health Organization, and many other immunization programs around the world."

The BBF foundation is now both an operating foundation and voluntary organization, using its funds and experience to "serve as a philanthropic broker for many countries, acting as a contact point between U.S. corporations and charitable or public institutions providing vital services to those in need." Their brokering includes in-kind gifts of food, books, medicine, seeds, tools, vaccines, hospital equipment and supplies, as well as the transportation necessary to get the supplies where they are needed.

Few of us knew or remember how much World War I shocked the American people. Those guns murdered and maimed so many men that there was an absolute determination that a war of this kind would never happen again. Many people expressed their horror, compassion and determination by forming or joining organizations designed to demonstrate "people-to-people" caring and service. Some of those efforts are described later in the chapter on "Cooperative Benevolence." Some foundations and wealthy individuals attempted to assist directly and personally. Curti's chapter, "The Great War," in *American Philanthropy Abroad*, includes this passage:

> The efforts of individuals or small groups, in contrast to the prevailing large scale and organized approach to the problems of war, represented a traditional American type of philanthropy in which only the very well to do could, if so minded, indulge. Mrs. Crocker and Miss Daisy Polk of California restored the completely destroyed village of Vitrimont in the Meurthe-et-Moselle. When George Ford visited it in October 1916, half of the former inhabitants had returned to the tottering walls that had been their homes and looked with some amazement at the fifty workmen on the scene. Houses were rebuilt, baths constructed, electricity installed. The Americans had left, but the attitude of the villagers

toward them was expressed in naming the principal street "la rue de Californie" and in making over to their benefactors any remuneration the French government might give: a tribute to the success of the Americans in doing what they did without cutting into the self-respect of the villagers. Mrs. Whitney Warren of New York adopted Cocy-le-Chateau. Kate Gleason, who had won engineering honors for the innovations she made in the tool machine factory of her father, sponsored Septmont. Miss Belle Skinner, daughter of a public-spirited philanthropist in Holyoke, Massachusetts, adopted Hattonchatel, an almost entirely ruined village. As houses were rebuilt she removed the manure piles from the fronts to hygienic storehouses in the rear. At a cost of a million dollars she built a school, town hall, public laundry, and modern water system. And all of this was done modestly and in a way to enlist the affection of those benefited.

These gifts were made out of a sense that if people were motivated to help one another, even in foreign lands, the world would not be brought to the edge of world conflict again.

Now, as then, many generous people and organizations help through organizations such as Save the Children that serve individual human beings. For example, that organization's recent gifts included the following:

- $3 million from Eastman Kodak and Burroughs Corporations for community development work in Zimbabwe and Zambia;
- $300,000 from Rafig Hariri for the organization's international training center;
- $150,000 of "in-kind" plane tickets from Pan American;
- a major gift from Sunoco to underwrite the printing and advertising of a holiday card campaign; and
- several hundred thousand dollars in a bequest from Mrs. Eli Lilly for central staff and plant expansion.

Funded by large and small contributions, Save the Children, like many other voluntary groups, is serving every continent of the world and almost every developing country. A recent report from Interaction (American Council for Voluntary International Action) describes the work of private voluntary organizations (PVOs) in Africa. The report, appropriately entitled "Diversity in Development," identifies more than 150 U.S. PVOs that provide assistance to people in Africa. The highest priorities for aid are in the areas of agriculture and food production, food stuffs, medical and general relief, water and other environmental problems, health, and education. Many organizations are also involved in longer-term development efforts. The report sums up:

> It is clear that the PVO's are making a long-term commitment to Africa. The commitment is one that moves once again from helping to alleviate suffering toward rehabilitation and development programs that address the root causes of drought and famine: poverty, poor sanitation, lack of clean drinking water, absence of primary health care, population pressure on limited resources, and environmental degradation. The PVO's are, as the study demonstrates, already focusing on these longer-term development issues and are substantially increasing their allocation of resources to Africa.

Africa was also the subject of a significant study by the Rockefeller Foundation. The study surveyed long-term needs on that continent and reviewed ways in which American individuals and groups could be of greatest assistance. Along the way the study created an unintended partnership with the Ford Foundation. Rockefeller's study was headed by Franklin Thomas who, early in the course of it, became the Ford Foundation president. Thomas has continued and expanded the Ford Foundation's long-standing assistance and development efforts in Africa.

Another Rockefeller philanthropy, the Rockefeller Brothers Fund, undertook a massive technical assistance program to assist development projects in Latin American countries that build local involvement and self-sufficiency. The fund provided primary support for the American International Association for Economic and Social Development "to encourage self-development in achieving better standards of living and in promoting cooperation and understanding among peoples throughout the world." Its initial work was in Brazil and Venezuela, spread to other Latin American countries, and was then extended to other countries of the world, notably India.

In an essay in *American Philanthropy Abroad*, Merle Curti traces some of the earliest efforts to build the capacity of communities receiving basic assistance:

> The carefully integrated community emphasis of the Rockefellers in Brazil and Venezuela was not, however, the first example of a technical assistance program in which the welfare of a specific area was advanced through coordinated services in agriculture, vocational training, home care, and health. Even before the Second World War far-sighted pathbreakers increasingly felt that no single program, whether in education, sanitation and health, or in agriculture, was in itself sufficient to improve substantially the living standard or to overcome the pull of tradition.

No agency did such effective pioneering in the improvement of community life as a whole and in developing the total personality of its inhabitants as the Near East Foundation did in 48 Macedonian villages in the 1930s and in its postwar programs in Syria, Eritrea, Iran and other countries. Under the leadership of Dr. Harold B. Allen, director of education in the Foundation, and a group of lieutenants who shared his vision and practicality, the principle was developed of bettering the community through improving the economy, health, the home, and recreational life. At every step, the objective was to help all age groups, but especially the young, to realize a larger measure of their potentialities. All this was done, not by imposing drastic changes from without, but by effecting gradual change from within. This involved the cooperation of the government—nothing was undertaken except on invitation and assurance of support and in the expectation that the government would in time take responsibility for programs that had proved successful. It also involved the idea of self-help. In the educational programs pupils quickly took on the role of teaching others. Nothing was given as charity, nor was there any paid labor. Working with the villagers and involving them in planning as well as in executing programs, the Foundation's field staff took into account local conditions, resources, and needs. It sent carefully selected young men to America for special training. It enlisted well-chosen Americans trained in nutrition, child care, and home making who worked with native women in the delicate task of improving family life. Boys and girls were encouraged to take part in organizations resembling 4-H clubs.

The Near East Foundation provided much of the blueprint for the "Point 4" program, the Technical Cooperation Administration, and later the Peace Corps.

This full book could be devoted to the work of the Rockefeller Foundation in China, including its development of the Peking Union Medical College and what that meant to so many human issues far beyond Chinese medicine and health. That gift ranks in the top five of those mentioned most often in response to my request for ideas. For example, Porter McKeever, longtime aide to John D. Rockefeller, 3rd, wrote: "Recently, in accepting an Asia Society award, John Fairbank said that if he were ever in an award-giving situation, he would make an award to the Rockefeller Foundation for its introduction of modern science into China."

McKeever also wrote of John D. Rockefeller, 3rd's generosity and courage in addressing the world's population problems: "While there were other and earlier pioneers, his early and persistent support has been pivotal in the subject of population becoming recognized as one of the key issues of human survival." Rockefeller organized the Population Council that was, according to Warren Weaver, "charged with hastening the development of the scientific knowledge and the trained personnel which were a prerequisite to effective solutions to national and international population problems." Speaking of this contribution, William Ruder, of Ruder and Finn, advised, "It would be the perfect chapter for you."

A smaller foundation with a record of impact on population and other international issues is the Jessie Smith Noyes Foundation. Among the fascinating efforts it has funded is the "Kenyan Family Planning Soap Opera Project" of the Center for Population Communications–International. The purpose of the program is described by the Center's president, David O. Poindexter:

> The purpose of the program in Kenya is to supply essential technical assistance so as to enable the government's Voice of Kenya to produce its own radio and telenovelas on family limitation in accordance with policies adopted by the government of Kenya.
>
> The use of family planning communications technology by way of the soap opera was first developed, applied and proven effective by Mexico's national broadcasting network Televisa.
>
> With soap opera, strong bonds are formed between viewers or listeners and the soap opera characters. Over the months, as these television "friends" find their way to family planning, large numbers of the audience follow their lead. In Kenya, it is expected that this program will provide a powerful family planning motivation driving force for Kenya's national population program. It will also provide a powerful tool to be applied in other crucial areas of development such as health, environment and reforestation. Kenya is an ideal base from which to move this technology into the other high population growth rate famine-threatened countries of East/Central Southern Africa.

Noyes has also funded novel and important projects related to global planning, open spaces, agricultural production, the development of art in different cultures, and the role of women in worldwide banking. They have also been a major backer of World Watch Institute.

Returning to China for a moment, in *Foundation Watcher*, Andrews includes a wonderful tale of one of the Russell Sage Foundation's gifts:

> I [received] a request which came to Russell Sage Foundation from Hung-chung Chang, of China's Ministry of Social Research, who reported that because of Japanese invasion China had for some years received no books from the outside world; what were late developments in relief policies, and could not some new books be

got to him? A selection committee picked pertinent material (including the whole of the latest *Social Work Year Book*). The Office of War Information was induced to photograph this material onto 35mm film, with 1,600 pages in each tiny roll. . . . The State Department let us use leftover corners in the diplomatic pouch. The "RSF Bulletin" carried the story:

"Silence for nearly a year. Then one morning came a sudden telephone call; would your Editor come in to lunch with Mr. Chang, who had just flown in from Chungking? Some fifty books, Mr. Chang reported, had come safely over The Hump. All had been read, and important portions translated into Chinese for further distribution. And from the light in his eyes and his almost embarrassing gratitude we learned anew how much the printed word can mean to a man and a nation starved for it."

An example of a very recent gift for a specific population and problem is the Koret Foundation's gift of $45,000 to Hadassah, the women's Zionist organization of America, "to provide instruction services for Ethiopian youth." Other grants and trends are reported in a story by Thomas Fox in the May/June, 1985, *Foundation News*. His article "A Rising Tide?" is subheaded: "Precise figures are elusive, but international grants appear to be growing steadily. In any case there's no doubt that the field is as vibrant and absorbing as any." Fox writes:

. . . highlighted by the Ford Foundation's recent announcement that it will increase its efforts in the family planning field, population activities continue to attract substantial foundation resources from Hewlett, Rockefeller, Ford and Mellon.

Particularly among foundations which define their priorities as their local community, there is keen interest in refugee resettlement and the preparation of local communities for accepting and integrating refugees. This is clearly another "growth area" in the international field.

The recent attention to Africa has been particularly noteworthy among individual donors, who have responded with unprecedented generosity. Although the "We Are The World" best selling album has generated the greatest publicity, individuals have contributed well over $100 million for African relief since late October 1984.

This attention is stimulating interest among foundations and corporations in establishing programs which can deal with long-range development programs in Africa. The Pew Memorial Trust and the William Penn Foundation, both Philadelphia-based private foundations, provide good examples of this development, as do several large corporations.

Another encouraging development is seen in the ability of the Council on Foundation's new unit, Grantmakers International, to attract the participation of 280 foundations and corporations which are interested in the rationales and mechanisms for international grantmaking.

International Peace and Understanding

At a panel on international grantmaking at a Council on Foundations meeting, I thought I heard Scott McVay, director of the Geraldine R. Dodge Foundation, say that there are more English-speaking people in China than in all of North America. Knowing that could not be so, but curious as to what he had intended, I asked him afterwards what he *really* meant. He *really* meant that there are more English-speaking people in China than in all of North America.

McVay's point, which his statistics underscore dramatically, is that other countries are preparing for their global opportunities and responsibilities, while the United States is not. For example, the number of Americans who speak Chinese is infinitesimal. To begin to correct the situation, McVay's foundation has undertaken:

> A Chinese language program which has led to the development of a network of 37 superb high schools which have a commitment to Chinese language instruction. We have gathered 31 of these teachers at Ohio State University in June for a workshop on teaching methods and curriculum development. This project will increase the number of American youth who are studying the Chinese language from 1,000 to, say, 5,000 and among those numbers may be critical mediators in the future who can contribute to our nation's survival. To date we've committed $1.3 million. . . .

Robert L. Smith, executive director of the Council for American Private Education, had called the same project to my attention:

> . . . critically important and having a wide impact is the Dodge Foundation's support of Chinese study in American high schools. By providing seed money in this area Dodge has enormously increased the number of high schools teaching Chinese and the interest of students in oriental studies generally. The orient is obviously of central importance to us as we increasingly become a smaller interdependent world.

Paul Simon, now in the Senate, was the sponsor of House legislation establishing the President's Commission on Foreign Language and International Studies chaired by James Perkins. Simon's experience with that Commission reinforced his concern that an increasing number of American students are going through high school and college with almost no exposure to foreign languages and international studies. He responded by writing a persuasive book *The Tongue-Tied American* and by assisting Perkins and others in the establishment of the National Council on Foreign Language and International Studies. The council, which received its principal funding from Chase Manhattan Bank, the United States Information Agency, and the Exxon Education, Hewlett, Luce, Ford, Mellon, and Rockefeller foundations, has as its main purpose the task of goading the American people into action.

The Carl Schurz Memorial Foundation developed one of the earliest and sustained efforts at promoting international understanding. The story is chronicled in Eugene E. Doll's book, *Twenty-Five Years of Service: 1930–1955.* Doll says that Americans of German birth were second only to the Quakers in their efforts "to bind up the wounds of victors and vanquished alike" after World War I. The foundation was established by American citizens of German descent just 100 years after the birth of Carl Schurz, who served as Secretary of the Interior in the cabinet of Rutherford B. Hayes. Doll records: "In the minds of the group nothing . . . could serve as a more appropriate memorial to this great citizen of two continents than a foundation dedicated to the promotion of cultural relations between the land of his birth and the land of his adoption."

The Schurz Foundation was the idea of Pennsylvania industrialist Ferdinand Thun, who along with his business associates Gustav Oberlaender and Henry Janssen, put up the first $150,000. Thun then undertook to solicit gifts from others he thought would want to strengthen the relationships between Germany and America. Doll writes: "The list of contributors reads like a directory of the German-American financial, social and intellectual elite."

For the next 25 years the foundation supported two-way student exchange, exchanges of English and German books and journals, a study of the degree to which schools taught English or German, a circulating film library, training of language and history teachers, an exchange lecture program, the exchange of art and artists, and much more. The foundation was considerably strengthened by its partnership with the Oberlaender Trust and together they established the journal, *The American–German Review.* During the late 1930s, the foundation and trust were considerably occupied with "helping German refugee professors, artists and writers to establish themselves in the United States." A major project during this period was establishment of the American–German Institute.

Doll mentions the following fact only briefly, but I found myself struck by it: the foundation, along with all German-American societies, had its tax exemption withdrawn automatically by the Department of the Treasury during World War II.

After the War, the trust was dissolved into the foundation which continued with the task of building relationships between the two countries. Years later, James Conant, the U.S. High Commissioner for Germany, said:

> This is also to express my conviction that the role of the private agency, such as the Carl Schurz Memorial Foundation, is an important one in this land at this time. Yours is the freedom to pioneer; to operate swiftly, unfettered by the cumbersomeness so often attending upon governmental operations; yours is the privilege of working intimately and personally with those whose influence is and will be great.
>
> Let me couple with my thanks for your past efforts the hope your work will bring closer together peoples of two great nations and may you continue to meet with deserved success.

The German Marshall Fund of the United States was formed in 1972 with funds from the German Federal Republic to:

> . . .commemorate American post-war assistance under the Marshall Plan (and) to foster intensified exchanges of ideas and practical experience between the United States and other countries on issues of common concern to modern industrial societies. Among its program interests have been the common problems of large cities in industrial countries, environment/land use, administration of criminal justice, a European-American studies program and an international problems program.

In 1981, the German Marshall Fund collaborated with Fred Bergsten, then the assistant secretary of the U.S. Treasury Department for International Affairs, to establish the Institute for International Economics "for policy-oriented research on the most important international economic issues." The fund provided close to $5 million for the first five years of the Institute "for attention to two kinds of issues: the international economic system and its institutions, rules, relations, and trade practices, with the goal of minimizing tensions and stresses flowing from unstable international economic developments; how the U.S. economy adjusts to these changes, and how U.S. domestic policies affect economic relations with Europe." Frank E. Loy, president of the Fund, reports that the project has been their largest investment by far, but he says, "We are in the business of making grants that make a difference. We believe the grant to the Institute meets that test."

A few years ago I attended a conference in England with an imposing title, something like "The Future of Philanthropy in the Western World." The conference was held at Ditchley Park, not far from Oxford. The U.S.

Ditchley Foundation and its counterpart in England had been established to develop understanding between the two countries. The mandate is now broadened to include other countries, but the focus remains on building ties between these two English-speaking nations.

Shortly before this book was written, the Hitachi Company of Japan announced establishment of a foundation in the United States "to promote better understanding between United States and Japan and increase cultural ties." A very different project relating to mutual Japanese-American understanding involved support of more than $1 million from the Mellon Foundation, with participation by the National Endowment for the Humanities and the Ford Foundation, to help solve a major problem in translation of scientific documents. As told in the October 1, 1985 *Ford Foundation Letter:*

> A scholar investigating educational reforms introduced during the postwar occupation of Japan wants to know the relevant sources in both English and Japanese. In the past, most large university research libraries could help the scholar with a computer search, but only data in Roman script could be processed. Titles in languages that do not use the Roman alphabet had to be listed in translation or in Romanization of the Japanese words.
>
> Now all this has changed. A new computer system has been developed by the Research Libraries Group (RLG), a consortium of universities and research institutions, that can retrieve information in Chinese, Japanese, and Korean scripts, as well as in Roman-alphabet languages. With the new system, called CJK for the three scripts, libraries can consult one national database representing twenty-two major East Asian library collections across the U.S.

One of the antecedents of the Mellon Foundation, the Old Dominion Foundation, helped to establish Dumbarton Oaks as "the center for Hellenic studies." Warren Weaver remarked, "Not often in recent years has anyone given $5 million to Greek studies!"

Thomas Fox, in the *Foundation News* article cited earlier, comments on the following educational efforts:

> Still, the major area of foundation and corporate international grantmaking activity falls in the general field of international education—educating Americans at all levels about a range of international issues and problems.
>
> One particularly interesting trend noted in a Carnegie-commissioned report is the growing tendency of foundations and corporations to fund independent research and educational institutions, somewhat at the expense of centers affiliated with universities and colleges.

For example, only one of the biggest 15 grants made by
foundations for international affairs in 1983 went to a university—a
Starr Foundation grant to New York University for its center for
Japanese studies.

In 1929, ten Pomona college students pooled their talent "to create the
Oriental Study Expedition. Each of them, with a particular area of interest, ingeniously sought and secured enough funding to spend one year
traveling throughout China. The people they met and the knowledge they
acquired during the trip left a lasting impression on them all." With that
preamble, the Durfee Foundation recently announced its "American/Chi-
nese Adventure Capital program . . . to recognize the exceptional spirit of
that original expedition, and to perpetuate its members' unique approach
to personal achievement. The program's sponsors hoped that by providing
this source of unusual project funding, people of bold curiosity and
determined ambition will be allowed to pursue fascinating interests and
innovative visions." R. Stanton Avery, one of the participants in that original expedition subsequently built Avery International and established the
Durfee Foundation, named after his original home base in Scotland.
Avery, feeling he has drawn so much on that China experience, is eager to
provide similar opportunities to others.

International exchange and study have long been primary ways that
foundations have helped to build tolerance and understanding. The Kellogg Foundation began its international program interest with exchanges
of health professionals with Canada, then reached southward into Latin
America and then to Central and South America. Almost all of the largest
foundations have also developed international programs, including scholarships, fellowships, special studies, and exchange programs. Many
funders have supported international programs because of an interest in a
specific country or special field, with the belief that such programs will
build better ways to deal with health, conservation, the environment, education, and maybe even peace.

International understanding received a major boost years ago when the
Rockefeller Brothers Fund helped develop the organization World Watch
and its publication of the same name. Its many publications on worldwide
problems, from population control to soil erosion, are respected around
the globe. More recently, in 1974, the relatively small Stanley Foundation
stepped in to become the publisher of *World Press Review*, which is
"published as a nonprofit educational service to foster international information exchange. The magazine is composed entirely of material from the
press outside the U.S. or by journalists affiliated with foreign press
organizations."

Increasingly, the mass media is being used to help build a sense of
world community. The Duluth–Superior Area Community Foundation

approved a grant from its Global Awareness Fund to the Northern Pine Girl Scout Council for an international education program called "It's Our World." The Carnegie Corporation awarded National Public Radio a three-year, $300,000 grant for reporting of Third World development issues. The Boehm Foundation awarded producers Robert Richter and Catherine Warnow a grant for production of "Do Not Enter: The Visa War Against Ideas," a film examining a U.S. policy that denies visas to foreign visitors with controversial views.

The March, 1985 Council on Foundations' *Newsletter* reports:

> Three films which focus on world peace and the specter of nuclear war have won $5,000 Media Production Awards from the Benton Foundation and the Film Fund. The three films, which will be completed under the new production grants are:
>
> "From the Hellfire," directed by John Junkerman, a film that examines the horror of nuclear war through the work of two Japanese mural artists whose paintings depict the aftermath of the bombing of Hiroshima;
>
> "How to Prevent a Nuclear War," directed by Liane Brandon, an upbeat film about the kinds of activities undertaken by ordinary people to help lessen the threat of nuclear war; and
>
> "Radio Bikini," directed by Robert Stone, a feature-length documentary about the consequences of America's first and largest nuclear war-game experiment.

Kathleen Teltsch interviewed Robert W. Scrivner, director of the Rockefeller Family Fund, about a year before Scrivner died, but not before he had helped convince the fourth and fifth generations of Rockefellers, whose philanthropic activities are administered by the fund, that they should turn their attention to the control of nuclear power and pursuit of world peace. Scrivner related:

> I told Eric Chivian I had the feeling a major movement would shortly begin. I felt as I had during the earlier civil rights days when Black clergymen organized, and then again in the 70's when the environmental movement started and a whole generation of public interest lawyers began making a case for clean air and clean water. In these three different instances three groups of leaders came along with a talent to get organized. This time the physicians were out front.

The Chivian about whom Scrivner spoke was the head of International Physicians for the Prevention of Nuclear War, the group that won the Nobel Peace Prize in 1985.

In her March 29, 1984 *New York Times* article headed "Philanthropies Focus Concern on Arms Race," Teltsch reported on the activities of a number of foundations and corporations of varying sizes and purposes. She begins:

> The nation's philanthropies, which in the past have concentrated on domestic social and educational projects, are now beginning to devote significant time and money to seeking ways of slowing the arms race and reducing the threat of nuclear war.
>
> . . . Many foundations contribute to nonprofit groups around the country that have organized to seek solutions to the nuclear arms race. Older organizations such as SANE and Physicians for Social Responsibility are now joined by newer organizations whose aim is to prevent nuclear war.

Teltsch goes on to describe recent support for projects dealing with the nuclear arms race. Among the grants she mentions are the following:

- The Hewlett Foundation . . . made the first grant of $600,000 for security issues . . . to Stanford University's arms control center and says it intends to increase support to $1 million for research and to train analysts . . . .

- The W. Alton Jones Foundation . . . decided to commit $1.2 million to projects on avoidance of war after three generations of the family agreed that nuclear war and depletion of resources were the nation's two overriding concerns . . . .

- Warren E. Buffett, board chairman of the Berkshire Hathaway conglomerate, said he and his wife, Susan, decided that their Buffett Foundation of Omaha would devote $1 million annually for three years to the "world's two biggest problems," preventing nuclear war and limiting population growth . . . .

- A group of older, smaller foundations that were among the first to make grants to prevent nuclear war have doubled or tripled their efforts. These groups such as the Kendall and Levinson Foundations of Boston prefer to spend money for field work. Many of their contributions go directly to advocacy and activist groups. The two-year-old Ploughshares Fund in San Francisco raises money from foundations and private donors and supports projects to reduce United States–Soviet tension . . . .

- The Field Foundation of New York is now giving $500,000 for peace and security projects and continues to be the leading foundation to support SANE, which since 1959 has been organizing grassroots groups to campaign for arms reduction. SANE, which gets grants from 20 foundations, has increased its membership to 90,000 from 35,000 in two years . . . .

- Other longtime supporters that increased grants include the Scherman and New World Foundations . . . and the Veatch program of the North Shore Unitarian Universalist Society of Plandome, L.I., which gave more than $400,000 for arms control and related activities . . . .

- The John M. Olin Foundation has contributed nearly $1 million to the National Strategy Information Center in Washington and New York whose publications maintain that a nuclear freeze now would leave the Soviet Union militarily superior . . . .

- The C. S. Fund of Santa Rosa, California . . . has increased contributions for peace and security projects to $500,000.

The mood of current times is not unlike that of 75 years ago when Edwin Ginn established the World Peace Foundation, originally known as The International School of Peace. Ginn's purpose was:

Educating the people of all nations to a full knowledge of the waste and destructiveness of war, its evil effects on present social conditions and on the well being of future generations, and to promote international justice and the brotherhood of man; and, generally, by every practical means to promote peace and goodwill among all mankind.

Ginn's efforts spurred Andrew Carnegie to establish his Endowment for International Peace. The Endowment was to have been the capstone of Carnegie's philanthropic endeavors, but even Carnegie's optimism and resources were no match for serious international problems. Philip E. Mosely, writing on "International Affairs" in Warren Weaver's *U.S. Philanthropic Foundations*, captures nicely the Carnegie spirit:

In establishing the Carnegie Endowment for International Peace in 1910, Andrew Carnegie sincerely believed that the permanent elimination of wars and prospect of wars might well be achieved in the lifetime of men then living. And he directed the Trustees, when that happy state had been achieved, to apply the Endowment's resources to solve other major problems of mankind.

Merle Curti in *Philanthropy Abroad* writes that Carnegie "stipulated that the Trustees should 'keep unceasingly in view . . . the speedy abolition of international war. . . .'" In the chapter "A Little War and New Disasters," Curti describes how the Spanish-American War and several other scrimmages sparked Carnegie's concern and his determination to seek peace.

What followed, of course, was not peace but two slaughtering world wars, the development of nuclear weapons, Korea, Viet Nam, the Middle East, and a whole world that could explode at any moment. Andrew Carnegie, where are you?

A new endeavor of the Carnegie Corporation shows promise of playing a prominent role in addressing some of the problems that concerned Andrew Carnegie. In a recent annual report, David Hamburg, president of the Corporation said:

> In a brief moment of evolutionary time—since the industrial revolution and mainly in the 20th century—we humans have thrust ourselves headlong into a world of enormous complexity, vast scale, unprecedented rates of change, technical and social transformation, brilliant new horizons, and weaponry of destructive power beyond previous imagination. Our power for better and worse suddenly dwarfs everything that went before in millions of years of human evolution. This power is rich in promise for the human future if we can at last come to master the pervasive tendency toward conflict in our species.
>
> The capacity for attachment and the capacity for violence seem to be fundamentally connected in human beings. We fight with other people with which we identify most strongly; altruism and aggression are thus intimately linked in war and other human conflicts.
>
> The underlying orientation of importance here is the ubiquitous human tendency toward egocentrism and ethnocentrism. We find it easy to put ourselves at the center of the universe, attaching a strong positive value to ourselves and our group, while attaching a negative value to many other people and their groups. It is prudent to assume that human beings are all, to some extent, egocentric and ethnocentric. But these tendencies, under certain conditions, can lead to violent conflict.
>
> The world is now, as it has been for a long time, awash in a sea of ethnocentrism, prejudice, and violent conflict. The worldwide historical record is full of hateful and destructive indulgences based on religious, racial, and other distinctions. What is new is the destructive power of our weaponry: nuclear, enhanced conventional, chemical, and biological. Moreover, the worldwide spread of technical capability, the miniaturization of weapons, the widely broadcast justifications for violence, and the upsurge of fanatical behavior are occurring in ways that can readily provide the stuff of very deadly conflicts in every nook and cranny of the earth. To be blunt, we have as a species a rapidly growing capacity

to make life everywhere absolutely miserable. As if that were not enough, two nations probably have the capacity to make human life extinct.

No longer have we the luxury to indulge in prejudice and in ethnocentric extremes. These are anachronisms grounded in our ancient past. There may be "tough-minded" people who believe that this is the human condition and that we must make the most of it. But technology has passed them by. The destructive capacity of modern weapons—large and small, nuclear and non-nuclear—has made the "tough-minded" view unrealistic, if not today, then tomorrow. If we cannot learn to accommodate each other respectfully—within nations and across nations—we will destroy each other at such a rate that humanity will soon have little to cherish, assuming there is any humanity left on earth.

When I read that, I responded to Hamburg:

> I find that I'm involved increasingly with organizations that are concerned about international issues, and I'm often surprised how many of the individuals involved have a rather naive view of what it will take to achieve lasting peace. I'm always delighted with their interest and go out of my way to encourage their efforts, but I try to add a note of realism about how terribly hard it is to create that "family of man." Your essay articulates how deep-seated the difficulties are, but it is clear to the reader that you go back to those basic points only for the purpose of helping build realistic efforts toward toleration and maybe understanding.

The Spring, 1985 *Carnegie Quarterly* summarizes the purpose of the Corporation's new program priority:

> A central aim of Carnegie Corporation's program called "Avoiding Nuclear War," now in its second year, is to strengthen the capacity of the scientific and scholarly communities to produce such analysis. It is an effort, in the words of David A. Hamburg, President of the Foundation, "to mobilize the best possible intellectual, technical and moral resources over a wide range of knowledge and perspectives and to address them to the threat of nuclear war."

The kinds of projects being funded by Carnegie as part of the new thrust indicate some of the new avenues that are being followed to prevent nuclear war and achieve lasting peace. The Corporation reported in 1985 that since it announced its new program in 1983, it has given 50 grants totaling $11,027,391 in this area alone. These grants include support for research and policy analysis on the nuclear arms race and on U.S.–Soviet relations and for media education. Among them are:

- *Harvard University:* for research and education on the avoidance of nuclear war, $1,600,000.
- *Massachusetts Institute of Technology:* toward support of the arms control and defense policy program, $1,110,000.
- *Stanford University:* toward research and training in international security and arms control, $905,750.
- *Cornell University:* for research and writing on the management of international crises, $400,000.
- *American Association for the Advancement of Science:* toward support of the Program in Science, Arms Control, and National Security, $256,500.
- *American Academy of Arts and Sciences:* toward support of a study of weapons in space, $250,000.
- *University of California, San Diego:* toward support of a study of warfare in space by the Institute on Global Conflict and Cooperation, $250,000.
- *Johns Hopkins University:* for a study of the effects of militarization of space on the likelihood of nuclear war, $240,900.
- *American Physical Society:* toward support of a study of the science and technology of directed-energy weapons, $200,000.
- *National Academy of Sciences:* toward a symposium on the medical consequences of nuclear war, $200,000.
- *American Civil Liberties Union Foundation:* toward support of the Center for National Security Studies Project on Government Secrecy, $150,000.
- *International Council of Scientific Unions:* toward a project on the environmental consequences of nuclear war, $150,000.
- *Columbia University:* for research and training on Soviet security arms control issues, $1,500,000.
- *Brookings Institution:* for research on international security issues as affected by U.S.–Soviet relations, $750,000.
- *University of California, Berkeley:* for research on Soviet foreign policy and behavior in selected regions, $599,675.
- *Harvard University:* toward research and training at the Harvard Negotiation Project on improving the U.S.–Soviet negotiation process, $250,000.

• *New York University:* toward research and training on news media coverage of international security matters, $250,000.

It is encouraging to see that another philanthropic giant, the John D. and Catherine T. MacArthur Foundation, has also moved into this area. According to a *New York Times* story by Kathleen Teltsch:

> A major philanthropic organization said yesterday that it will spend $25 million over the next three years on the study of international security and prevention of nuclear war.
>
> The grant almost doubles the privately contributed money for research in this field according to the group, the John D. and Catherine T. MacArthur Foundation of Chicago.
>
> "No issue threatens the collective destiny of humankind like the menacing threat of nuclear war" said John E. Corbally, Foundation President. He said a study had found a "disturbingly small cadre of individuals devoting their efforts to these problems."

MacArthur provided grants totaling several million dollars to found and help develop the World Resources Institute. We are fortunate, too, that other giants such as Ford and Rockefeller have maintained and increased their attention to nuclear issues and peace.

The field has not been left only to the major foundations. As previously noted, the Rockefeller Family Fund is an example of a smaller foundation that devotes a considerable percentage of its attention to the nuclear threat. Many people with whom I have corresponded give substantial credit to the relatively unknown W. Alton Jones Foundation for its leadership in this field. Scott McVay of the Geraldine R. Dodge Foundation wrote:

> . . . the single most important grant in my view was the W. Alton Jones Foundation of Charlottesville, Virginia to fund the conference on "Long-term Biological Consequences of Nuclear War" last fall in Washington. That conference led to a telecast involving Russian and American scientists confirming the consensus of the scientific community which led to the publication of two papers in *Science*. In early July, military experts testifying at a Senate hearing accepted the "Nuclear Winter" scenario that, given certain assumptions including even attack by only one country, the Earth will become a dark, cold place for a long time, snuffing out the possibility of photosynthesis since the sun's rays could not penetrate the soot mantle that will girdle the Earth. Only with this dire recognition can we develop plans for a more stable less threatened world.

To give another sense of the range of possible efforts, the following is a list of organizations the Jones Foundation has funded:

Federation of American Scientists
American Friends Service Committee
Arms Control Association
Harriman Institute for Advanced Study of the Soviet Union
Center for International Security and Arms Control
Committee for National Security
Educators for Social Responsibility
Harvard Center for Science and International Affairs
Lawyers Alliance for Nuclear Arms Control
League of Women Voters Education Fund
National Public Radio
Natural Resources Defense Council
Nuclear Control Institute
Peace Links (Woman Against Nuclear War)
Peace Through Law Education Fund
Performing Artists for Nuclear Disarmament
Physicians for Social Responsibility
Scientists' Institute for Public Information
Union of Concerned Scientists
United Campuses to Prevent Nuclear War
Woodrow Wilson Department of Government and Foreign Affairs
World Policy Institute

The annual meetings of the National Network of Grantmakers bring together many of the smaller and change-oriented funders, and are always substantially devoted to international considerations ranging from human rights to outlawing nuclear power. Attendance at any one of those meetings provides an orientation to the breadth of grantor concerns relating to equality and quality of life everywhere.

The George Gund Foundation of Cleveland, which has generally focused on local and regional issues, now devotes sizable attention to "arms control research and East–West tension reduction." A March 9, 1984 story in the *Christian Science Monitor* quotes foundation officials:

Heightened interest in the issue stems from the chill gripping U.S.–Soviet relations and increased international tension in the wake of new U.S. missiles in Western Europe, the Soviet destruction of the Korean airliner in September, and conflict in the Middle East. Also playing a role were President Reagan's speech on what has been dubbed "Star Wars" weaponry and the televised movie "The Day After" which attempted to dramatize the aftermath of a nuclear strike.

When queried as to what all this had to do with the foundation's interest in Ohio, Associate Director Henry Doll said: "Since we're concerned with the quality of life in northeastern Ohio, and since the threat of nuclear war impinges on that life, we decided to make grants toward the pursuit of peace." Gund has also been a funder of International Physicians for the Prevention of Nuclear War.

I indicated earlier that the Kettering Foundation, one of the earliest to be concerned about international issues, is now giving priority attention to the mechanisms by which citizens can become informed and involved with even the most complex international subjects. One of its challenges to community-related foundations is to invest in organizations and activities that will, in Thomas Jefferson's words, "enlighten the electorate." Jefferson and Kettering can take encouragement in the closing story of the Thomas Fox article on international philanthropy:

> Finally, since this magazine regularly features smaller foundations in a column called "Small Wonders," it should be noted that the New Hampshire Charitable Fund has recently established an international fund, to promote world peace and international understanding through educational, cultural, social, economic and legal programs of nonprofit organizations that directly involve New Hampshire residents.

9

To Remember the Dead

I. IN MEMORIAM
II. "USEFUL EVEN AFTER DEATH"
III. IN PERPETUITY OR JUST FOR A WHILE?

In Memoriam

In his sophomore year at Dartmouth College, Richard Drew Hall, class of 1927, died, leaving everyone who had known him shocked that such a promising life could be cut short. His parents were beyond consolation until another grieving father sent them a note from the White House which read, "In recollection of his son and my son who have the privilege by the Grace of God to be boys through all eternity."

President and Mrs. Calvin Coolidge had lost a son while they still occupied the White House. Because they had been helped to bear their grief through the help of others who had lost children and by the thought of young Cal as a happy boy forever, the President wanted to try to comfort his friend Edward Hall in the same way. Hall and his wife began to think of an appropriate memorial to their son, and this project, along with the President's words, began to pull them out of their anguish. They decided to build an infirmary at Dartmouth and to endow it so that it could provide warm hospitality and care to young men at the same stage in life as Dick. The gift document said, "We are especially anxious that everything possible be done to create and maintain in the House and all its surroundings, the cheerful atmosphere of both home and college." Dick's House has already served Dartmouth students for 60 years; it has become a permanent part of the campus. Each visitor is greeted with the inscription:

In recollection of his son and my son who have the privilege by the
Grace of God to be boys through all eternity.

—Calvin Coolidge

The same pain and poignancy were at the heart of the Stanford story,
told more fully in Chapter 2. That great university was founded in memory of Governor and Mrs. Leland Stanford's only child, Leland Jr. During
the boy's last illness, Governor Stanford stayed by the bedside, and when
death finally came to the 15-year-old, his father insisted on remaining
right there through another long night's vigil. In the morning, with
remarkable composure and vision, he said to his wife, "The children of
California shall be our children," and the two proceeded to spend their
grief in building Stanford as a lasting monument to their only child.

A different institution that has served as a memorial to a son and as a
perpetual service to society is the John Simon Guggenheim Memorial
Foundation and its Guggenheim Fellowships. John Simon Guggenheim
was 18 in the summer of 1922. He had just graduated from Exeter and
was planning, with great anticipation, to attend Harvard in the fall. He
suddenly developed the combination of pneumonia and an inoperable
mastoid condition and died. His father wrote:

> In this great sorrow, there came to Mrs. Guggenheim and myself a
> desire in some sense to continue the influence of the young life of
> eager aspiration by establishing a foundation which in his name
> should, in the words of the charter "promote the advancement and
> diffusion of knowledge and understanding, and the appreciation of
> beauty, by aiding without distinction on account of race, color or
> creed, scholars, scientists and artists of either sex in the prosecution
> of their labors."

Gordon N. Ray, who served as president of the foundation for several
years, added the following, in his 1978 "Summary Report":

> The Fellowships thus envisioned would be awarded "to provide
> opportunities for both men and women to carry on advanced study
> in any field of knowledge, or in any of the fine arts, including music,
> . . . under the freest possible conditions." It was hoped that they
> would operate both "as to the educational, literary, artistic and
> scientific power of this country, and also to provide for the cause of
> better international understanding."

Milton Lomask's *Seed Money: The Guggenheim Story* includes this further
description:

> Such rules as the John Simon can be said to follow are those dictated
> by its purposes. Moe [Henry Allen Moe, Guggenheim mentor and

early foundation officer] believes that brain power is America's "most critical need," and he describes the underlying purpose of the John Simon as an effort to help "stock pile" this precious commodity for the future. Obviously a John Simon grant is seed money; it is reserved for the person who has arrived at a stage in his field sufficiently advanced to justify the assumption that, given a "leg up," he can scale the further heights on his own.

Guggenheim Fellows are given financial support to sustain them for a year. The money was once intended only to work abroad but now fellows can also spend their year in this country. The foundation has also instituted a Western Hemisphere program providing assistance to Latin and South Americans. There is no longer any age limit.

The foundation was established and gave its first grants in 1925 after three years of extensive research on the very best way to fulfill the Guggenheims' dream. Their first gambles netted Purcival Bailey and Aaron Copland. Gordon Ray reports that the second class included Steven Vincent Benet, Margery Nicolson, Linus Pauling, and Roger Sessions. Ray's 1979 "Summary Report" contains fascinating totals for both dollars and fellows:

> I shall now skip ahead to 1979, pausing only to note that in the interval, the Foundation's endowment has grown from $3 million to $93 million, the culminating increase being the $40 million we received after the death of Mrs. Simon Guggenheim in 1970. . . .
> . . . In the 55 years of its existence, 1925 to 1979, it has made some 11,500 awards totalling more than $80 million. Its fellows have received 41 Nobel prizes and 102 Pulitzer prizes. Of the 1303 members of the National Academy of Sciences 452 (or 35%) are Guggenheim Fellows.

The names of just some of the stars listed by Ray take up several pages and are truly a "Who's Who" of arts, letters and science. Among them are:

> Saul Bellow, Arthur Compton, Henry Kissinger, Linus Pauling, Gian-Carlo Menotti, Gunther Schuller, William Schuman, Ansel Adams, Richard Bentsen, Aaron Siskind, Conrad Aiken, W. H. Auden, Hart Crane, e.e. cummings, James Dickey, Alan Ginsburg, Randall Jarrell, Robert Lowell, Langston Hughes, Marianne Moore, John Crow Ransom, Theodore Roethke, Allen Tate, Richard Wilbur, James Baldwin, John Cheever, John Dos Passos, Joyce Carol Oates, Philip Roth, John Updike, Kurt Vonnegut, Jr., Robert Penn Warren, Eudora Welty, Thomas Wolfe, Irvin Howe, Ada Louise Huxtable, Dwight Macdonald, Lewis Mumford, Susan Sontag, Lionel Trilling, Edmund Wilson, and on and on.

In that same report Ray adds:

> By limiting myself to lists of names, I have had to forego any
> mention of what our Fellowships have meant in human terms to
> those who have held them. There are many such stories, from
> among which I'll select three. Our awards have often been turning
> points in the lives of those receiving them, permitting hazards of
> new fortunes that would otherwise have been inconceivable. When
> James Dickey became a Fellow in 1961, he was creative director
> for an Atlanta advertising agency, composing copy for Coca Cola,
> potato chips, and fertilizers. His grant not only made it possible for
> him to write *Helmets,* his third book of poems; it also enabled him
> to give up advertising for poetry. I find in our records that he once
> thought of calling his Fellowship volume *Goodbye to Serpents.* It is
> not clear whether or not he finally came to regard this title as too
> pointed an allusion to his former employment. When Pauline Kael
> received her award in 1964, she was in Berkeley devoting most of
> her attention to film advertising and programming for colleges and
> theatres. Not only did she write *I Lost It at the Movies* on her
> Fellowship; she also moved to New York, there to embark on her
> remarkable career as a professional film critic. In 1957 Lynn White,
> who had been the highly effective president of Mills College for 14
> years, grew tired of the endless battle with his trustees which was
> necessary to keep his institution on the right track. He had earlier
> had a notable career as a historian of medieval technology,
> exploring areas where there are few documents or none, his head
> "full of horse collars and windmills, cranks and spinning wheels."
> The Foundation heeded his appeal for a year to get back to
> scholarship, and during it he wrote *Medieval Technology and Social
> Change,* a book notable for its mastery of the interaction of culture,
> technology, and sweeping historical trends. Thus he was enabled to
> embark on a second scholarly career which has proved to be even
> more remarkable than the first.

In his 1964 report, Ray quoted a letter from Linus Pauling stating that his
Nobel prize in chemistry was awarded for work directly related to his fellowship studies in 1926 and that his Nobel Peace Prize in 1962 stemmed
from an awareness of world problems that he developed during his 19
months abroad as a fellow in 1926 and 1927.

Lomask, in *Seed Money,* includes this quite different testimonial from
"the now famous short-story writer and novelist Katherine Anne Porter [a
1931 winner]," who explained:

> . . . I wrote to Mr. Henry Allen Moe full of contrition that I hadn't
> turned out a book in that year. And Mr. Moe wrote that nobody had

expected me to! That the grant was not just for the work of that year, but was meant to help me go on for all my life. And this has been true—without that grant, I might have just stayed in Mexico, or here at home! I should certainly not have gone to Europe when I did; and so in the most absolute sense that Guggenheim Foundation Fellowship has helped to nourish my life as a writer to this day . . . .

Perhaps the very best testament to the success of the memorial is also provided by Lomask when he quotes Brand Blanshard, Sterling Professor of Philosophy at Yale University and a Guggenheim Fellow:

The Foundation is the Socratic midwife of American scholarship. It has helped bring to the birth all sorts of insights, theories, and systems, scientific hypotheses and works of art. I cannot think how anyone could have made a more imaginative or decisive contribution to American scholarship than Senator Guggenheim did in his memorable letter of gift. He was moved to make the gift because he had lost a son. He gained some thousands of sons and daughters who will always think of his name with thanks and honor.

The tragic loss of a child has often led to the combination of memorial and public service. When the only child of Mr. and Mrs. Michael L. Benedum was killed in World War I at the age of 20, the parents established the Claude Worthington Benedum Foundation in his memory to support human service institutions in western Pennsylvania and West Virginia. William Donner gave more than $2 million for the study of cancer, which took his son's life. Mr. and Mrs. Hugh Roy Cullen lost their only son in an oil rig accident, and turned their attention to the development of the University of Houston, including the Roy Gustav Cullen Memorial Building, with the stipulation that "the University of Houston must always be a college for working men and women and their sons and daughters. . . ."

Some individuals who had not previously been unusually public-spirited were moved to greater charity by family tragedy. The Geraldine R. Dodge Foundation was established after the only child of Geraldine Rockefeller Dodge and Marcellus Hartley Dodge, who was an heir to the Remington Arms fortune, died in an automobile accident. Mrs. Dodge devoted the rest of her life to public service, including the establishment of the foundation that bears her name. After Gladys Brooks Thayer's son died a tragic death, Mrs. Thayer also turned to charitable activity including the establishment of the Gladys Brooks Foundation.

Walter Wilson Jennings' book, *A Dozen Captains of American Industry,* describes how tragedy inspired Henry Clay Frick's generosity: "When the Pittsburgh Bank of Savings closed in 1915 and approximately 5,000 children were about to lose their Christmas savings, he telegraphed his bank to advance hundreds of thousands of dollars to pay depositors in full. . . . Each check bore a cut of his beloved (daughter) Martha who died at the age of 6."

In Baltimore, the Jill Fox Memorial Fund was created "to finance extraordinary medical needs for individuals who cannot find the necessary funds elsewhere." Known as a "fund of last resort," it was established in 1978 by Mr. and Mrs. Lewis J. Fox in memory of their daughter and is designed to "make the difference between leading an active life in the community or confinement to bed, home or residential institution. Funds have been provided for medication, artificial limbs, rehabilitation equipment, braces and specially designed wheelchairs."

Jill Fox shared her family's commitment to those less fortunate and was especially interested in working with the physically handicapped. Though she died during her college years, her interest lives on through the fund established in her name, which aids such people as these:

- A 23-year-old man with a progressive neurological condition which affected his ability to speak was furnished with a portable, battery-operated electronic voice system with which he was able to communicate.

- A 16-year-old boy with a developmental disability was furnished with special lift equipment enabling him to leave his home and travel to school and activities rather than requiring him to be educated at home.

- A 27-year-old man who suffered head injuries and leg fractures in an accident was provided with special experimental electrical-stimulation equipment from a New York research program. Subsequently, he was able to return to work.

- A 30-year-old quadriplegic man, unable to write or use dictating equipment, was provided with a special electric typewriter that enabled him to further his academic studies.

In many cases it was children who memorialized their parents. Keele and Kiger's *Foundations* indicates that the Josiah Macy, Jr. Foundation was established by Kate Macy Ladd as a memorial to her father who had "died of typhoid fever in 1875 at the age of 37." His daughter was determined that such diseases be prevented in the future. Keele and Kiger also record that the Henry J. Kaiser Family Foundation emphasizes medicine and health because "Kaiser's life long interest in medicine reflected his belief that his mother, who died when he was 16, might have lived longer had medical care been more readily available and more effective."

Sometimes money is left to memorialize a mentor. William S. Barstow was a protegé of Thomas Edison. A New York Community Trust description of the Barstow Fund explains Barstow's motives in establishing the fund:

[When] Mr. Edison decided to move his New Jersey laboratory from Menlo Park to West Orange, he picked young Barstow to supervise the installation. This was the beginning of a close friendship between the two men that was to last until Mr. Edison's death. Reminiscing on those days Mr. Barstow later commented: "There was no such thing as electrical engineering then; it was not taught in the colleges and little was known of the subject; the Edison Machine Works issued loose-leaf pamphlets every week explaining new developments and these constituted the principal text-books then available."

. . . he never forgot the man who launched his career: at Menlo Park in New Jersey he built the Edison Tower, a 131-foot steel shaft in Mr. Edison's memory topped with a three-ton enlarged replica of Edison's incandescent lamp.

George A. Howles, like William Barstow, felt indebted to his mentor; in this case, his friend Addison Rand of the Ingersoll-Rand Company. He left his money "for the establishment of the Addison C. Rand Fund (of the New York Community Trust) so the help Addison Rand had extended to so many during his lifetime might be carried on in the generations that came after him."

Friends established the Philip Murray Memorial Foundation to honor the humanitarian and labor leader. Seventy-five friends of Edmund L. Godkin, Editor of *The Nation*, established "The Godkin Lectures" at Harvard in 1903, a continuing lecture series "upon the essentials of free government and the duties of the citizens."

Sometimes the donor wants to memorialize himself. One of the candidates for the "Remember Me" award would have to be James Lick, who spent so many years trying to establish a monument that would call attention to himself in perpetuity. He settled for the Lick Observatory, which, though enormously important, is now being eclipsed by bigger and better facilities.

"Useful Even After Death"

". . . I wish to be useful even after death. . . ."

This was the principal message in Benjamin Franklin's will, written in 1790. In it, Franklin reviewed his past and his hopes for the future. He wrote: "Having myself been assisted to set up my business . . . by a kind loan of Money . . . which was the foundation of my Fortune, and of all utility in life that may be ascribed to me, I wish to be useful even after my death, if possible, in forming and advancing other young men that may be serviceable to their Country."

Forty years later, when another wealthy and generous Philadelphia citizen, Stephen Girard, passed away, the city anxiously awaited report of his last will. As the newspaper put it: "Curiosity is on tip-toe to know what he has done with his money." In death, as in life, Stephen Girard arranged to have his usefulness continued. In *Noblesse Oblige*, Kathleen McCarthy reports that upon his death:

> Girard bequeathed a substantial amount to his adopted city for
> municipal improvements and founded the celebrated Girard College
> for Poor Orphan Boys. In appraising Girard's bequest, Hunt
> [Fremont Hunt in *Lives of American Merchants*] commented
> approvingly, "The savings of the years of toil were . . . dispensed in
> bulk upon the community in the midst of which he had gathered
> them." But it was clear that Girard had also been singled out for
> his extraordinary personal charity during his lifetime. "What is a
> man worth?" queried Hunt. "He is worth precisely just so much as
> he has capacity and inclination to be useful."

McCarthy also provides an enjoyable follow-up: "Men of prominence knew that at life's end their achievements and shortcomings would be candidly dissected and reviewed in pulpit and press. In his excellent study of philanthropy in Tudor–Stuart England, Wilbur K. Jordan suggests the significance of funeral sermons in spurring emulative charities."

Bequests can be pretty specific and clever. In *American Philanthropy*, Bremner provides this example: "It is easy to laugh at the highly specialized and seemingly trivial purposes of many philanthropic activities. Yet who can deny, for example, that old people often suffer from a failing eyesight? And who but Elias Boudinot, first president of the American Bible Society, was thoughtful enough to leave money in his will for purchasing spectacles for the aged poor?"

George Adams Boyd picks up the story and expands on it in *Elias Boudinot: Patriot and Statesman:*

> Boudinot's will, made shortly before his death in 1821, serves as an
> index to his more formal benefactions. Some of the smaller
> bequests displayed unusual imagination. The New Jersey Bible
> Society was to expend $200 "in the purchase of spectacles, to be
> given by them to poor old people, it being in vain to give a Bible to
> those who cannot obtain the means of reading it." The Public
> Hospital in Philadelphia was granted the use of 3,270 acres in
> Bradford County to enable poor foreigners and persons from states
> other than Pennsylvania to meet the requirements for admission.
> The Mayor and Corporation of Philadelphia were allowed the use
> of 13,000 wooded acres along the Susquehanna River to provide
> the indigent with fuel. The Magdalen Societies of Philadelphia and

New York were left $500 each. Dividends from fifteen shares of stock in the Burlington Aqueduct Company were to be devoted to the relief of "poor females" in and about Burlington, and Susan was to distribute $200 at once among at least ten poor widows.

Boudinot's interest in the red man, manifested in *A Star in the West*, was reflected a number of times in the will. The American Board of Commissioners for Foreign Missions received the use of 4,542 acres in Lycoming County, Pennsylvania, especially for Indians, and a gift of $5,000 after Susan's demise. To the United Brethren of Moravians at Bethlehem went $2,000 "for the purpose of endeavoring to civilize and gospelize the Indian nations or any others destitute of a gospel ministry." The sum of $500 was to be paid to the Institution for Instructing and Educating the Heathen in Cornwall, Connecticut, otherwise known as the Foreign Mission School. It was here that the young Cherokee, Galagina or "The Buck," had come in 1818 to take the name of Elias Boudinot and to learn to be leader of his people.

Mae Dorland McCoy married an army officer, and they decided to stay in the Philippines when he reached retirement age. He died before World War II, and she was left alone to face the Japanese invasion. The New York Community Trust tells her story in a special pamphlet dedicated to the Colonel and Mrs. Henry Bayard McCoy Memorial: "Mrs. McCoy was imprisoned in a concentration camp with other survivors of the invasion. Like the other prisoners, she was treated cruelly. Malnutrition resulted in failure of her eyesight and she became almost totally blind." Reflecting on their years of service to the country, she decided that their money should go to help young men interested in history and public service. The fund was established to foster "particularly among boys, interest in and respect for the traditional ideals of American life and the Constitutional representation form of government under which the United States has endured."

In Perpetuity or Just for a While?

In his "Principles of Public Giving," Julius Rosenwald acknowledged that Alexander Hamilton was a wise man, but he added:

> Yet it was Hamilton who drafted the will of Robert Richard Randall, who in the first years of the last century left a farm to be used as a haven for superannuated sailors. A good many years ago the courts were called upon to construe the word "sailor" to include men employed on steamships. Even so, the Fund for Snug Harbor, I am assured, vastly exceeds any reasonable requirement for the care of retired seafarers. The farm happened to be situated on Fifth Avenue, New York. Today it is valued at $30 or $40 million.

Rosenwald's "Principles" were first published in *The Atlantic Monthly* in May, 1929, and drew considerable response, with particular focus on Rosenwald's opposition "to gifts in perpetuity for any purpose."
Rosenwald offered these additional examples to make his point:

> I have heard of a fund which provides a baked potato at each meal for each young woman at Bryn Mawr, and of another, dating from one of the great famines, which pays for a half a loaf of bread deposited each day at the door of each student in one of the colleges at Oxford. Gifts to educational institutions often contain provisions which are made absurd by the advance of learning. An American university has an endowed lectureship on coal gas as the cause of malarial fever. . . . The list of these precisely focused gifts which have lost their usefulness could be extended into volumes, but I am willing to rest the case on Franklin and Hamilton. With all their sagacity, they could not foresee what the future would bring. The world does not stand still. Anyone old enough to vote has seen revolutionary changes in the mechanics of living, and these changes have been accompanied and abetted by changing points of view toward the needs and desires of our fellow men.
>
> I do not know how many millions of dollars have been given in perpetuity for the support of orphan asylums. The Hershey endowment alone is said to total $40,000,000 and more. Orphan asylums began to disappear about the time the old-fashioned wall telephone went out.

True to his convictions, Rosenwald directed that his own fund should be entirely spent "within 25 years of the time of my death." The trustees obviously caught Rosenwald's spirit, for the fund was fully expended in 14 years and closed in 1946.

Rosenwald's daughter, Edith R. Stern, and her children carried on the example of time-limited trusts. A May 19, 1986 *New York Times* story told of the closing of their fund:

> After a half-century of philanthropy, the Stern Fund of New York has spent itself out of existence and has thrown a party to celebrate.
>
> The ending had been planned from the beginning, in 1936 in New Orleans. The founders, Edith and Edger Stern, did not want their fund to spend money perpetuating itself.
>
> . . . The ending was in keeping with a family tradition. Mrs. Stern, who died in 1980, was a daughter of Julius Rosenwald, a founding partner of Sears, Roebuck & Company.

The Rosenwald and Stern Funds represent one alternative to perpetual trusts, but there are many other variations and models. For instance, Mr.

Rosenwald, along with Calvin Coolidge and Alfred E. Smith, was a trustee of the Hubert Fund, which decided on immediate distribution of the assets.

Frederick P. Keppel, in *The Foundation: Its Place in American Life,* reports that:

> The trustees appointed by the late Payne Whitney, instead of creating a foundation, as they might have done under the terms of Mr. Whitney's will, announced the immediate distribution of the principal sum entrusted to them, amounting to nearly $20–$36 million, among certain institutions in which Mr. Whitney had already shown an interest and had supported with characteristic generosity.

Edward A. Filene gave his trustees the option to spend part or all of the principal. Several years ago, the Rockefeller brothers decided to direct approximately half of the assets of the Rockefeller Brothers Fund to the favorite institutions of each brother and their sister. The Fleischmann Foundation grew to more than $100 million before the trustees began to fulfill the request of the donor, Max C. Fleischmann, who asked that the fund be expended within 20 years after the death of his wife.

A compromise between a perpetual fund, with the disadvantages Rosenwald foresaw, and indefinite investment, is the gift to a community trust. Frederick Goff, founder of the community foundation movement, was motivated in part by his dislike for self-perpetuating philanthropy. His solution was to encourage leaving money in perpetuity, but to a board that was not self-perpetuating and indeed was designed to reflect contemporary community priorities. As Goff put it: "The community foundation is the best way to defeat the 'dead hand.'"

When I compare all of the good arguments against perpetual trusts (the foundation's purpose gets out of date, the staff becomes so professional that the original purposes are suffocated, control of the foundation by "the dead hand," and so on) with the relatively few foundation dollars there are—certainly compared to government expenditures, I tend to come down on the side of perpetuity. In this study, for example, I have repeatedly come across the enormous current impact of such foundations as Ford, Carnegie, Rockefeller, Commonwealth, and Kellogg. Had they all gone the way of Rosenwald, Fleischmann, Hubert, and Whitney, I wonder if there would be nearly the positive influence of this "extra dimension" in society today. In the face of today's relatively low birthrate of new foundations, which barely keeps the total number constant, it would be particularly unfortunate to accelerate foundation closings.

I find myself wishing very much that the General Education Board were around today to deal with the issues of racism and unequal opportunity.

When I look at the growth of the John Simon Guggenheim Memorial
Foundation, which still has more than $100 million of assets (after spend-
ing even more than that in interest) and which still has great influence on
scholarship and international understanding, I wonder if the case really
holds up that we would have been better off if that money had all been
spent by 1950.

Pluralism is one of philanthropy's most attractive assets. Certain donors
may want their estates to be dispersed immediately; others may wish to
establish time-limited trusts; while still others may prefer gifts in perpetuity. All of these should be options for giving money to strengthen the
future fabric of society.

In *Trails Plowed Under*, Will Rogers provided the best motivation for
remembering the dead: "Course we are all just a-hangin' on here as long
as we can. I don't know why we hate to go, we know it's better there.
Maybe it's because we haven't done anything that will live after we are
gone."

PART III
Unique Dimensions
of Philanthropy

10

Unique Opportunities of Corporate Philanthropy

At a Council on Foundations meeting, about three years ago, Alex Plinio, then Director of Contributions for Prudential Insurance Company, gave a paper with a title something like "Fourteen Ways that Companies Provide Non-Cash Assistance to Voluntary Organizations." I urged him to expand it into a more formal article, and told him that INDEPENDENT SECTOR would be pleased to publish it as part of a series of Occasional Papers. About a year later, I asked Alex how it was coming, and he said he had run into the interesting problem of finding new examples that should be included. By then he was up to "Twenty-Nine Ways. . . ." He had also been promoted to Vice President for Public Service, and President of the Prudential Foundation, so he would have even less time to work on the paper. Finding the idea more interesting than ever, and sharing his frustration with the time constraints he faced, I said INDEPENDENT SECTOR would provide him some research and editorial assistance.

Another year went by, and I explained to him that we really should be getting something published. This time Alex said that between his own efforts and those of Joanne Scanlon, the part-time research assistant, he was coming across all kinds of new information that really should be included. By then he was up to "Forty-One Ways. . . ." Six months later, out of eagerness to have this important resource document published, and seeing my offer of modest help reach a not-so-modest level, I said we absolutely had to go with what we had. The result was Plinio and Scanlon's excellent *Resource Raising: The Role of Non-Cash Assistance in Corporate Philanthropy,* which contains, in six categories, forty-nine types of assistance and more than one hundred examples. At that, Alex Plinio still says, "You know Brian, I wish we hadn't rushed that into print, because it's still very incomplete!"

Resource Raising contains information about an extraordinary variety of in-kind gifts or subsidies that corporations are currently providing to nonprofit organizations. These include gifts of land, computer tie-ins, piggyback advertising, dispute resolution/negotiation services, energy conservation audits, product and marketing consultation, survey development and analysis, gifts of trees, horses, and seeds, no-interest or low-interest loans, meeting and conference facilities, and staff and volunteer training. The list is very long.

Their paper illustrates graphically how corporate philanthropy differs from the work of private foundations. This difference is not yet fully understood by either the grantmaking or grantseeking community. In a Council on Foundation's 1982 publication, *Corporate Philanthropy,* I tried to address some of these differences between foundations and corporations:

> To a much greater extent than private foundations, corporations have a range of opportunities to influence change. Indeed, those opportunities are exactly why John Kenneth Galbraith believes that corporations should not be allowed to make contributions—he says it gives them the chance to exercise undue influence. One of the discouraging things about the efforts of many companies is that they try to emulate their counterparts in the foundation world. They do the same things, they even organize themselves the same ways, and so they lose the chance to capitalize on their uniqueness. . . . Conversely, good corporate efforts play to that special role and make the most of a corporation's many opportunities to effect change. . . . The best company programs are those that encourage employee giving and volunteering, sink the company up to its neck in public/private partnerships, provide program-related investments, and in every other way use their dollars and other assets to increase the ability of people to solve problems.

The unique ways in which corporations make useful contributions to causes and communities are extraordinarily varied. For example:

- The Atlantic Richfield company provides $500 grants to be presented by employees to organizations with which ARCO's personnel have done substantial volunteer work.

- Aetna Life and Casualty established a National Urban Neighborhood Investment Program through which it contributes and invests in inner-city neighborhoods. The program includes a combination of grant funds, corporate investment dollars and technical assistance to promote the revitalization of these communities. The "intent is to build an ongoing management capability to implement local rehabilitation efforts, package information necessary to obtain mortgage financing commitments, monitor construction and serve as a liaison for neighborhood leaders, property owners, developers, government agencies and lending institutions."

- The Baltimore Resource Bank is a cashless bank that enables businesses to be involved at the grassroots level. A neighborhood organization needing materials or technical assistance to undertake a self-help project submits a request to the Resource Bank. Acting as a liaison, the Resource Bank then matches resources with worthy community projects. Once a match is made, the Resource Bank provides oversight to make certain that the aims of both partners are being achieved. Existing matchups, unmet needs and available resources are listed in the Resource Bank's quarterly newsletter, "The Bank Statement."

- The agri-business Partnership known as "The Andersons" in Maumee, Ohio, makes substantial gifts to colleges and other grant recipients, and to make part of the gift last, they ask that "at least one-third of the contribution be invested in the Partnership, creating a continuing source of endowment income for these limited partners." Over a two-year period, a half-million dollars was given to the University of Ohio; the University was so impressed with this investment opportunity that it asked that the full gift be reinvested in the Partnership.

- In its annual evaluations of executives, General Mills includes involvement and effectiveness in community service among its five areas of review.

- The Gary-Williams Oil Company of Colorado has created an Employee Advised Fund administered by employees drawn from all parts of the company. The employees have sole responsibility for selecting the Denver-area charities that receive Gary-Williams corporate contributions each year. They do their own assessment of community needs and of agency effectiveness. No one in management signs off on their grant decisions. The result has been a substantial increase in the number of employees who participate in the company's volunteer and matching gifts programs—a corporate public service program that has its own built-in multiplier effect.

- The Trailways Corporation established a "Home Free" program that provides free bus trips home to runaway youth.
- When the Southern Railway System phased out its old steam engines, it donated the more than one hundred bells to small urban and rural churches.

One company that is conscientious about applying its total business resources to its philanthropic program is AT&T. For example, their support of ten historically black engineering schools combines cash assistance, the full-time in-residence teaching of one or more Bell Laboratories scientists each year, and computer/product/laboratory and library equipment and resources. Another example involves support of minority medical institutions where AT&T has advanced substantial challenge grants for endowment scholarship support at Howard, Drew, Meharry, and Morehouse, combined with equipment gifts and with a board of directors appointment.

In these and thousands of other cases, companies are finding ways to use their talent, experience, knowledge, facilities, money, trained people, and concern to support and strengthen the communities and causes with which they are involved.

In that same Council on Foundations' publication on *Corporate Philanthropy*, Cecile Springer, Director of Contributions and Community Affairs at Westinghouse, writes about the opportunities for corporations to exercise real leadership through their public service efforts:

> Business leadership exerts itself in many ways in the stimulation of innovation through corporate research and development; in the support of university research; in innovative product design as well as in techniques of manufacturing, marketing, and sales. Business leadership also expresses itself as investment in new facilities and programs.
>
> Leadership in giving can adopt these same characteristics, stimulating innovation in funded programs and investment in new facilities and programs. Business can seek out approaches that solve critical community problems, enrich communities, and foster the creative use of technology and professional advice.
>
> . . . The challenge to corporate philanthropy is to apply business expertise and leadership to contribution efforts, to respond more effectively to changing social trends. But challenges are also opportunities. The coming years offer a unique opportunity to enrich the relationship between those who give and those who receive; let's take advantage of it.

Leadership works best when it involves the experience, overview, and leverage of the chief executive officer. In the publication, "Corporate Community Involvement," developed by the President's Task Force on Private Sector Initiatives, there is this good example of top level involvement and influence:

A group of top corporate executives—principally from high-technology industries—engineering college administrators and minority leaders met in 1972 to plan a program to increase the number of minority engineers. Of 43,000 graduates that year, only 1,300 were Black, Hispanic, or American Indian.

The National Academy of Engineering (NAE), an affiliate body of the National Academy of Sciences, assumed primary responsibility in 1973 to establish a program that would lead to a substantial increase in the number of minority engineers. In January 1974, Reginald Jones, chairman and chief executive officer of the General Electric Company, spearheaded the creation of the National Advisory Council on Minorities in Engineering (NACME, a committee of NAE) and endorsed the goal of achieving a tenfold increase in minority graduates in the next decade.

Mr. Jones, aware that this was a shared concern among high-technology firms, approached corporate leaders to participate in NACME. He succeeded in recruiting 16 top officers of major corporations. By 1979, NACME included top-level corporate representation from 37 leading technology-based firms, plus educational institutions, technical societies, minority organizations and cabinet-level federal government advisors.

NACME's activities include: student identification to locate prospective engineers (handled through contract with the College Board and the American College Testing Program), research and planning to track minority enrollments, technical assistance performed with the aid of five regional corporate chief executives who are charged with promoting local programs between industry and schools, and fundraising, primarily for scholarship programs (in 1980–81, $3.8 million was raised). While NACME sees a long road ahead to achieve its goal, by 1980 enrollments had tripled.

In 1981, NACME was folded into a new nonprofit organization—the National Action Council on Minorities in Engineering, Inc., which is a combined private and public group comprised of 100–200 chief executives and others having equivalent leadership roles in education, government, minority organizations and professional societies.

Mr. Jones' leadership did not stop with the creation of NACME.

Within GE, he initiated the Program to Increase Minority Engineering Graduates (PIMEG). Programs were targeted where there was a company presence and a large minority population. As of 1980, GE had 80 programs in 48 cities and 22 states. These programs range from meeting with pre-college (as early as elementary school) students, to comprehensive efforts linking schools, employers, parent associations and other interested parties. In 1980, PIMEG had reached approximately 30,000 minority students. Since 1972, GE has allocated over $7 million toward increasing enrollments.

PIMEG is a decentralized program and local executives are given significant discretion in designing strategy. Stress is placed on attracting local groups who have a vested interest in the concept of increasing minority enrollment. GE's success with PIMEG is based on the same ingredients that were applied to NACME: CEO involvement and self-interest.

Reginald Jones, in his role as head of the Business Roundtable, had said: "Public policy and social issues are no longer adjuncts to business planning and management. They are in the mainstream of it. The concern must be pervasive in companies today, from board room to factory floor. Management must be measured for performance in economic and non-economic areas alike. And top management must lead."

Often the leadership is collaborative as business executives join together to address community needs. The San Francisco Bay Area Business Task Force was established in 1982 when a group of Bay Area business leaders met to discuss ways in which the business community could become more active in community affairs. They were particularly concerned about regional employment trends and strategies, summer jobs for youth, and health cost containment. They decided, after examining other collaborative efforts, that they should take the initiative in bringing together for-profit and nonprofit interests so that, with the leaders of community organizations, they could begin to devise new strategies to address these problems. The Task Force's report, "Rethinking Corporate Involvement: Some New Sector Roles in the Bay Area," observes: "Business cannot solve every local problem, but for some issues it can provide part of the solution by contributing to a new style of local problem solving that is collaborative, pragmatic and issue oriented."

In 1978, Weyerhaeuser conducted what is still one of the most comprehensive studies of a company's public service program. Prompted by concerns that the corporation had been donating money to projects too far removed from the company's identifiable interests and strengths, the review gave Weyerhaeuser the opportunity to study possible configurations for its future program. After hearing and considering varied advice about being truly eleemosynary or truly self-serving, the company concluded that it should focus its giving "at the crossroads where company and public interests intersect." William Ruckelshaus, then Weyerhaeuser vice president, described it as "the intersection of corporate self-interest and societal need." Since then, the company has moved "toward topics of unique concern to the Company, but important to the larger society as well." The company's position on grantmaking and other public service was revised to read:

> To increase understanding of and provide leadership for significant issues at the intersection of industrial and societal interests, with initial attention to the use of the forest land base; and
> to improve the quality of life in communities and regions where Weyerhaeuser Company has a significant number of employees.

Corporations initially became involved in the support of voluntary efforts through this same enlightened self-interest. In his chapter, "How Giving Grew," in *Corporate Giving*, F. Emerson Andrews recalls a case in which there was a literal and figurative crossroads involving the railroads. The railroad companies found a need to help develop local YMCAs to provide "supervised, economical accommodations and some of the advantages of a club. . . ." Both sides saw a distinct advantage to the relationship. Andrews reports that "in 1868, the YMCA's annual convention, held in Detroit, passed this resolution":

> *Resolved*, that the manufacturers of our country can make no investment that will bring them greater dividends than that of contributing largely to the aid and formation and sustaining of Young Men's Christians Associations within their various localities

Andrews adds, "The same 1868 convention authorized employment of a director to undertake religious work among laborers on the Union Pacific Railroad, pushing westward from Omaha." He continues: "By 1890, Associations were reported at 82 divisional and terminal points and in every instance railroads helped financially. The usual practice at this stage was for railroad corporations to pay about 60 percent of the operating budgets for railroad YMCA buildings, the employees making up the remainder."

The tension that can exist in defining the intersection of corporate and public interests was apparent from the beginning. Andrews says: "The Movement, highly evangelistic in its early period, accepted these funds first with some questioning. Says the YMCA *History*:

> The conscience of the Movement was not clear at the beginning on the acceptance of corporation funds, but the practice was soon rationalized. "The shrewdest men, the most careful managers, are

now ready to appropriate money for the purpose," declared a speaker at the conference of 1882, "and the response they make to their stockholders is 'we are making money for you by it.'"

Andrews reports that the next step was the expansion of Ys into most metropolitan areas. This broadened their base of support but they still appealed to business on the basis of providing a place where its workers would find low-cost housing and also receive attention to their recreational and spiritual needs.

I've heard people describe B. Dalton's philanthropic focus on literacy as either the smartest corporate giving program or the most self-serving. B. Dalton, one of the country's largest book store chains, has an obvious interest in literacy. The company makes no bones about its interest: "Dalton Bookseller is firmly committed to increasing functional literacy in the United States. As a national full-selection, full-service bookseller, we recognize our responsibility to help solve the illiteracy problem, which affects not only our business, but also the quality of life in the communities we serve." The company argues that just as Weyerhaeuser knows something about and has a stake in forests, and health insurance companies know something about and have a stake in longevity of life, so too B. Dalton Booksellers knows something about and has a stake in literacy. That is their "crossroads."

The Boeing Company provided its largest gift ever—$5 million to the University of Washington—"to fund endowed chairs and professorships in several of the college's departments in such areas as artificial intelligence, aerospace controls and space systems, structural analysis, semiconductor electronics and parallel processing, and advanced materials." In presenting this award, Boeing's Chairman, T. A. Wilson said: "From this company's earliest days, when Claire Egtvedt and P. G. Johnson left the University to become Bill Boeing's 'idea men,' until today, we have relied on technical leaders trained at the University of Washington."

In its September 21, 1981 issue, *Fortune* carried an article by Lee Smith, "The Unsentimental Corporate Giver," that provided these additional glimpses of how the "intersection" is perceived:

> Some large companies give money to causes that at a glance seem remote from the company's day-to-day concerns but on examination turn out to be important to them. Xerox, for example, lends money to provide housing for the poor in Stamford, Connecticut, the company's headquarters town. The money earns no interest for Xerox, but it earns the company a reputation as a good neighbor. Similarly, Atlantic Richfield helps support native artisans in Alaska partly because the company is the largest oil producer on the North Slope and wants the goodwill of the local population.

At a recent conference on corporate philanthropy sponsored by the Public Affairs Council, Gerald Gendell of Procter and Gamble poked fun at the group by suggesting that maybe the joining of the words corporate and philanthropy would qualify as an "oxymoron." He may have had even more doubt about the phrase "business idealism" used by Robert Curtis Ogden as the title of an article for *Business World* in 1905.

As told by C. Vann Woodward in *Origins of the New South: 1877–1913,* there was a major effort to convince northern businessmen that they had a stake in helping develop the education systems of the South. The successful launching of the campaign was the result of the combined efforts of concerned southerners and northern philanthropists. The man chiefly responsible for bringing the two groups together was Robert Curtis Ogden, wealthy merchant, capitalist, and churchman of New York City, who preached a gospel of "business idealism." At that point, it was not corporations that were directly involved but business leaders, and the appeal was more to their moral and religious motivations than their business responsibilities.

Irving Kristol is pictured, in an April 10, 1981 *Business Week* article, as "a vocal critic of philanthropy." He is described as believing that companies have to be extremely cautious in using company money to "just do good. . . . When you give your own money, you can be as foolish as you like. But when you give away your stockholders' money, your philanthropy must serve the longer-term interest of the corporation. Corporate philanthropy should not and cannot be disinterested."

In the same piece, Robert Bothwell of the National Committee on Responsive Philanthropy is quoted: ". . . The fundamental issue is whether corporations take long- or short-range viewpoints—whether they are simply looking for today's PR value or are thinking about what America needs." Bothwell was not arguing that companies should ignore their self-interest: "I don't think there is any room for most corporations to support, say, environmental or consumer groups that are challenging corporations' practices. And I think that most of those groups would reject such support even if it were offered." He does argue that too much self-interest and too little public interest are not good for the country and in the long run would cause Congress to limit opportunities for corporate grantmaking.

The advantage to some corporations can be advertising. Mobil even takes from its advertising budget its support of such public television efforts as "Masterpiece Theater."

There is other evidence of companies trying to be at "the crossroads where company and public interests intersect":

- In his *Fortune* article, Lee Smith says that because Interpace deals with clay, steel, and aluminum, it is natural that the company would contribute to the development and display of sculpture. He also reports that in the mid-1970s General Motors, seeking to improve its management/recruiting program, decided to concentrate most of its generous education grants on 13 business schools and 14 engineering schools it deemed crucial to its own future.

- In an October, 1980 *Nation's Business* piece, Kenneth L. Albrecht, then Vice President at Equitable, is quoted: "There is really no point in any corporation wasting its time on matters in which it has no interest and with which it is not equipped to deal. For example, Equitable—as a life, health and pension company—will almost always have a segment of its program devoted to health. If we made musical instruments, our interest in the performing arts would likely be great."

- The Pillsbury Company applies its experience to several programs in relation to nutrition. It was honored in 1986 for its role in the development of the applied nutrition program in Bolivia, spearheaded by Meals for Millions/Freedom from Hunger Foundation. Pillsbury is among the several food manufacturers and retailers that formed and support the Food Industry Crusade Against Hunger, which grants funds to humanitarian organizations in under-developed countries. Closer to home, Pillsbury puts to work its food distribution know-how through its concentration on combining emergency food assistance with public education to identify conditions which cause hunger and malnutrition. As part of this program, the company supports the Advertising Council's Food Stamp Information Program.

- General Foods provided $1.7 million to establish the Nutrition Center at Meharry Medical College. David Brush, President of the General Foods Fund, provided this background information:

  While the health status of Americans generally is improving, this is not the case for blacks and other minority groups. Fewer than 10 percent of U.S. health professional schools in the United States are believed to have nutrition as a formal part of their curriculum. Nutrition related diseases, still among the most prevalent health problems in the U.S., disproportionately affect blacks and other under-served minority groups. . . . As a focal point for minority health professions education, Meharry is in an ideal position to educate current and future physicians, dentists and other health professionals on the importance of nutrition in disease prevention, the techniques for health promotion and the need for patient responsibility in improving health status.

In 1984, Congress faced a brouhaha over a bill that would have made an exception to the laws governing corporate charitable deductions, thus allowing the Apple computer company to deduct contributions of almost a billion dollars of computer equipment to elementary and high schools. Other computer manufacturers, fearing that Apple would be given too much of an advantage in name identification, cried "foul," and won the day. Earlier, the companies, working together, had convinced Congress to ease the law governing deduction of products rather than cash. The law had been tightened in 1969, when it was discovered that some companies, including drug companies, were giving away outdated products and deducting full market value. Their egregious practices caused an overkill solution and efforts are now underway to develop rules that will again encourage maximum, but realistic, non-cash support.

One of the largest donors of equipment has been the Hewlett Packard Company, which provides approximately $50 million a year in gifts of computer, electronic, chemical, and medical equipment, primarily to institutions of higher learning. Emery Rogers, Executive Director of the Hewlett Packard Foundation, wrote to me:

> There is one aspect of our philanthropic effort which has proven to be exceptionally rewarding. It is summed up by the following axiom:
> The surest escape route from deprived surroundings in today's changing world is the acquisition of a scientific, engineering or medical education. Equipment grants to minority colleges and to inner-city high schools have proved the validity of this maxim over and over again.

In *Resource Raising,* Plinio and Scanlon report these other gifts of "products, supplies and equipment":

- Clorox gives cleaning materials, such as liquid bleach, to the Red Cross for use in relief efforts after floods and other disasters.
- Hallmark donates cards, paper plates, posters, jewelry, and other items to such agencies as the Red Cross and the Salvation Army.
- Merck gives health products to developing countries and sites of medical emergencies.
- In Wadsworth, Illinois, Temple Farms presented 15 Lippizaner horses to a therapy program for the physically handicapped.
- General Mills has donated trainloads of cereals, mixes, and other products to food banks identified by local plant managers, often based on employees' volunteer involvement with a feeding program.

- Kraft distributed over 2 million pounds of food to 43 Second Harvest outlets in 1982.

- David Johnston, writing in the *Los Angeles Times,* pointed out: "Even seemingly useless items sometimes can have value to a nonprofit. When United California changed its name to First Interstate Bank in 1981, it donated 83 tons of stationery with its old name to the Skid Row Development Corporation. The gift allowed the nonprofit agency to start a paper recycling program which now gets computer and other paper from about 10 downtown firms."

Some companies are recognized for both the breadth and excellence of their public service programs. In 1985, IBM won the first Harvard/Dively Award for Corporate Public Initiative. The award is named for George S. Dively, who was chairman of the Harris Corporation, and the program is administered by the Center for Business and Government at Harvard's John F. Kennedy School of Government. A sampling of IBM's activities cited in the award were:

- *Job Training Programs:* Since IBM began its affiliation with job-training centers in 1968, more than 12,000 people have graduated from 57 major centers throughout the U.S. And, perhaps more importantly, more than 80 percent have found jobs with a variety of firms.

- *Social Service Leaves:* This program enables an IBM employee to take a paid leave of absence to work for a nonprofit, tax-exempt community service organization, which encourages volunteering. Since the program began in 1971, more than 800 employees have been granted leaves, usually for one year and with full pay from IBM.

- *Computer Literacy Program:* In 1983, IBM conducted an $8 million model computer literacy program in California, Florida, and New York. IBM donated 1,500 personal computer systems to 89 high schools and set up centers to train teachers in using the systems. The program was expanded for the 1984–85 school year to 26 states, Puerto Rico and the District of Columbia.

- *Education Executive Programs:* IBM introduced this program in 1984 to help school district superintendents, principals, and other senior administrators more effectively manage the personnel and financial resources in their school systems. More than 1,300 educators from nearly 200 communities throughout the United States participated with IBM paying all program costs except transportation and personal expenses. An earlier, similar program had 1,500 executives for nonprofit urban serving groups participating.

A February, 1982 *Newsweek* story had this unusual heading: "Doing Good—At A Profit." It reported on the City Ventures Corporation, created by Control Data Corporation:

> Building plants in poor, urban areas, in fact, has become a substantial part of the big computer manufacturer's business. CDC now has six other inner-city facilities, three in the Minneapolis–St. Paul area and one each in Washington, D.C., San Antonio and Toledo. In 1978, the company expanded on the idea by joining a consortium of corporations and church groups that plans major business developments in blighted areas. City Ventures Corporation hopes, for example, to create 2,500 jobs in Baltimore's Park Heights neighborhood—the home of Maryland's largest concentration of welfare recipients. Control Data has opened a bindery in an old warehouse in the area, and it plans to lure other businesses there by offering them managerial and technical help— and even office space—until they can get established.

Control Data's City Ventures Corporation is just one type of Program Related Investment (PRI), a growing means by which companies and foundations are attempting to be of greater service. Many PRIs come under the heading of "socially responsible investments." The Weyerhaeuser Company Foundation produced a report, "Non-Cash Corporate Philanthropy: A Report on Current Practices with Annotated Bibliography," which defines investments such as PRIs as "those investments that were made for socially desirable purposes and would not otherwise have been made under the company's customary lending standards; or social considerations played a substantial part in investment decisions." In turn, many such programs come under the heading "community economic development" (CED).

One of the largest of the economic development programs was established in 1980 under the title Local Initiatives Support Corporation (LISC). On May 23rd of that year, *The Washington Post* carried the story, "Business Sows Seed Money to Aid Urban Neighborhoods," reporting:

> . . . LISC will make investments in the form of loans below market rate or loan guarantees, but will also make modest grants—not exceeding about $50,000 a year. It also will provide technical assistance to help the local leaders find financing and put together business deals. The project is based on the premise that local groups working in deteriorating urban neighborhoods cannot prosper without a combination of private and government assistance.

Mitchell Sviridoff, the first president of LISC, told me that the first million dollars to get LISC off the ground came from John Filer and the Aetna

Foundation. With that signal from the business community, the Ford Foundation, which worked with Sviridoff to develop the idea, put up $5 million with the understanding that other businesses would quickly add support. These corporate supporters were forthcoming: Atlantic Richfield, Continental Illinois National Bank and Trust of Chicago, International Harvester, Levi Strauss, and Prudential Insurance. Four years later, Sviridoff reported that Aetna's first million dollars had provided the initial impetus to reach an investment program of more than $100 million a year, and that this sum had leveraged more than a billion dollars in community economic development loans and other funds.

By 1983, Robert Lilly, LISC's volunteer chairman, reported in the May issue of *Response:*

> LISC deals in investments of the most tangible kind: putting capital to work at below-market rates to build self-supporting, income-producing ventures in real estate, housing, industry and commerce. The partnership is just as tangible. One hundred forty-eight corporations and 54 foundations have taken the initiative (with 53 donors giving $100,000 or more) to create pools of investment funds in 24 cities and regions and to make loans and grants to 197 community development organizations.
>
> Typical projects are a $12.5 million, 190-unit federally subsidized housing development run by a Boston-based Puerto Rican group, for which LISC provided a crucial front-money loan of $250,000; a plan to acquire, develop and run a currently vacant neighborhood shopping center in Liberty City, Miami, for which LISC loan and grant funds, totaling $300,000, will leverage $2.125 million in other private funding; and the acquisition and conversion to commercial office space by ASIAN, Inc., of a currently vacant San Francisco building, funded by $150,000 from LISC and a concessional loan of $800,000 from The Equitable Life Assurance Society.
>
> LISC chooses and structures these and all of its 200 or so loans and grants to help recipient developmental organizations pursue three goals important to their survival and long-term growth: 1) to attract new sources of private and public capital and to show those sources that they can find community development investment opportunities of acceptable risk and high social return; 2) to build up the community organization's assets and income to lessen its dependence on unpredictable and transitory grants; 3) to increase its managerial capacity, and business discipline so that it can raise and invest its own funds most effectively.

Lilly emphasized how important the insurance industry's financial participation has been. He indicated that since 1980, Aetna and Prudential had been followed by major support from CIGNA Foundation, General American Life Insurance Company, John Hancock Mutual Life Insurance Company, Metropolitan Life Foundation, Mutual of Omaha Insurance Companies, New England Mutual Life Insurance Company, New York Life Foundation, Penn Mutual Life Insurance Company, the Provident Foundation, and the Ryan Insurance Group, Inc.

Five years after its inception, LISC was able to report: "By the end of 1985, LISC was operating in 27 cities nationwide and had committed or dispersed over $30 million in loans and $10 million in grants to 370 community development organizations to support 700 projects. The loss or failure rate on its loans has been encouragingly low, at less than 5 percent." By 1985, General Electric, SOHIO, and BankAmerica had also become major national funders.

On Sunday, September 1, 1985, *The New York Times* carried a Kathleen Teltsch story beginning: "The Metropolitan Life Foundation . . . has created a $25 million loan program to encourage business ventures that meet 'significant needs'. . . . The loans will be made, for example, to assist community groups in housing, rehabilitation, or to help minority-owned commercial undertakings. Other loans will improve the delivery of health services. . . . The loans will be made at below-market interest rates."

Self-Help Ventures is a subsidiary of the Fund for an Open Society, a national nonprofit mortgage pool. The publication *Response* reported that "the CIGNA Corporation recently approved a mortgage loan to Philadelphia's Self-Help Ventures . . . to rehabilitate an abandoned school building and 27 units of cooperatively leased low-income apartments. . . . Issued through CIGNA's investment program, the $450,000 loan will help SHV leverage funds from private equity investors for the project."

Resource Raising divides program-related investments into several categories. Here are two of them with examples:

1. *Investments:* . . . A nonprofit group sold "air rights" above its buildings so that an apartment condominium complex could be built. An educational institution became a corporate investor as partner in developing rental property on the institution's land. A self-help human service delivery organization found an investor to back its entry into a neighborhood fast food business. . . . Allstate has an urban committee that invests funds in a variety of urban development projects at a positive anticipated return. Allstate's interest is in projects that create new jobs, primarily in manufacturing.
2. *Loans:* . . . Bank of America established a revolving loan fund of $10 million as part of the BankAmerica Neighborhood

Partnership. CitiBank set aside $10 million in loan commitments, $600 in operating expenses and $50,000 in grants as well as the services of seven bank offices for its Community Banking Pilot Program. This program will test methods of financing housing improvement and promote the commercial revitalization of Flatbush in Brooklyn, New York. Coca-Cola, USA has begun a National Hispanic Business Agenda, a marketing program which sets aside funds to be spent to conduct business with Hispanic banks, advertising agencies and other businesses. Five cities with Coca-Cola offices are also involved in an Hispanic Recruitment and Hiring Program. General Mills reinvested the proceeds of one housing investment into a new interprise called Alt-Care, an experimental system that provides senior citizens with alternatives to institutional care. The options include purchasing chore services, Meals on Wheels, neighborhood health care and visiting nurses services. Giant Foods entered into a partnership with the District of Columbia and a citizen's group to build the inner-city's first supermarket since the 1963 riots. Monsanto is involved with the Missouri Neighborhood Assistance Program. The company is working with the state and a community development organization to build low-income housing. Prudential provided $70 million over four years in below-market-rate loans to projects in disadvantaged areas, and has invested in a variety of enterprises, including housing, supermarkets, nursing homes and a catfish processing plant.

I was rather surprised when John Phillips, then President of the National Association of Independent Colleges and Universities, responded to my request for illustrations of "great gifts" by submitting, as his top nomination, "the whole matching gift concept for support of higher education." When I looked into the specific figures, I understood why. The program was started by General Electric in 1955, matching approximately $200,000 in employee contributions to colleges. By 1980 more than 900 companies were participating in an education "match," producing almost $40 million for higher education that year. The total in matching funds donated to these and other nonprofit organizations was more than $100 million.

According to Lee Smith in the *Fortune* article, General Electric started the matching gifts program "as a fringe benefit meant to attract and retain employees." Andrew Heiskell, a former Time CEO, described matching gift programs to me as one of the best means of boosting employee morale and building good feeling about working for an organization that supports causes chosen by its employees. Heiskell argues that about 50 percent of a corporation's giving should be "employee driven." Others argue that a company should target less than that for matching gifts and more for special projects where large sums can make a real difference.

Many companies conduct "in-plant solicitations," also a unique feature of corporate charitable effort. This has been a major source of help to federated campaigns, particularly United Way, and is spreading to include a broader group of umbrella organizations and individual charities.

In 1983, Frito-Lay, Inc. received one of the President's Volunteer Action Awards for a program described in INDEPENDENT SECTOR's *Corporate Philanthropy:*

> When Braniff International Airlines filed for bankruptcy in May 1982, the Dallas/Fort Worth area faced its greatest unemployment crisis in recent history. Over 5,000 workers were suddenly out of work in an already tight job market.
>
> In order to help the former Braniff employees find new employment, Frito-Lay, Inc., a subsidiary of Pepsico, developed an employment assistance program that included information gathering and dissemination, education and public awareness components. The company established a communications center that was staffed around the clock by 34 company volunteers. The center organized job opportunities on a day-to-day basis and fielded questions from the unemployed workers. Frito-Lay sent 5,500 letters to the unemployed Braniff employees and 51,000 questionnaires to potential employers. This information was tabulated and prospective employees were paired with employers.
>
> The company sponsored a three-day job readiness seminar with sessions on résumé writing, interviewing and job counseling and three Job Fairs that were open to all the Dallas–Fort Worth-area unemployed. The fairs gave 8,700 individuals the opportunity to meet with representatives of over 200 companies.

Honeywell was also a 1983 winner of the President's Volunteer Action Award for its support and encouragement of volunteering by employees and retirees. Among the strategies Honeywell uses to increase involvement as volunteers are:

- Community Service Awards: once-in-a-lifetime grants of $500 to organizations with which employees are active volunteers.
- Management Assistance Project (MAP): volunteers provide technical and management assistance to area nonprofit organizations.
- HELP (Honeywell Employee Launched Projects): provides a way to respond to community needs in a small group environment. Depart-

ments or groups of employees use their skills and energies to solve problems.

- Honeywell Retiree Volunteer Program: retired employee volunteers coordinate recruitment activities, organize and develop the programs, administer the office and train and place other retired volunteers.

A year later, Tenneco received a Volunteer Action Award for its Volunteers in Assistance program. The program, started five years earlier, includes over 1,600 Tenneco employees serving 40 agencies in the Houston community. They help the elderly, the mentally handicapped, the Hispanic community, the Red Cross, and many other organizations. The award also saluted Tenneco's first corporate volunteerism conference, and its joint national volunteer program with the Red Cross.

A 1985 winner of the same award was Allstate Insurance for its corporate efforts to encourage volunteering. The keystone of the company's volunteer efforts is the Helping Hands program, in which 75 percent of Allstate's employees nationwide have participated in more than 10,000 community projects. "Allstate decided that there were some excellent reasons for any company to be involved in its community," said Donald F. Craib, Jr., Chairman. "The first is quite simply corporate self-interest. When corporations help to improve social conditions, they are working to enhance their own profits as well."

There are an increasing number of corporate programs that encourage volunteering. For example:

- Philip Morris, Inc. has taken out full-page ads to recognize and encourage the good volunteer work of Philip Morris employees. Headlined "Good People Do Good Things," the ads included a picture of Philip Morris volunteers with copy that read: "They look quite ordinary and they are, in reality, quite extraordinary. They work hard for a living, and then, in their off time, they work hard for nothing. They want to help those who are less fortunate than themselves and in doing so they help all of us. For the hard fact is that without these people, our societies and our lives would be a lot less livable."

- On the occasion of National Volunteer Recognition Week, General Mills held a reception honoring employee volunteers. As a sidelight, there was a contest to guess the number of hours that General Mills employees gave to the community during 1984 and the winner received $500 for his or her favorite charity. The five runners-up were able to give $100 each. The correct answer: 28,289 hours.

- "A Citizen Wherever We Serve" is the title of a colorful magazine dedicated to the men and women of the Georgia Power Company who "give countless hours to volunteer their talent, creativity, hard work, love and care to the people of Georgia." The publication features particular employees who are involved in a wide variety of community concerns and organizations throughout the state.

- Avon products produced a different kind of pamphlet, "Caring is Everyone's Business," describing the "Caring Spirit" program. That program includes recognition for volunteering, awards, financial assistance for nonprofit organizations served by Avon volunteers, and technical assistance described as "helping the helpers."

- In 1983, PepsiCo introduced a new program for its employees— "A2V" or Awards to Volunteers. The PepsiCo Foundation provides as many as ten awards, each for up to $1,000, payable to the organization to which the employees volunteer their time. Donald M. Kendall, Chairman and CEO of PepsiCo, stated upon presenting the awards that "PepsiCo people have demonstrated that they care about their community. In honoring these employees, we are celebrating the spirit of voluntarism in America."

- Levi Strauss is one of the companies that have led the way in encouraging employee public service. They developed the concept of "community involvement teams" composed of employee volunteers who identify local community needs and design projects for the active intervention of volunteers. According to Ira Hirshfield, former Levi Strauss Corporate Affairs Director: "The team concept includes direct volunteer service, local fundraising efforts and follow-up grant support from the Levi Strauss Foundation. The needs identified by the team are frequently representative of major concerns in a community and often are social issues that affected the lives of employees and their families."

- At Westinghouse, every three years, there is a "Community Involvement Survey" to determine the levels of employee participation. In 1981, 44 percent of the employees were active volunteers. Twenty-two percent of Westinghouse employees volunteered 2–4 hours per week and 12 percent volunteer more than 4 hours each week.

    The Westinghouse Electric Fund has established a Gift Matching Program to encourage employees, retirees and directors to share in the support of nonprofit organizations. The fund also supports a Volunteer Training Program developed within the company.

    Cecile M. Springer, Director of Contributions and Community Affairs, summarizes: "What we have done at Westinghouse has been first, identify the level of volunteering; second, develop a Gift

Matching Program to support voluntarism; and third, develop a training program to equip our employees with advanced abilities to assist in community development."

Beyond encouragment of a company's own employees, many other companies attempt to motivate, support, and honor volunteering by everyone in the community. For example, Rexnord has a program and publication, "Activate Someone," that provides "how-to" information about "identifying community problems, determining which needs best suit the volunteer's talents and getting started." Robert V. Crecorian, the company's CEO says: "We're convinced that no business can prosper for long in a community that does not enjoy the enthusiastic involvement of its citizens. . . . The best thing business people can volunteer is how-to and leadership. It is the largest most talented pool of expertise in the nation which, unfortunately, remains underused."

TRW selected three Cleveland organizations to receive grants totaling $65,000 "to underwrite three manager of volunteer positions. The organizations will use the grants to develop positions to recruit, organize and manage volunteers more effectively." Security Bank in California has no trouble enlisting employees to welcome each contestant at the finish line in events of the Summer Special Olympics. Their volunteers are even called "huggers." Conoco does the same for the Winter series in Colorado.

A major effort has been underway in Minnesota for several years under the heading of Corporate Volunteerism Council of Minnesota which involves 44 corporate members. The *Christian Science Monitor* reported that "instead of just posting flyers from the local Volunteer Center, more than 450 corporations are actively recruiting their employees to volunteer for community organizations in the Twin Cities area. . . . For incentive, some offer release time, corporate recognition, extra vacation days, donations to employees' favorite charities and added points on employees' annual reviews."

Metropolitan Life developed a "skills bank" to help broker the needs of community agencies and abilities of persons willing to volunteer. *Volunteers From the Workplace*, first published in 1979 by VOLUNTEER: The National Center, was an excellent resource for such programs. Their new edition published in 1987, is even better. Called *A New Competitive Edge*, it sets forth the rationale and program descriptions for many leadership efforts of corporate and labor encouragement of volunteering. Here is their table of contents:

CHAPTER 1
Creating A New Competitive Edge: The Rationale by Kenn Allen
  Profiles
  Levi Strauss & Co.: Preserving a Tradition of Community Involvement

Ben Bridge Jewelers
Casa Sanchez

(*A New Competitive Edge* is edited by Cynthia Vizza, Kenn Allen, and Shirley Keller and includes a foreword by George Romney.)

VOLUNTEER and United Way of America also carry on another helpful resource, this one begun by President Reagan's Task Force on Private Sector Initiatives, chaired by William Verity of Amoco. It's called Partnerships DataNet, and includes close to 5,000 examples of public/private partnerships that address community needs.

Some corporations and foundations have programs to encourage volunteering as a national value. For example, there is the "Hearts of Gold" awards of the Gannett Foundation. Also Mutual Benefit Life's "Give America a Hand" advertising campaign is designed "to help strengthen and expand this partnership by encouraging businesses and individuals to increase their levels of involvement and support of community programs. Robert V. Van Fossan, Mutual's Chairman, said: "With more than 6 million volunteer associations in our country, there is ample opportunity for business and individuals to 'give America a hand.'"

In their encouragement of volunteering, many companies include their retirees. The Corporate Volunteerism Council in Minnesota even conducts training courses on corporate retiree volunteer programs. Bell Telephone's "Pioneers" program was the first and probably still is the largest of deliberate efforts to help match able, experienced volunteers with community needs. Kodak, G.E., and Republic Steel have also been long involved in such efforts.

This aspect of corporate community service has become so pervasive that Plinio and Scanlon divided the subject into ten sub-categories with several subdivisions each. Among the more unusual categories or examples were:

- *Corporate Support for Volunteer Activities*

  The Manville Corporation, NB Corporation, and Pacific Power and Light Company are among many which allow nonprofits to recruit volunteers on company time and property.

  Rohm and Haas Company, Smithkline, Beckman Corporation and the Kroger Company, among many others, maintain a clearinghouse within the companies, staffed by corporate personnel, to match individual employees with community volunteer jobs.

  The Sun Company, United Telecommunications and the Wisconsin Telephone Company are examples of groups which encourage volunteer involvement of retirees using pre-retirement seminars to help orient and train persons who are scheduled for retirement.

• *Loaned Executives*

Xerox, IBM and Wells Fargo Bank all have Social Service programs to enable employees to receive their regular salaries and benefits while working full time for nonprofit organizations.

• *Employee Committees and Cash Grant Linkages*

Aetna has a "Dollars for Doers" program which provides grants of $50 to $500 to support agencies with company volunteers.

Chevron has an Employee Involvement Fund in four cities where a committee of workers reviews applications for contributions up to $250 to nonprofits that have had company volunteers for at least three months.

Dayton Hudson maintains an Employee Involvement Program and provides grants of $50 to $1,000 for projects sponsored by non-profits in which employees are active.

Prudential Insurance Company has an extensive employee structure to advise on company and foundation grants.

As long ago as 1914, the rationale for corporate public service and employee involvement was stated by Thomas J. Watson of IBM:

We want you to take time off from IBM to do a good job as citizens because communities will only be as good as the citizens make them.

We want IBM to be a real part of the citizenship of this country and the world. Keep that in mind. That is one of your duties. We are trying to develop not only IBM and develop people for IBM, but we are trying to help in our small way to develop this great country of ours.

We all owe a duty to the community in which we live, to society at large. Aside from that, it is a fine thing for a person to participate in things of worth while outside his business.

Many years later, in 1981, about the time that the Business Roundtable came out with its important position statement, "Corporate Philanthropy —An Integral Part of Corporate Social Responsibility," I was part of a small meeting with Clifford Garvin, then chairman of the Roundtable and of Exxon. The subject was corporate public service and someone took the occasion to chide Garvin that businesses were a long way from the 5 percent of profits that they were then allowed to contribute. At first Garvin turned cold, then angry, and finally just exasperated. He asked us to think of which group from society could routinely be identified in leadership roles in every community and as part of every community's nonprofit boards, fundraising campaigns, and every other form of public service. He

didn't wait for anyone to answer. "Who does all of those things everywhere and all the time?," he more implored than asked, "business people,
business people, and more business people."

When Garvin got that off his chest, he talked about percentages, but we
each recognized that to approach from the negative side the matter of the
involvement of businesses and business people is not fair and, based on
Garvin's reaction, not likely to induce positive results! Even for those
present who very much believed that business should be doing more,
there was greater appreciation that business people are owed respect and
appreciation for all the leadership and community service they are
providing.

Although it seems unproductive to prod companies with the 5 percent
argument (since 1981 the legal limit is now 10 percent), it is not fair to
those who give at that level to suggest that their leadership efforts are not
terribly significant. For example, even though only 10 percent of companies contribute 5 percent or more of their profits, this adds up to 160,000
businesses, and they contribute one-third of all that is given by corporations. There are 272,000 companies that give 2 percent or more. This
group is 17 percent of all business but they donate two-thirds of all that is
given by corporations.

Perhaps the last unique opportunity for corporations is to get credit for
their efforts. In a fascinating piece, "Public Invisibility of Corporate
Leaders" in the *Harvard Business Review*, David Finn of Ruder and Finn
laments that corporations and their leaders don't get nearly enough credit
for what they do for society and that out of fear of criticism, they don't
make more of an effort to tell what they and their companies are doing for
their communities and the nation. He concludes:

> I believe that executives have a great potential for inspiring
> leadership in contemporary society. But they need to let people see
> what kinds of human beings they are, what they believe in, what
> they want to accomplish through their business activities, and what
> values they want to achieve for society through their efforts. To
> accomplish these objectives, business executives with a talent for
> leadership should:
>
> 1. Integrate their communal and business lives so they can gain
> credit for their public services and be credible when making
> statements about their businesses.
>
> 2. Develop an appetite for being in the public eye as individuals
> who represent the character of their companies.
>
> 3. Speak publicly and convincingly about human needs and values
> as well as economic benefits when discussing business policies.

4. Have the courage to initiate company programs that grow out of their personal interests, and become the public spokesperson for those programs.

5. Develop their own sense of style about the conduct of their businesses without worrying that they may be catering to idiosyncratic tastes.

6. Persuade their stockholders that it is important for managers to be human beings who have deep concerns about the health and well-being as well as the material comfort and financial security of their fellow citizens.

The public may approve or condemn a specific corporate action, but if it knows what kind of person is responsible for the company's policies and what values he or she believes in, it is possible to be responsive to that leadership. Instead of being anonymous instruments of impersonal corporate interests, top executives can be understood as conscientious individuals doing their best to fulfill responsibilities to society which they believe to be of great importance.

Occasionally questions are raised whether it is the business of business to give anything away and whether such behavior doesn't work against the interest of stockholders. The best answer to that was provided by James Burke, Chairman of Johnson and Johnson, when he and his company received the Advertising Council's 1980 Public Service Award. As described in INDEPENDENT SECTOR's *Corporate Philanthropy*, Burke said:

"Those companies that organize their business around the broad concept of public service over the long run provide superior performance for their stockholders."

Burke's comments and the research behind them represent an important new statement on the positive relationship between corporate public responsibility, including corporate giving, and financial performance.

Burke's findings are from a survey of the companies that have received the Ad Council award. He narrowed this list to those that have been in existence at least the 30 years the award has been given; that have a "written, codified set of principles stating the philosophy that serving the public is central to their being"; and that have "solid evidence that these ideas had been promulgated and practiced for at least a generation of their organizations." He noted that: "These companies showed an annual 11 percent growth in profits compounded over 30 years! That happens to be better

than three times the growth of the Gross National Product, . . .
which grew at 3.1 annually during the same period.

"If anyone had invested $30,000 in a composite of the Dow Jones
30 years ago, it would be worth $134,000 today. If you had
invested the $30,000 . . . $2,000 in each of these companies instead
. . . your $30,000 would be worth over $1,000,000! . . . $1,021,861
to be exact!

"I have long harbored the belief, that the most successful
corporations in this country—the ones that have delivered
outstanding results over a long period of time—were driven by a
simple moral imperative—serving the public in the broadest
possible sense—better than their competition. . . . We as
businessmen and women have extraordinary leverage on our most
important asset . . . goodwill . . . the goodwill of the public. . . . If
we make sure our enterprises are managed in terms of their
obligations to society . . . that is also the best way to defend this
democratic, capitalistic system that means so much to all of us."

One of the earliest industrialists to be greatly involved in philanthropy
was Charles Pratt, who carried his corporate pragmatism into his
approach to giving. According to F. Emerson Andrews, when Pratt
designed the buildings for Pratt Institute he did it "such-wise that in case
his educational purpose failed, he might readily convert the premises into
a factory."

This chapter has, by definition, dealt with the unique opportunities for
corporate philanthropy, and therefore is not focused on corporate cash
donations. I am reminded, though, that during a public meeting of the
Minnesota Council on Foundations, one of the corporate speakers went
on and on about how much was being done by a growing number of companies to provide non-cash support. The lively discussion ended with
applause and whistles when one of the voluntary agency representatives
rose to observe: "With all due respect for your in-kind help, don't forget
the cash!"

11

Unique Opportunities of Community Foundations

Kate Bohm was a fairly typical immigrant to the United States in the late 1800s. She and her mother arrived from Germany and found their way to Cleveland where both worked as domestics. From age 16 that was Kate's life. By today's standards, she might be thought to have had little to be thankful for, but from her point of view, the freedom and security she found in her new community allowed her to lead a privileged life.

While she was employed by the Samual Mather family, she heard a guest, Frederick H. Goff, describe the Cleveland Foundation and its purposes. She was particularly struck by the idea that through such a foundation people could pay something back to their adopted communities. When Mather, her employer, died and left a sizable legacy to the foundation, the idea of making a similar gesture began to take root. Years later when, almost blind and crippled, Kate Bohm died at age 80, she left her entire life savings of $6,500, with no strings attached, to the Cleveland Foundation for the purpose of improving the quality of life in the city that had welcomed her.

Since her death in 1936, interest from the Katherine Bohm Fund has supported scores of special projects. Her first grant went to the Cleveland Society for the Blind, to buy artificial eyes and glasses for those who could not afford them. Among other things, through her fund Kate Bohm has:

- paid for the training of volunteer leaders to work with black girl scout troops.

- given a scholarship to a paralyzed boy who wanted to study building repair.
- paid for the Post-War Planning Council to plan for Cleveland's transition in the mid 1940s.
- expanded the home services of the Visiting Nurses Association.
- underwritten a study of Cleveland's nursing homes.

With all of that, Kate Bohm's $6,500 is still growing and will work to her credit and that of her adopted community for all time.

In an earlier chapter, I described how a small Cleveland Foundation grant of $15,000 allowed a team to study the ways by which European cities have transformed their waterfronts into places of beauty and how that grant eventually led to a multi-million dollar project that improved Cleveland's own lakefront. Not all of its grants are so modest. For example, the foundation gave more than $350,000 to develop a Mediation Program so that the city could provide swifter justice and thereby help unclog the courts.

The first gift to the newly established New York Community Trust in 1924 was $1,000 in honor of the donor's early mentor, Teresa Bernholz, the principal at Public School #9. Each year a prize in Ms. Bernholz's name is presented to the girl who "has earned the highest respect of her teachers." Like the Cleveland and other community foundations, the New York Community Trust handles many small funds, but it also operates larger programs such as the Neighborhood Revitalization Project which gives New York's 75 diverse neighborhoods the opportunity "to submit proposals for neighborhood revitalization, meaning structural rehabilitation, economic development or improved services."

These brief glimpses of the Cleveland Foundation and New York Community Trust illustrate just two of the unique opportunities represented by such philanthropies: the pooling of large and small gifts for the good of the community and a vehicle for leadership to deal with the community's problems and aspirations. In a fascinating article, "The Community Foundation Connection," in the *Foundation News* of April 1982, Lois Roisman, then of the Council on Foundations, illustrated several of the roles this way:

- A resident of Hartford, Connecticut wanted to give the community $6.5 million; the donor also wanted to remain anonymous.
- The people of Atlanta needed a place to put contributions that were pouring in to aid in the investigation of the murders of 28 black youngsters.
- The Lechmere Corporation wanted to clean up the toxic waste site blighting the town of Woburn, Massachusetts.

- New Hampshire corporations wanted to work with the state's non-profit institutions to help them improve their management skills.
- A man in San Francisco created a fund to memorialize his wife and benefit the needy elderly of that city.
- The parents of a preschool teacher's students wanted to create a fund in her memory to benefit preschool education in Oklahoma City.

In each instance, the donor's intent became reality because community foundations existed to manage and assign the funds.

Roisman believes that, in the aggregate, these roles and impacts add up to a quintessential dimension of leadership. "Through their participation in the lives of their communities, serving the interest of both donors and providers of public services, community foundations have gained key positions in civic life, allowing them to be forces for public good in ways that no other entities can duplicate."

In a 1981 meeting of some of the larger community foundations, Paul Ylvisaker, one of the most perceptive observers of both foundations and urban needs, outlined some of the problems which add up to horrendous crises for our cities. He separated the problems into these categories:

- The movement of jobs and people out of the cities;
- The growth of an urban under-class;
- An increasingly dilapidated infra-structure;
- Increasingly complicated relations between governmental jurisdictions involving cities, counties, metropolitan regions, states, etc.;
- An inadequate supply of housing, particularly for low-income persons.

These problems are compounded, he said, by consequences of deferred maintenance and a lack of confidence in the governance and governability of our cities.

In my presentation at the same gathering, I tried to make the point that community foundations have a unique obligation and responsibility to address the fundamental issues of their communities. I told them that one of the problems with many community foundations, just as with many corporate giving programs, is that they have tried to emulate private foundations—for example, by identifying certain program areas such as housing and then waiting to respond to applications that come to them in these areas. To try to make the point that community foundations are and should be different, I said:

I spend a good deal of time consulting with foundations and corporations and, like this session, the topic generally relates to the

changing or future role of philanthropy. In most of these sessions, I
attempt to lay out the major needs of our times including such
urgent issues as governance of our cities, structural unemployment,
strengthening public education, persistence of poverty,
neighborhood deterioration, conservation of land and water, etc.
The usual response I get is that each of these problems is utterly
beyond the capacity of the foundation and that indeed almost all of
them are so large in scope that costs of addressing them have to be
left to government. This usually brings the discussion right back to
the question, "What can we do that is unique and important?" My
answer in all such cases is, "Use your power and influence to make
our government more effective, including its capacity to deal with
the big issues." Making government work is almost always far more
important than all the other worthwhile things we do. It is certainly
clear in my mind that it is the primary function of *community*
foundations.

To help put the role of community foundations in perspective, I said,
"The fundamental institutions of our communities can function without
foundations but they will function ever so much better when foundations
are at their best." Also, as a matter of perspective, I tried to lay out what I
consider to be the unique assets of community foundations:

- A board, committee members, and other citizen leaders who partic-
  ipate in the work of the foundation;
- The unique opportunity to gain an overview of the community and
  of specific problems;
- The aura of influence as perceived by most people outside the
  foundation;
- Some degree of objectivity and neutrality;
- Influence with other donors;
- Greater continuity of leadership than is likely to be the case among
  the political leadership of the community;
- Money

After reviewing the relative sizes of community governments and community foundations I observed: "The annual expenditures of community
foundations are so small as to be inconsequential measured against the
budgets of our communities. Nonetheless, to the extent that they help
empower the fundamental institutions and processes that exist in all your
communities, community foundations can have significant influence." I
concluded:

Community foundations have a unique opportunity and obligation. They are not indispensable, but they can make a very large difference in solving the agonizing dilemma of how to organize and govern our communities. These can be very significant years for the aggressive and effective community foundation, and what seems to be needed is not impossible to achieve. It comes down to more of the best.

When a community foundation is involved and involves others, the results are impressive. I included examples of such foundations and their work in the chapter, "To Make Communities Better Places to Live." Other illustrations are given here:

- The cutback in public funds for service provided by Chicago agencies and institutions increased the need to leverage private dollars and to encourage public/private partnerships for their service. The Chicago Community Trust, working with the Illinois Department of Children and Family Services (DCFS) established the Joint Day Care Facilities Improvement Project. The project provides loans to day care programs in Cook County that serve low-income families. This collaborative project worked because it combined the Trust's ability to respond quickly to needs to improve and expand facilities and the capability of DCFS to adjust its rate of reimbursement to the day care centers at a sufficient level to allow them to repay the loans.

- The San Francisco Foundation has provided or brokered Program Related Investments (PRIs) to several community development efforts. The foundation provided the funds so that a community development corporation could acquire a desirable commercial site adjacent to the low-income community of Marin City. As the community development corporation reaches milestones such as ground breaking, construction and occupancy by commercial tenants, its debt to the foundation will gradually be forgiven.

- The Cleveland Foundation developed a management training program for city officials to help them become better planners and managers.

- The New York Community Trust established a camp management project to strengthen camp management by agencies which owned and operated summer camps in the greater New York area. A decade ago, there were 75 such camps operated by public service agencies that were having to close an average of five a year. After the Trust organized the project, management procedures were improved, common purchasing introduced and other services provided. In this way the operations were streamlined while overhead costs were lowered and the survival rate among these camps increased accordingly.

• The California Community Foundation provided funding to Tree People to support its efforts with school children to plant a million trees in Los Angeles.

• The Minneapolis Foundation, assisted with a $5 million grant from the McKnight Foundation, established a "Designated Area Fund, dedicated to the development of Twin City Neighborhoods."

• The St. Paul Foundation established the Emergency Care Fund to help provide shelter, food, clothing and other emergency services for people impacted severely by the depressed economic conditions, beginning in 1982.

• The Denver Foundation helped develop the Teen Parent Education Network of Human Services Inc./Florence Crittenden, designed to give teenage parents a better chance for employment.

• The New Haven Foundation, combining its interests in community arts and education, provided a large grant to the New Haven Board of Education to bring community artists into the schools and involve students in community based arts programs.

• An increasing number of community foundations are involved in community education. To help them learn from one another and to pass their experience on to others, the Kettering Foundation helped form the Network of Community Foundations Interested in Community Education. One of its early projects was "An Executive Summary of Twelve Case Statements" edited by Leonard P. Oliver of Kettering.

(The following additional examples of community foundation activity are drawn from these case statements.)

• The Rhode Island Foundation provided leadership funding for the public education program of Save the Bay "to generate substantial public interest in local environmental issues" and to develop "understanding, and the methods in which civic skills could be developed to participate fully in the decision-making process."

• The Oregon Community Foundation has provided funding for several years for the Center for Urban Education and its Columbia Willamette Futures Forum to engage as fully as possible the citizens of Greater Portland in identifying and understanding immediate and long-range "critical choices" for their community.

• Another statewide community foundation, the Community Foundation of New Jersey, is helping with dollars and other assistance to develop the Network Collaboration which brings together over 200 corporate, labor, education, government, and community leaders "to analyze Newark's problems, encourage broad-based discussion of these problems, and to work for cooperation and concerns to revitalize Newark."

- The Milwaukee Foundation has had a leadership role in sponsoring and funding a three-year project to involve the broadest possible array of Milwaukee organizations and citizens to help identify "Goals for Greater Milwaukee 2000." Their documentation of formal goals lists 68 recommendations on the issues of jobs, recreation, schools, health, housing, public safety, transportation, and land use.

(The following additional examples of the work of community foundations are drawn from Lois Roisman's article in *Foundation News.*)

- The Hartford Foundation for Public Giving has helped to fund the Citizens Committee for Effective Government, a corporate-sponsored study group that has used volunteer teams from the private sector to complete management studies of the Hartford City government and the public school system.

- The Chicago Community Trust spent two years developing systematic policy for grant allocation in the health field in order to identify priorities. It began with an analysis of the problems and needs of Chicago-area hospitals and grew into an examination of the entire range of health care service. This investigation not only expanded the Trust's own grantmaking process, it expanded cooperative funding with local and national foundations and enabled the Trust to participate effectively as an intermediary or broker with other area funding sources.

- The Lincoln Foundation is acting as agent for the city of Lincoln, the University of Nebraska, the Natural Resources District, the Railroad Transportation Safety District and the Nebraska State Highway Department to negotiate the purchase of the Rock Island Railroad right-of-way property within the city limits of Lincoln.

- The Greater Atlanta Community Foundation was the first to develop the "Leadership" programs that have become popular throughout the nation. Called "Leadership Atlanta," the program brought together potential leaders from all sectors of Atlanta to study the city in detail and to get to know one another. The networks and friendships that developed have served Atlanta well through difficult times, and the model has been emulated by other cities.

- The Peninsula Foundation in California sponsors special conferences and meetings, bringing together people who, although they have common concerns, have never met. One such affinity group centered on dance—modern as well as ballet. Teachers, students, and interested patrons met together and created the Mid-Peninsula Center for Dance Development to which the foundation gave $42,000, the first collaboration effort among dancers in the area.
- The Akron Ohio School System was closing Grace School. To make the transition as humane and comfortable as possible, the Akron Community Trust funded the Grace Model Program. It involved the parents and children in meetings to orient them to the new school, smoothing the way in a potentially troublesome time.
- The Minneapolis Foundation's Equal Opportunities Fund provides creative opportunities and emergency funding to agencies and programs that address the needs of disadvantaged people within the metropolitan community. It also coordinates joint funding ventures and the search for alternative financial resources.
- The Boston Foundation, responding to its city's troubled race relations, funded the Boston Committee which was convened in 1980. Its task was to move the city toward racial peace. To that end, the committee is working on an ambitious program to create jobs in the city's most economically depressed neighborhoods; it is also establishing eight neighborhood task forces, composed of community leaders and residents, to foster inter-neighborhood collaboration on housing, employment and gang activity.

After giving these and other examples, Roisman writes:

> For each of these examples, thousands more exist. As donors and board members become more aware of such challenges, they are coming to expect their community foundation to provide mechanisms and leadership to help them meet those challenges. Through the community foundation, the city's people wrestle with difficult issues—drug abuse, unemployment, teenage pregnancy, refugee immigration, women's rights and the problems of the elderly—as they work continually to build endowments that will secure the future of their community's culture, social welfare, health, education and governance.

Community foundations get their funds in several ways. They have a *general fund* that receives and pools contributions from individuals and other sources. This money is allocated by the board or distribution committee according to its view of current priorities.

Community foundations also have *trust funds*. These are administered separately but in many cases are available for distribution committee allocation. For example, the San Francisco Foundation has the Adelle M. Moore Cahill Foundation which is an "unrestricted fund." Some of the trust funds given to the San Francisco Foundation have more specific instructions and others are quite directive, ranging from the Wilhelimina N. Bossana Trust, "an unrestricted trust with certain preferences mentioned by the testatrix," to the Scanlon Scholarship Fund "primarily for tuition at Shattuck School, Fairbault, Minnesota with preference for California boys."

A third category involves *donor-advised funds*, described by the Chicago Community Trust as "an option available for those donors who wish to actively participate in the grantmaking process. . . . the Trust accepts these contributions as endowment funds subject to the terms and conditions set forth in the Declaration of Trust. The written recommendations made to the Executive Committee by the Donor/Advisor are advisory only, and must be consistent with the purposes of the Trust, and the Executive Committee must have the final decision regarding all disbursements. Jack Shakley of the California Community Foundation says: "Donors of these funds, while irrevocably giving away control over the money to the community trusts, maintain an advisory position with the fund."

A recent 1985 report of the San Francisco Foundation lists several hundred "Donor Designated Gifts," such as stipulated gifts for the San Francisco Conservatory of Music ($27,500), St. Mary's College of California ($65,000), Monterey Bay Aquarium ($50,000), Cogswell College ($10,000), and United Way of Cincinnati ($1,000).

There are also *field of interest funds*. As described by the Chicago Community Trust, "these funds are also tailored to the needs of those who wish to contribute smaller amounts to the Trust but who want to restrict the use of the income for a particular purpose. Contributions to any of these funds are added to an endowment from which the income is used to meet the changing needs in these particular fields of interest: The Children and Youth Fund, the Concern for the Aging Fund, the Cultural Arts Fund and the Concern for the Mentally Disabled Fund."

There are also *agency endowments* given to the trust with the interest specified to specific organizations.

Within all of these and other income-pooling and service arrangements, the community foundations have opportunities ranging from informal consultation to court relief in order to be certain that the funds entrusted to it are targeted now and in the future to needs that are consistent with the donors' wishes and to needs that are not out of date. In the extreme, the foundation can gain the right of *cy pres* which was described this way in a March/April, 1976 *Grantsmanship Center News* article, "Community Foundations," by Jack Shakley of California Community Foundation:

A trait shared by all community foundations and one of the major
factors that led to the creation of the community foundation concept
itself is the legal doctrine of *cy pres*.

Literally meaning "as near as," the *cy pres* doctrine had long been
applied by the courts to amend a trust whose originally-specified
purpose was impossible to accomplish. For example, if a trust
specifies that it is to be used to help daughters of civil war veterans
get an education, a court may modify the trust to allow it to be
used to help daughters of veterans of a more recent war. . . .

It should be pointed out, however, that while *cy pres* still plays a
role in all community foundations and is touted by community
foundation people as one of their strongest points . . . the current
emphasis on unrestricted, no-strings-attached funds has gradually
diminished the importance of the doctrine.

Cy pres was used to modify the terms of the prize associated with that
first gift to the New York Community Trust. Public School #9 no longer
exists, but the Trust was able to broaden the program restrictions to carry
forward both the wishes of the donor and the memory of her principal.
The Bernholz Prize is now given in other elementary schools serving the
same part of the city. Even if that neighborhood were to lose all its schools
to commercial or other development, the trustees would be expected and
empowered to find the closest possible way to carry forward the intent of
the gift.

Specifically, Federal regulations stipulate that the governing board of a
community foundation has the power to modify charitable distribution
restrictions only if they become "unnecessary, incapable of fulfillment, or
inconsistent with the charitable needs of the community or area served."

Beyond these advantages, the legal standing of a community foundation
and the way it is organized provide very real assurance that the foundation will remain in tune with the times. The founder of the movement,
Frederick H. Goff, who established the Cleveland Foundation in 1914,
was himself opposed to private foundations operating in perpetuity
because he felt this arrangement was not flexible enough to be certain that
the management and objects of trusts could change with the times.

Goff believed that a community foundation could work against "control
by the dead hand" if it was established with authority to make appropriate
adjustments and with a board of trustees and/or a distribution committee
whose membership is changed periodically. For most community foundations, these bodies are made up of a rotating membership appointed by
specific public officials such as the mayor, chief judge, head of the city
council, and the like. Jack Shakley writes that a grant recipient in Ohio
said: "Let me tell you, the Cleveland Foundation Board is more represen-

tative of Cleveland than Cleveland is representative of Cleveland." More fully, he notes:

> To their credit, most community foundations go out of their way to set up board selection procedures that address not only the letter, but the spirit of those vague regulations. As already mentioned, the Cleveland Foundation enjoys a reputation of having a governing body that not only represents the community, but reflects it as well. "Their meetings look like a microcosm of the city itself," said one grant recipient who had been invited to discuss a proposal. "I thought I was going to make a presentation to a bunch of bank presidents, but when I got in there I found rich and poor, men and women, ethnic representatives and special interest people all talking at once, pointing their fingers at each other and really communicating."

Community foundations have an enormous opportunity to serve their communities through day-to-day, informal consultation and assistance to other funders in the area. Recently, I was invited to speak at one of the luncheon meetings of the Cleveland Grantmakers Forum. During lunch I was fascinated to hear the give and take between Steven Minter of the Cleveland Foundation and the others at the table who represented business organizations, banks, attorneys, and other foundations. It was about the most intense, albeit informal, consultation I have ever heard. Almost everyone was asking questions—whether Steve knew this particular group, whether Steve had ideas about what to do about a particular school problem, whether he had any up-to-date information on the annexation issue, and so on. Some of the questions were as blunt as "do you think we should fund 'X'?" Even a couple of the larger foundations and corporations used the opportunity to explore opportunities for collaborative funding. It was obvious they would feel more comfortable if their trustees and directors could be assured that the Cleveland Foundation would participate. I came away with much greater appreciation of the informal but important leadership that a community foundation exerts with other funders.

Roisman writes that "the larger a community foundation becomes, the more valuable its staff becomes to donors who lack the staff's sophisticated knowledge of the community. The community foundation's staff is paid to know *all* about the region's life: health, education, culture, the arts, social welfare, and governance. This broad staff knowledge, the experience of a diverse board of directors, and sound management—all packaged in a legal entity that affords maximum tax advantage to donors —makes the community foundation an attractive partner for all manner of philanthropists."

The community foundation also represents a valuable service to bank trust officers and to attorneys who need the same guidance but who are often at a loss to know how to use smaller funds, particularly if they are designated to an end not well known to the executors. These same individuals and institutions may sometimes stand in the way of development of the community foundation. They are covetous of their authority and their fees and are unwilling to surrender these prerogatives to a community foundation that can clearly do the job far better. Some banks and trust officers handle their responsibilities so poorly that they encourage lack of confidence in the trust system. If this persists, it will become obvious how much this responsibility is better left to a community trust.

Community foundations may also lead the way for national funders. In its Community Priorities Program, the Gannett Foundation eagerly seeks the advice and assistance of community foundations. Ford, Kellogg, Mott, Rockefeller, Robert Wood Johnson, Commonwealth, and other large foundations routinely seek local collaborators to test ideas for local application.

The local trusts are also of great service to voluntary agencies in ways far beyond cash grants, though this, too, is a little-known aspect of community philanthropy. More and more community foundations accept and invite nonprofit groups to have the foundation invest reserves and endowments. In many cases, individuals give endowment funds to the foundation earmarked for a specific community group. The McClew and Roxe Randolph Trust of the San Francisco Foundation is one such endowment: "The net income is to be distributed to Masonic Old Folks Home, Masonic Children's Home and Womens Overseas Service League."

Some community foundations are now offering pooled-investment accounts which take advantage of the community foundation's experience with investments. Roisman says:

> Virtually every community foundation's annual report shows strong cooperation between that organization and the basic nonprofit institutions of its community. The Greater Charlotte (North Carolina) Foundation holds endowments worth more than $2 million for more than 30 of the city's arts organizations, social welfare agencies and youth programs. Earnings are distributed yearly to the agencies giving them the security of a permanent source of income. Some of these endowments were begun by the community foundation, but many were begun by the agency itself or by a donor wishing to endow that agency. United Way, 4-H, YMCA, the Community Health Association all have had funds established in the Greater Charlotte Foundation, and anyone can add to these funds at any time.

The United Way of the Bay Area (San Francisco) was attempting to bring many new organizations into its annual campaign but did not want to create too great a loss for existing participants. It found itself unable to invite as many new groups as it felt were deserving. The San Francisco Foundation worked out an arrangement whereby the foundation put up 100 percent of the initial allocation for 15 new agencies per year, two-thirds the second year, and one-third the third. Thereafter, the groups were fully assimilated in the United Way campaign. The agreement resulted in the addition of 15 new groups for each of the three years of the program: most of those 45 groups now remain part of the United Way.

Many local foundations have set up or helped organize technical assistance programs for nonprofit organizations. Some local funders even run regular orientation sessions for nonprofit groups on ways to seek foundation and corporate support, including community foundation grants.

The California Community Foundation is helping set up community foundation services in Orange and Venture Counties. Years ago the new York Community Trust did the same for Westchester County and Long Island.

Coming full cycle, community foundations have assets and leveraging opportunities far beyond those available to private foundations and even corporate giving programs. Even where money is not involved, the foundation can make an enormous difference. Before the Cleveland Foundation had any funds to speak of, it arranged to survey that community's needs. As Nathaniel R. Howard tells it in a history of the foundation, *Trust For All Time:* "The ink was not dry on the resolutions creating the Cleveland Foundation before Mr. Goff had moved in two directions to make the new agency an active thing. He determined on the most striking promotional program he could envision to make Cleveland aware of it—a series of community-wide public surveys through which the city would learn something about its principal problems and then, with no funds in sight of the foundation's own, he proposed to the bank directors that he and the bank share the expense of the program."

The first study concerned welfare services; the second, the public school system; the third, the city's recreational programs and facilities; and the fourth, the criminal justice system. In Howard's view: "The 10 years of community surveys and their helpful results stand almost alone in the history of the good accomplished across this country by community trusts. It is hardly too much, in hindsight, to judge that they rescued the city of Cleveland on several frontiers." On the subject of the studies, he quotes Raymond Moley, the foundation's first director:

The pattern of the Foundation's concerns served as an agency which endeavored to concentrate on city-wide problems, consider them from a measurably detached position, and create a climate of opinion in which improvements could be made. Whether with larger funds it would have been prudent to continue the surveys, I hesitate to venture opinion. I was in an excellent position to realize such surveys arouse controversy; old habits and old forms of institutional life had of necessity to be criticized. But in general the Foundation had public opinion on its side.

There were problems, when I left [1923], appropriate for Foundation research. The development of Cleveland's lakefront needing planning and large government and philanthropic money; a need for planned smoke abatement; and overhaul of property assessment to create a more orderly and beautiful metropolitan area. In some of these, other institutions made contributions. I do venture to claim the Foundation's explorations did a great deal to awaken the city to the need for self-appraisal, however painful.

It is interesting that Moley mentions lakefront development which, 50 years later, became one of the foundation's major achievements.

At the heart of success of most community foundations is a sense of obligation to and pride in a community. For most donors, the idea is to make gifts to the community where they live or to leave the city better off for those who come after them. And though the town or cause that bene-fits is usually local, some donors also remember other places in their bequests or contributions. Nathaniel Howard tells this good story:

Every year the New York Community Trust finances the town fair of the tiny community of St. James, in the Missouri Ozarks, and sees that the fair maintains prize competitions for the best quilts and the best women's dresses made from flour and farm sacks; this under the instruction of the Lucy Wortham James Trust set up for philanthropy in the village where her grandfather had an iron works in 1826 which was the foundation of three generations of an iron and ore fortune. St. James has a model modern library and a recreation park from the Trust. But the best part of this story begins with the company doctor of the iron works who brought Lucy Wortham James into the world, Dr. Samuel H. Headless. The niece with whom he lived, when she died, sent the New York Community Trust a cocoa tin containing $1,080 in currency and note asking that this be added to Miss James' philanthropy for St. James, Missouri. Among other benefactions, Miss Headless' bequest has furnished andirons for the model library and a bible for the Episcopal church of the village.

A typical but still moving example of the usefulness of gifts to community foundations is captured in the background of the John and LaVerne Short Memorial Fund of the Cleveland Foundation. The Shorts of Lakewood were poor but, after 40 years of hard work and saving, built a nest egg which they wanted to turn to charitable ends. They searched for a way they could leave it "to repay the community that had given us the means of a good life." When they died they left their entire estate, then grown to $1 million, to the Cleveland Foundation to establish a capital fund for "the advancement of medical science, the assistance of young men and women in procuring a medical education, and the improvement of hospitals or health institutions." Since 1973 the Short Fund has supported such projects as:

- A $132,000 leadership grant to the medical school of Case Western Reserve University to increase its minority student enrollment.
- A $225,000 grant to the same medical school to develop a range of mental health services to troubled children and adolescents.
- A $40,000 grant to create special out-patient services for the victims of spinal cord injuries at Cleveland Metropolitan Hospital.
- A large grant to the Westlake Health Campus Association to integrate health and human services.
- A large grant to the Cleveland Clinic to fund a study on the rehabilitation of elderly patients.
- A series of grants made in 1983 and 1985 to the Free Medical Clinic of Greater Cleveland to improve services to those unable to pay.

In its brief existence, the Short's one million dollar gift has already provided more than a million dollars for health care in their city of Cleveland, and the fund itself has more than doubled. That's what Goff intended when he proposed that Cleveland and every community should have "a trust for all time."

12

Unique Opportunities of Cooperative Benevolence

It's a bit of surprise to hear one of the best associations of givers referred to simply as "The Joint," but after the shock of irreverence wears off and after one begins to know "The Joint's" courage and accomplishments, the nickname becomes endearing. It's an organization that has head, heart, and soul, and one soon becomes proud to speak knowingly of "The Joint."

Even its full name, The Joint Distribution Committee, doesn't provide much indication of what it does, and its earlier name, The American Jewish Joint Distribution Committee, only begins to do so. It is called "The Joint" for two reasons. First, it was formed from three separate organizations that operated at the time of World War I to provide relief to European Jews. Its nickname also derives from its function as the principal distribution agent for funds collected by the Council of Jewish Welfare Federations and the United Jewish Appeal for charities overseas. These funds are administered "jointly."

Most of all, "The Joint" means 75 years of generosity and service by American Jews to assist Jews in other countries with human needs and human rights. In *My Brother's Keeper*, an excellent history of JDC, as "The Joint" is also called, Yehuda Bauer concludes:

> It tried to meet the emergencies as they arose. JDC, together with HICEM [an emigration association] and others, was involved in the emigration of some 440,000 Jews from Central Europe: 281,900 from "old" Germany, 117,000 from Austria, 35,000 from the Czech

lands, and 5,500 from Danzig. It had relieved the suffering of many
more in Europe. It proved to them that the Jewish people in
America cared, that they were not alone. It answered the voice of
conscience—which is more than can be said of many in that time.

In briefest history, JDC originally provided relief—basic food, clothing,
and medical supplies—during and after World War I. Then it began to
assist in essential economic development for displaced and oppressed
Jews during the late 1920s and the early 1930s. It returned to basic assistance for Jews facing persecution, imprisonment, and death in Germany,
Austria, Poland, Russia, and other parts of the world during the late
1930s. After World War II, JDC once again emphasized economic development, particularly assistance to those being resettled, especially in
Israel. In recent years it has increased attention to human rights and
empowerment.

Throughout, "The Joint" has attended to direct intervention for those
in greatest need, and to the preservation of Jewish religion and culture. In
1916, the JDC convinced President Wilson to declare January 27 "Jewish
Sufferers Relief Day" when more than $1 million was collected. In 1985,
the JDC Jerusalem Project received a quarter of a million dollars to help
form neighborhood committees so that, for the first time, residents will
have community-based mechanisms "to influence their own futures," and
to influence planning, oversight, and evaluation of human services that
are designed to serve them.

JDC has established health clinics, milk stations, orphanages, soup
kitchens, food banks, low-interest and no-interest loans, gifts of religious
materials, refugee and resettlement services, training programs, housing
construction, the creation of public/private partnerships, and an almost
never-ending range of services and influence that match and in may ways
have shown the way for U.S. philanthropy. It was and continues to be joint
philanthropy—or cooperative benevolence—at its best.

One of the reasons for JDC's establishment and success is given by Philip Bernstein in *To Dwell in Unity*, a history of the Jewish federation movement in America: ". . . The federations were an expression of ancient
Jewish principles, of which one was that the administration of charity is a
communal, rather than personal and individual responsibility. For thousands of years, there has been a tradition in Jewish life for people to make
their charitable gift to a community committee . . . for distribution to the
poor."

Part of that tradition involves gifts that build self-sufficiency and prevent hardship. Yehuda Bauer points out that increases in food production
became one of the main objectives of a special JDC project known as
"Agro-Joint":

Rosen [Joseph A. Rosen, JDC representative in Russia] thought of a way to increase food production without actually increasing the acreage sown. This could not be achieved by the traditional methods of sowing wheat or barley, especially since the seed was lacking owing to the droughts. With full Soviet support, therefore, Rosen began the importation of seed corn from the United States and 2.7 million acres in the Ukraine were sown with that crop.

One of JDC's "failures" foreshadowed the eventual development of the State of Israel. To try to deal with the growing oppression of Russian Jews, JDC tried to establish a major agricultural colony, which would have almost been a separate state for Jews in the Crimea. This project was well under way and had already attracted several hundred thousand Jews "when the rise of the Bolsheviks brought an end to the project, including a complete eradication of all their private business by means of excessive taxation, confiscation of property, arrests and exile."

During the 1930s, and indeed all through World War II, American Jews attempted to provide whatever relief they could to Jews still living in occupied and aggressor nations and to provide services and support to those who had been able to get out and were in need of resettlement. During these years, JDC representatives used overt and covert means to help other Jews. The history of their work during this period, which often involved extreme danger and thus required courage and dedication, continues to inspire the organization's activities today.

After the war, much of JDC's work focused on helping to bring displaced Jews to Israel and on aiding the development of the new state. That emphasis continues to the present. In addition, the organization serves the needs of Jewish people and the vitality of Judaism in 30 countries. JDC's annual giving stands at approximately $50 million. According to Bernstein:

> By the end of 1981 the JDC had spent $1.355 billion; the bulk of the funds came from the federations. Expenditures in 1981 alone totaled $44.5 million, of which the federations supplied $37.8 million. . . . The JDC has assisted more than three hundred thousand people in more than thirty nations, including Jews in Western and Eastern Europe, Moslem countries, Israel, India, and Latin America. Aid has been in the form of cash relief, feeding and nutrition programs, medical treatment, care for the aged, child welfare, Jewish education, vocational training, community center and youth activities, and religious and cultural programs.

On the occasion of the organization's 70th birthday in 1983, its Executive Vice President, Ralph I. Goldman commented:

It was in Morocco that the young student greeted me in Hebrew with the quote of Joseph: "It is my brothers I am seeking."

Joseph's words seemed to me to be an apt expression of the JDC purpose. In country after country on almost every continent JDC reaches out to provide help and hope to Jews in need. We are there, throughout the Jewish world—to help them live and to help them live as Jews. This is a responsibility we assumed voluntarily—and willingly—as a fulfillment of our Jewish tradition that we are our brothers' keepers.

This illustration of cooperative benevolence would not be complete without further information about the Jewish federation movement. It started in 1895, when, almost simultaneously, in Boston and Cincinnati, organizations were created to collect funds from Jews to help Jews and Jewish causes. Today there are 200 local federations serving 800 communities, and the total amount of money they raise is approaching one billion a year. These funds support many of the organizations whose names represent Jewish charity: Hillel, B'nai B'rith, JWB (formerly Jewish Welfare Board), Jewish Vocational Service, Jewish Board of Family and Children Services, Jewish Family Service, Jewish Immigrant Aid Society, and many, many others. At the community level, local federations provide much of the funding for Jewish community centers, homes for the aged, and the full range of human services. They also are in the thick of community relations; they are involved in defending civil rights and in maintaining relationships with the black and Hispanic communities. They attend to Christian–Jewish relationships, affirmative action, human rights, the needs of immigrants and refugees, the separation of church and state, anti-Semitism, and far more.

In explaining the title of his book, Bernstein gives one of the best indications of the meaning of cooperative benevolence.

> The title *To Dwell in Unity* was chosen because unity is the hallmark of the federations. It is taken from Psalm 133: "Behold how good and pleasant it is for brethren to dwell together in unity." The federations, uniquely among Jewish organizations, have brought together the broadest range of people with the most diverse philosophies, views, and priorities, to work together for purposes and needs they all share. In their combined power the federations have found unparalleled strength.

If the Aid Association for Lutherans (AAL) were an insurance company it would be one of the dozen largest in the United States. If it were a foundation it would also be among the top twelve. What AAL is, however, is a fraternal society of 1.3 million members, organized into 6,000 local branches in every state. Like most fraternal organizations, AAL encourages public service, but they have made cooperative benevolence a focal point of their being. To read its publications is to be reminded of the essential values of helping other people, whether they are neighbors, members of the same community, or other Americans. Every issue of their several different publications emphasizes service and doers.

Though the national philanthropic program is a giant of itself, most of the giving and volunteering occurs within their local branches. AAL tries to keep track of as much of this community service as possible and to spotlight model programs and leaders. Branch activity is encouraged and kept track of under these categories of "benevolent activities":

- *Community Action Benevolence.* AAL grants up to $2,500 to a branch which wants to purchase supplies, materials, and equipment, and provides most of the labor from its own membership to construct or improve community facilities such as recreational buildings or playgrounds, community parks, and the purchase of sports equipment.

- *Helping Hands Benevolence.* AAL grants up to $250 to buy supplies and materials for branch members who want to help others through building a wheelchair ramp, painting a home for a person who can't do it and can't afford it, or making toys for hospitals.

- *Disaster Response Benevolence.* AAL provides up to $2,500 to a branch that wants to help its community or others after a disaster by cleaning up after a tornado, helping to harvest crops, or rebuilding the riverbanks.

- *Co-operative Benevolences.* AAL will provide up to $5,000 in a supplementary grant to assist a branch to raise money for individuals or causes; for example, to provide laundry equipment for a home for battered women or medical equipment for a community hospital.

AAL provides thousands of small gold hearts to members in hundreds of branches as a way of recognizing community service. The Heart of Gold is sought after and worn proudly; it is often seen at regional and state conventions where the message is clear—every branch and every member should strive to receive them.

The national organization provides millions of dollars in support of these branch efforts, but it also has its own national programs. Although AAL is not a part of any church body, "support is provided regularly for the efforts of various Lutheran organizations." The following organizations and institutions are among those benefiting from AAL support:

- Fifty-two Lutheran colleges and universities share at least $1 million each year in various types of support.
- Sixteen Lutheran seminaries share in grants of almost $1 million annually.
- Ninety-eight Lutheran high schools get more than half a million dollars each year.
- Grants to projects proposed by various church bodies to serve their communities and strengthen their education efforts are about $1 million a year.
- The national auxiliaries, agencies and institutions receive about $500,000 a year for special projects or efforts not related to on-going expenses.
- Auxiliaries such as Lutheran Church Women and the Lutheran Women's Missionary League receive grants as do Lutheran camping associations and Lutheran social ministries.

AAL also has an extensive scholarship program, including: the All-College Scholarship Program, the Competitive Nursing Scholarship Program, the Vocational/Technical School Scholarship Program, the Lutheran Campus Scholarship Program, the Lutheran American Minority Scholarship Program, and the Seminary Scholarships Program.

One of AAL's largest national programs is the encouragement of volunteering, including support for the President's National Volunteer Awards Program, VOLUNTEER: The National Center, many local Voluntary Action Centers, Association for Volunteer Administration, and others.

While the term "cooperative benevolence" may have been coined elsewhere, I first heard of it in the description of AAL's program and philosophy. It seemed an apt description of one major aspect of philanthropy in action.

There are thousands of fraternal organizations in the United States and, like the rest of philanthropy, most of their charitable effort is too little known. The Knights of Columbus has the largest number of members and a multi-million dollar public service program, but even many of the smaller fraternal organizations emphasize charitable activity. Here is an interesting assortment of examples:

- The Catholic Association of Foresters provides college scholarships.
- Danish Brotherhood in America also provides scholarships, runs a summer camp for needy children, and provides financial assistance to aged members.
- The Grand Court Order of Calanthe, which has 442 lodges, runs a home for delinquent boys and has a "progressive adolescent service" that was founded by the Order, "Calanthe House of Bees."

- Independent Order of Vikings has the Viking Scholarship Fund and provides grants to "subordinate lodges to aid aged or needy members."
- Neighbors of Woodcraft operates Woodcraft Home to "provide comfort, care and security for aged members."
- Royal Neighbors of America (which has almost 3,000 lodges) maintains a national home for aged members, sponsors a national "help to hear" project and "dogs for the deaf," and encourages local units to give aid to speech and hearing handicapped persons.
- S.P.R.S.I. Conselho Supremo DA, which has 116 lodges, operates a scholarship program and provides financial grants to universities for scholarships in Portuguese language and culture.

A large proportion of fraternal groups have some religious affiliation. Religious motivations and practices have enormous bearing on the charitable giving of the majority of Americans. Indeed, almost two-thirds of all funds contributed by individuals goes to religious organizations and their affiliated schools, hospitals, and service agencies. Approximately 45 percent of all the money given by individuals goes directly to the church or synagogue itself. Another 20 percent goes to service organizations identified with religious groups such as Catholic hospitals, Lutheran colleges, and Jewish homes for the aged. Of the 45 percent given directly to the churches, synagogues or mosques, approximately one half supports the nonsacramental activities of the minister and congregation. Most personal giving therefore has some religious basis. The church bodies which this giving supports represent a very large part of the service structure of our communities.

Beyond this, many churches have formal grantmaking programs and behave very much like foundations. The total amount of dollars they donate exceeds the combined grants of foundations and corporations. In its February, 1985 *Newsletter,* the Council on Foundations reported on its survey of religious giving, a study that was supported by the Lilly Endowment, Pew Memorial Trust, and McKnight Foundation:

> Religious philanthropy surpasses corporate and foundation giving combined and has become increasingly targeted toward social change. Moreover, according to a special report just published by the Council, religious bodies are becoming more sophisticated about charitable giving. . . . Through religious philanthropy every conceivable need in society is being addressed—from soup kitchens in urban areas to making films about social justice, from building wells in the Sudan to emergency food aid in Ethiopia, said Council President, James A. Joseph. In announcing the publication of the

new report, he estimated that religious philanthropy totals $15–$16 billion annually.

Beyond the staggering sums of money collected and granted by churches, religious training and orientation seem to influence charitable behavior generally. In 1980, Research and Forecast, Inc. conducted a study for the Connecticut Mutual Life Insurance Company on "American Values in the 80s." The final report, appropriately entitled "The Impact of Belief," indicated that the 45 million Americans who are "intensely religious" (as measured by regular church going) "are far more likely to be volunteers active in the community, and contribute far more than average to charity." Three findings illustrate this strikingly:

- The most religious are far more likely to do volunteer work for a local organization.
- The most religious are much more likely to attend neighborhood or community meetings.
- Those who are most committed to religion are more likely than the least religious to feel that they "belong to a community."

In a *Foundation News* article, "A Metaphor Carried Too Far," John F. Wilson, Professor of Religion at Princeton and Director of the Project on Church and State, took as his topic the separation of church and state.

We have also lost the subtle understanding of how religious groups operate in American society. As de Tocqueville saw so clearly, religion was the most pronounced strand of the new nation's voluntary behavior. It formed mores, educated citizens, and in general exercised a civilizing influence.

Tocqueville thought religion played this role effectively only because it did so voluntarily. This was, for him, a point of marked contrast with societies of the Old World.

We, of course, tend to forget that religion was in the 19th century (and continues in the 20th) the most pronounced form of voluntary behavior in American society.

Wilson's piece was part of a September/October, 1984 issue of *Foundation News* devoted to "The Philanthropy of Organized Religion." In another article, "Hand in Hand," Martin E. Marty, Professor of History of Modern Christianity at the University of Chicago and author most recently of *Pilgrims in Their Own Land: 500 Years of Religion in America*, helps explain the relationship of voluntary activity in churches with religious motivation and support for community groups.

American religionists did not invent almsgiving or charity. In

Europe, Jews in shtetl and ghetto knew that they had to take care of their own.

For centuries, Catholics and Protestants had built, run and financed the hospitals and charitable institutions—but usually through their alliance with the state, as most churches were governmentally subsidized.

Separation of church and state forced them to invent new systems of philanthropy in America.

Most clergy were dragged screaming and kicking into the new era. The Reverend Lyman Beecher, the powerful Connecticut cleric who vehemently opposed separation in his state, soon turned around and boasted that American churches, thrown "wholly on their own resources and on God" would do more and were doing more through voluntary efforts, societies and the like than they did in the day of privileges for church, a day of cocked hats and gold-headed canes.

Voluntary societies became the main agency of philanthropy, beginning with the birth of the nation. They needed the support of motivations and givers.

Marty also reminds his readers that early religious training and continuing religious orientation had a great deal to do with the philanthropic behavior of such early philanthropists as Carnegie, Rockefeller, and Rosenwald.

In the same issue of *Foundation News*, Lester M. Salamon and Fred Teitelbaum begin their article with a reminder: "Religion," historian Henry Allen Moe has written, "is the mother of philanthropy." Moe was the early head of the John Simon Guggenheim Memorial Foundation and author of "Notes on the Origins of Philanthropy in Christendom."

One fascinating tale that captures the religious motivation behind gifts and giving was told by William M. Danner, Secretary of the American Committee of the Mission to Lepers, in the May, 1915 edition of *The Missionary Review*. It begins with an excerpt from a letter to the Mission.

> "Wife and I are about to sell our farm, and want to help your work. If you will send us your correct address, we would like to make a gift to your Society for the Lepers."
>
> Thus ran a letter that was received a few years ago at the Edinburgh office of the Mission to Lepers. It was postmarked at a small town in Kansas, U.S.A., and came from a farmer with a German name. The Secretary forwarded the desired information, expecting that a few dollars might come from some one whose heart had been touched by the lepers' needs. No one connected with the mission had ever heard of the farmer or his wife; but a surprise awaited them, for not long after a check came for $7,500, and the

check was genuine. Every year since there have come added gifts of $100 or $200 prompted by the same generous impulse and sympathy for the work.

A request came to me from the Edinburgh office, asking that when convenient I would call on the Kansas farmer and his wife and tell them a little more of the work, and express appreciation for their generous support. Last year an opportunity came during a tour through the South and West. Arrangements were made with the Methodist minister of the little Kansas town for me to speak in his church on a Sunday evening, and I determined to look up our generous friends.

Imagine my surprise, on reaching the town, to learn that the Methodist minister had never heard of Mr. and Mrs. P. D____. Inquiry among several members of his church brought no more enlightenment. We called on the Dean of the Mennonite College, and after four fruitless telephone calls on people who knew a number of D____'s but no P. D____, the fifth man gave us the desired information. Following his directions I walked, with the Methodist minister and the Dean of the College, to the edge of the village, and there stopt in front of a small frame cottage. It was a very modest little four-roomed house that could not have cost more than $700. The blinds were drawn, but the Dean knocked at the door. After repeated knocks, the door was opened by a pleasant-faced old German, with hair and beard as white as snow. He stood in the doorway, greeting us with a pleasant smile, and awaited a statement as to our mission.

The Dean explained to him in German that we came from the Mission to Lepers. Immediately the door was pushed wide open, and without having spoken a word he smilingly pointed toward the kitchen. As I passed through the front room I made a quick inventory of the furniture. Luxury was evidently a stranger to that home, and there was not even any intimation of comfort. If the furniture had been offered at auction the first bid would have been about 25 cents for the lot.

When we reached the kitchen we found the wife, a plainly clad little German woman, whose hands and face gave evidence of years of sturdy toil. On her neck was an unsightly swelling, perhaps a goiter, which caused her head to lean over on her shoulder. The marks of patient suffering were plainly visible. On being introduced to us she shook hands, and in the process we made practical acquaintance with the horny hands of toil. She skirmished through the three other rooms of the cottage and managed to find five straight-backed kitchen chairs of the plainest type. On these the three guests and the two old people sat down for the interview that followed. I could only gaze in wonder as I thought of the thousands of dollars that these two old people had given to help the lepers. In a few moments we learned that the husband had been paralyzed in speech some years before, and could not speak a word. From his cheerful smile and nods of approval, however, it was clearly evident that he was in hearty sympathy with all that had been done.

After we had exchanged friendly greetings and had engaged in a bit of general conversation, I asked our interpreter to express as fully and strongly as possible the appreciation of the officers of the society for the generous support they had given to the lepers' work, and to assure them that the lepers also were deeply grateful for the help they had received.

The interpreter took some time to make this plain to the old lady, who received the expressions of gratitude with apparent indifference. The husband smiled and nodded, meanwhile, to show that he quite understood everything. After the wife had said a few words to him, and had received another nod of approval, she turned to the interpreter and in a few words quickly spoken in German, with apparent indifference, ended all that she seemed to wish to say. Then, resting her face on her hand, she looked down at the floor, as if to say, "Do not bother me any more with the subject." Her words were uttered so brusquely that I almost feared that they were in some way displeased by my message. Then the interpreter turned and translated to me, "Mr. Danner must not come here to thank us for what we have done. It was God who put it in our hearts to help the lepers. Go and thank Him, for all the glory belongs to Him. We have been very glad to help the work."

There was nothing more to be said. The fine old couple, like Mary of old, sought no further recognition of the costly gifts they had made to their Lord.

Finally, after we had knelt in prayer, which the Dean of the College had led audibly, the interview closed. In clasping hands as we said Goodby, we could only think of these two aged and infirm Christians as true disciples who were meeting the test of love by seeking not their own welfare but the comfort and salvation of their less fortunate brothers and sisters. Inasmuch as ye have done it unto one of the least of these my brethren ye have done it unto Me.

In *Philanthropy in Negro Education,* Ullin Whitney Leavell writes: "The first efforts exerted in the colonies toward the education of the Negro were prompted by religious motive." He points out that: "The Society for the Propagation of the Gospel in Foreign Parts was the first

benevolent organization created to give enlightenment to the Negroes in
this country. It was formed in the Established Church of England in 1701.
It began its work for the Negroes in Goose Creek Parish in South Carolina." He then goes on to outline the work of the Quakers and later "Bap-
tists, Methodists, Presbyterians and other sects." Leavell writes:

> The Methodist church was especially energetic in this regard,
> having more than 300 workers in the field in the year 1860. During
> the 15 years of its separate existence before the Civil War, this body
> expended upon Negro missions the sum of $1,500,000. These
> missions almost without exception maintained schools and taught
> thousands of pupils to read and write. From these schools came
> many of the literate Negroes who appeared after the Civil War.

In his article, "Hand in Hand," Marty writes: "Today it is hard to
remember how religious were the roots of philanthropy for more than a
century. Pious Protestants, orphaned Quakers, people with names almost
forgotten, names like Isabella Graham and John Briscom, used their faith
to raise funds and start societies." Marty reminds us that many of the
efforts of such people were chronicled by Charles Foster in a book with
the wonderful title, *An Errand of Mercy*. Among the organizations Foster
cited were the Society for the Relief of Poor Widows with Small Children;
the Female Assistance Society; the Association for the Relief of Respect-
able, Aged, Indigent Females; and the Association for Relief of Indigent
Wives of Soldiers and Sailors.

In that special issue of *Foundation News*, Lawrence M. Jones, Dean of
the Divinity School and Professor of Afro-American Church History at
Howard University, has an article called "Serving 'The Least of These.'"
His apt summary is:

> Black churches have historically shouldered many more
> responsibilities than their White counterparts—and have thus
> emerged as the central force in their congregants' lives. . . . The
> benevolence of Black religious institutions has shared in the intent
> of philanthropy in that its ultimate goal is the empowerment of
> individuals to take responsibility for themselves and for their
> communities.

In the mid-1800s, the Protestant church in America was undergoing a
schism not unlike that which began to occur a hundred years later. Con-
fronted by so many problems and human needs and with little social
structure to deal with them, Protestant churches began to recognize a
need for their intervention and what developed became known as "The
Social Gospel." In *American Philanthropy*, Robert Bremner says: "The
1830s, an era of religious, political and economic ferment, was the age of

the 'Benevolent Empire,' a coalition of separate but closely related inter-denominational religious societies."

In a University of Wisconsin dissertation, "Protestant Stewardship and Benevolence, 1900–1941: A Study in Religious Philanthropy," John Errett Lankford wrote:

> Arthur M. Schlesinger, Sr. appraised the closing twenty-five years of the nineteenth century as the "critical period" for American religion. The older orthodoxy was hard pressed to adjust to pressures from the world of science. The rise of cities and the rapid development of the industrial economy presented challenges which shook the rural, pre-industrialist religious synthesis to its core.
>
> Out of this process came the social gospel with its emphasis on the fulfillment of the Kingdom of God in the immediate historical context. The social gospel was a relatively new emphasis in American theology. It attempted to come to grips with the immigrant, the robber baron, and the manifold problems presented by the rapid urbanization of America.

Among the many illustrations presented by Lankford are the Student Volunteer Movement for Foreign Missions and the Layman's Missionary Movement. He quotes frequently from a publication whose title describes the moving force of cooperative benevolence. It was called "The Living Church."

With the expanded agenda came a need for increased funds, and the answer for many churches was to invoke more strongly the expectation of tithing. Lankford quotes *The Continent*, the northern Presbyterian weekly: "There is no reason why anybody but a miser, who of course doesn't count, should fear in any church the appeal for Christians to adopt the tithe (as a method) and at least the initial measure, for fulfilling the Christian's duty to share for Christ's sake with others, the substance with which a bountiful God blesses him."

A century and more later, America's churches are struggling again with what their social role should be. At the extremes, conservatives point the finger at the black churches which supported Jesse Jackson's campaigns and liberals point to evangelicals such as the Moral Majority to sound the alarm that such bodies are interfering with public policies and elections. "The Impact of Belief" report found that:

> Today it is once again moral issues that have, via religion, vaulted to the forefront of the political dialogue, and suggest that this reawakening of moral activism carries a special significance as the United States enters the 80s. Moral issues have become the leading political issues. It appears that our society is at a transition point,

and that the public may be willing, under almost imperceptible influences, to throw its entire weight behind the leader who strikes the correct "moral" or "reaffirming" tone. This new trend is both heartening and potentially frightening. Since the injection of faith into politics via religion is capable of creating a single powerful voting block, this suggests the opportunity for a truly visionary leader, or a dangerous demagogue, who, by striking the appropriate religious–moral notes, could be swept into a position of awesome power.

Still, there is the question about what is the right philanthropic interpretation of separation for church and state. Henry C. Doll of the Cleveland Foundation urges foundations and even corporations not to lean too far to avoid encouragement of religious bodies. In the religious issue of *Foundation News*, his article, "Why Foundations Should Support the Projects of Religious Organizations," argues: ". . . Given the agendas of most philanthropic bodies, there are persuasive reasons for supporting the projects of religious groups." The points he makes can be summarized as follows:

- Religious organizations address human needs. In many ways they reach out more effectively than many other agencies.
- They are often in the forefront of addressing pressing societal issues.
- They have their own resources, unlike many social service institutions which depend almost exclusively upon foundation assistance.
- They can call upon an army of volunteers.
- They create and preserve many of our society's cultural treasures. . . . Much of our cultural diversity stems from the artistic contributions of churches and their members.

Doll cites these examples of collaboration in Cleveland:

- Without the help of Cleveland's Catholic diocese, which has parishes in most of Cleveland's neighborhoods, the Gund Foundation's desire to assist in the process of neighborhood rehabilitation and improvement might not have been fulfilled. . . . Our grants enabled organizers trained by the diocese to help neighborhood organizations which now have sufficient influence to prevent banks and insurance companies from red-lining and have spawned effective local development corporations.
- The Greater Cleveland Interchurch Council's (our Council of Churches) early stand in support of the court's desegregation order for the Cleveland schools undoubtedly contributed significantly to

what has been a remarkably peaceful desegregation process. . . .
Throughout the process the Gund Foundation and other local foundations supported the Council's efforts along with those of the Catholic diocese, which sought to assure that parochial schools would not be used as havens for families who wanted to escape from the Cleveland schools.

- Cleveland's Inner City Renewal Society, a church-based organization, has sponsored a training program for minority ministers for the past five years, implemented in conjunction with Ashland Theological Seminary and Case Western Reserve University and supported by foundations. The course has helped more than 250 clergymen become more effective church leaders.

The Lilly Endowment is one of the few major foundations that actively seeks collaboration with church bodies and projects. Indeed Lilly spends about $5 million a year on such efforts. In another article from that special edition of *Foundation News*, Richard J. Margolis quotes Robert Lynn of Lilly: "I'm really astonished at the number of people in private foundations who think they have to observe separation of church and state. They are completely misreading history." Margolis writes "The obstacles to cooperation between corporate, foundation and religious grantmakers may be more a matter of perception than reality." Margolis gives these illustrations:

- In Minneapolis and St. Paul, food producing corporations like Pillsbury and General Mills have teamed up with local churches and foundations in a massive, long-term effort to feed the hungry.
- In Cleveland, the George Gund Foundation and the United Methodist Church have joined forces in a local campaign for gun control.
- In Denver, Fern Portnoy of the Piton Foundation has organized a series of monthly "brown bag" lunches where leaders of corporations, religious groups and foundations discuss a broad range of community issues.
- In Boston, the monthly newsletter on civil rights and fair employment practices is being developed by a coalition of churches, businesses, foundations and community-based organizations under the coordination of Joan Diver of the Godfrey S. Hyams Trust.

The different philanthropic interests of churches are probably well illustrated by the Catholic church. Each parish, according to its orientation, is involved in some kind of education and social service. Some parishes have been in the forefront of food kitchens and resettlement of refugees. The organization Catholic Charities attempts to provide community-wide services, both for Catholics and the community at large, not unlike the role of the local Jewish federations. The Campaign for Human Development, an activist arm of the church, deals with such issues as social change and empowerment. Catholic Relief Services is one of the oldest organizations in international service. There are many other bodies, but these illustrate how pervasive are the philanthropic efforts of most of the major denominations.

Religion has quite clearly had an enormous influence on our philanthropy. In the opening chapter,"Our Religious Heritage," from my book *America's Voluntary Spirit,* I tried to put it in perspective:

> A very large part of America's attractive voluntary spirit stems from our religious heritage. The lessons are as varied as the religions of the hundreds of groups that came and still come to our shores. The common root of these varied testaments is an awareness that service beyond self is both an obligation and a joy. It is the ultimate universal truth.
>
> Even the new religions share the belief taught by Jesus, Moses, Mohammed, and Buddha and expressed in the Bible, Old Testament, Koran, commandments, Torah, or any contemporary equivalent, that of all the virtues to be made part of each of us, the greatest is charity.
>
> Even those who find meaning in life without religion have a grasp of these lessons. Confucius articulated this belief when he said that "goodness is God," by which he meant that God may not necessarily be a supreme being apart from us but at least is a supreme state of being within us. . . .
>
> Perhaps the most familiar of all the theological references is the following selection from I Corinthians 13:1–13 (as interpreted here by Catholic Gospel):

> > "And I point out to you a yet more excellent way. If I should speak with the tongues of men and of angels, but do not have charity, I have become as sounding brass or a tinkling cymbal. And if I have prophecy and know all mysteries and all knowledge, and if I have all faith so as to remove mountains, yet do not have charity, I am nothing. And if I distribute all my goods to feed the poor, and if I deliver my body to be burned, yet do not have charity, it profits me nothing.
> >
> > "Charity is patient, is kind; charity does not envy, is not pretentious, is not puffed up, is not ambitious, is not self-seeking, is not provoked; thinks no evil, does not rejoice over wickedness, but rejoices with the truth; bears with all things, believes all things, hopes all things, endures all things.

"Charity never fails, whereas prophecies will disappear, and
tongues will cease, and knowledge will be destroyed. For we
know in part and we prophesy in part; but when that which is
perfect has come, that which is imperfect will be done away with.
When I was a child, I spoke as a child, I felt as a child, I thought
as a child. Now that I have become a man, I have put away the
things of a child. We see now through a mirror in an obscure
manner, but then face to face. Now I know in part, but then I
shall know even as I have been known. So there abide faith, hope
and charity, these three; but the greatest of these is charity."

Henry Allen Moe concluded his "Notes on the Origins of Philanthropy
in Christendom" this way:

So it is with the law of philanthropy: starting with the Gospels, it
has survived wars and upheavals, schismatic popes and conquering
kings, Dark Ages, Renaissances, and Reformations.
It has survived because the necessities of the human race—
material and spiritual—have not changed.

There is a good deal of cooperative benevolence that has no apparent
relationship to religion. Much of it began with Benjamin Franklin who
established various joint philanthropies and societies in Philadelphia to
put out fires, build streets, and foster ideas. A little later when the government in Boston refused to appropriate money for the Bunker Hill monument, people did it themselves, raising more than $100,000 in voluntary
contributions and far more in uncompensated services and in materials,
including the granite. Boston had been aided by other towns and colonies
in 1774–75 when its port had been blockaded; they sent gifts of money,
grain and livestock for relief of the people of that city.

Charles Loring Brace formed the Children's Aid Society in New York in
1853 "to better the living conditions of children" and over the years it has
broadened its base of support to become one of the largest service societies supported by a large number of funders. Similarly, Josephine Shaw
Lowell established the Charity Organization Society for the city of New
York and set it on its course of diverse supporters and programs.

Boston's oldest social service agency, the Children's Mission to the
Children of the Destitute of the City of Boston, was founded by nine-year
old Fannie Merrill. The story is recounted in the Mission's history:

Fannie, who deplored the plight of many of the poor, neglected
children on the streets of Boston in 1849, was determined to find a
way to help them. Out of her determination (and the sympathetic

support of her parents) the Unitarian Church organized a society dedicated to rescuing "morally exposed" children from "vice, ignorance, and degradation." During its early years, the Children's Mission depended largely upon funds donated by Sunday School children such as Fannie.

The work of the Mission is still carried forward by its predecessor organization, the Parents and Children's Service of the Children's Mission.

An even longer record, of a different sort, was celebrated in 1985 when Catholic Charities observed its 300th year of continuous service in the United States.

Organized labor began its support of charitable activities to help workers and other needy people, and today, almost every major drive and charity involves not only volunteer leadership from labor unions but cash and in-kind assistance as well. Several unions have foundations such as the David Dubinsky Foundation of the International Ladies Garment Workers Union. The AFL–CIO has organized and operates several special funds. For example, in 1961 they established a foundation "for the development of union leadership in Latin American countries."

The Chamber of Commerce of the United States has a foundation as do many service and professional societies. The Rotary Foundation was founded so that "each individual might assume the perpetuation of the ideal of service and so make his membership in Rotary a continuing force." The American Association of University Women has its AAUW Foundations to provide graduate and research fellowships, fellowships in selected professions, grants for public service, and grants for women re-entering the work force.

There is the Permanent Charities Committee of the Entertainment Industry, Council for Financial Aid to Education, NOW Legal Defense and Education Fund, National Fund for Medical Education, Council for the Advancement of Science Writing, Citizens' Scholarship Foundation of America, and even the Herb Society of America for "furthering the knowledge and use of herbs and contributing the results of the experience and research to the records of horticulture and science."

People join together for many different causes. The Clinton Community Garden in New York was purchased at public auction by the Trust for Public Land after the Trust sold square inch plots for $5 apiece to finance the purchase.

There are thousands of alumni associations devoted at least in part to raising funds for their institutions, and there are college funds such as the Pennsylvania College Fund that raise money from corporations and others to support their member institutions.

Combined fundraising or federated campaigns got their biggest boost during World War I. First there was the international campaign for the YMCA, then the Red Cross campaigns. Later, broader federations were formed to address needs associated with the war. In Curti's *Philanthropy Abroad,* he writes:

> The most characteristic feature of American giving in the first years of the war however, was the increasing reliance on large-scale, highly organized, business-like approaches to the problem. Also, the role of members of the American Foreign Service in philanthropies overseas was greater and more sustained than ever before. In the scale of magnitude what was done exceeded any earlier overseas effort. It was ironical that a vast war, highly destructive of life, brought forth such devoted efforts in providing money, supplies and services to lessen the force of the disaster.

In the 1920s, Herbert Hoover proved himself the great organizer of relief efforts, culminating in his massive Commission for Relief of Belgium. The post-war period also saw the development of the Community Chest, now the United Way, a giant of cooperative benevolence. In 1986, United Way raised more than $3 billion in 2,300 local campaigns serving thousands of agencies and millions of individuals. The United Negro College Fund is another prominent example of cooperative benevolence at its best.

In 1961, Richard Carter wrote a book whose title captured the essence of people joining together in giving and volunteering. The title was *The Gentle Legions.* It told the story of the organization of the major voluntary health agencies such as the March of Dimes, American Heart Association, American Cancer Society, and the National Mental Health Association. It makes the point that large numbers of people working together in charity dwarf the work of any single individual or even any one major foundation. Today, we continue to organize to address every conceivable aspect of the human condition, ranging from improving our neighborhoods to protecting the ozone layer. In the exercise of cooperative benevolence, the "gentle legions" are America's largest philanthropic force.

In a recent campaign conducted by the Advertising Council, INDEPENDENT SECTOR attempted to help the American people understand and take pride in the breadth of giving and volunteering in our society. To help make that point, the volunteer advertising firm, Ogilvy and Mather, produced a number of illustrations, but none better for the message than "J. Robert Anderson" who appears on the next page.

Meet J. Robert Anderson, philanthropist.

He's not a millionaire. In fact, he's not even rich. But he gives.

Most of the giving in this country doesn't come from the wealthy. Almost half of it comes from people who earn less than $20,000 a year. Everyday, ordinary people. Like the guy down the street. Or your next-door neighbor. Or 100 million others who, every year, give unselfishly just to help people.

And while those who give may sometimes go unnoticed, their contributions don't. Because in this country, when a lot of people give, it adds up to a lot.

It helps fund important research. It helps run community church programs. It helps support local charities.

It helps people out.

There are so many things in this country that could use your hand. Your time, your tal-

ents, your money. What you give isn't so important. That you do give is. Because you don't have to

be rich to be a philanthropist. You just have to care.

 A Public Service of This Publication

INDIVIDUAL GIVING/VOLUNTEERING CAMPAIGN
MAGAZINE AD NO. IGV-1625-84—7" × 10" (110 Screen)
Volunteer Agency: Ogilvy & Mather, Inc., Volunteer Coordinator: Maureen Hartigan, TRW

CM-1-85

13

The Most Unique Opportunity and Obligation: To Lead

The Social Service Review of September, 1958 published an article, "The Reputation of the American Philanthropist—A Historian's View," by Irving Wyllie. In it Wyllie wrote:

> One of the most significant questions we can ask about the philanthropist is: How did he stand with his constituents—What was his reputation among the men he professed to serve? . . .
>   . . . Americans have always used hard yardsticks in taking the measure of their philanthropists, standards that have been articulated time after time in the massive and discriminating public commentary on the lives and deeds of the benefactors. There is no mystery about it. Before he can win a place in the philanthropic hall of fame the benevolent American must convince his beneficiaries that 1) his charity flowed from love and not from vanity or self-interest, 2) he accepted the dominant values and aspirations of his society and identified himself in a personal way with his city or the nation, and, 3) he contributed something toward the solution of one or more of the significant problems of his age.

Toward the end of that paper, Wyllie asks and answers:

> Did America ever produce a perfectly reputable philanthropist, a man who embraced in his person all the virtues and attitudes here described? She did, and his name was Peter Cooper. His

reputability cannot be measured in quantitative terms, for others gave more than he, others received more publicity, others are better remembered today. But no benefactor ever stood closer to the people he tried to serve than he, and none ever received so much reciprocal love from his fellow men. It could not be said that his charity, like Girard's, offset a forbidding personality; or that, like Rockefeller's, it helped him live down his business past. Cooper lived the stewardship of wealth. He gave the bulk of his fortune, not just the surplus, and he gave it while he lived. Occasionally he gave to the poor, but through his Union he tried to supply opportunities that would make such aid unnecessary. Recognizing the limits of charity, he turned in his old age to political reform and to thoughts of a benevolent state. Shallow men have viewed his campaign for the presidency as a Greenbacker in 1876 as an unaccountable aberration, when it was in fact a logical extension of his philanthropic career. Cooper was, in every sense, a public-spirited man. His sense of debt to the city of his birth and his love for the nation were boundless; his identification with both was complete. He put full-length portraits of Washington, Franklin, and Lafayette in the main lecture room of the Cooper Union, for the heroes of the republic reminded him of all his brightest hopes for the renovation and improvement of the world. When word of Cooper's death spread through New York on April 4, 1883, flags all over the city dropped to half-mast, and shops were draped with black. On the day of his funeral the busiest thoroughfares were closed to business. Countless thousands wept in the streets. New York mourned as it had not mourned for eighty years, when the body of George Washington passed through the city. No one needed to ask for whom the bells tolled. By some intuitive process, Peter Cooper's neighbors seemed to understand that America had lost a philanthropist who was worthy of the name.

Doing good in the right ways often provides the rewards, even if not intended, of appreciation and some degree of immortality. In James W. Wooster, Jr.'s biography, *Edward Stephen Harkness: 1874–1940*, there is this reproduction of an editorial from the *Yale Daily News*.

A great man has died. We walk through the halls he built. We live in the comfort and luxury he provided. We learn from men he endowed. Much of the graciousness and beauty of our life here is his creation. For all this, men of Yale feel a gratitude beyond the power of articulation. In the death of this man Yale feels the loss of a son whose loyalty, devotion, and generosity knew no bounds.

It is hard to believe that we are only one of the host of groups

whose lives were made richer, happier, and more pleasant by this
man's benevolence. Countless places of learning, vast medical
centers, great charitable organizations—scarcely any form of
constructive human endeavor was without his aid. Here and abroad,
thousands of institutions were brought into being, developed, and
enabled to survive by the grace of his philanthropy. Thanks to him,
millions of his fellow men came to know a fuller life.

It was given to him to realize the dream shared by all men: to see
the world made better by the fact of his being. In great and
thankful communities like this one the memory of Harkness can
never be extinguished.

But more than buildings, lectureships, medical centers, and
charity funds survive. There is the story of a man. There have been
men of greater wealth. There have been men of private station who
knew greater power. During his lifetime greater commercial
empires than his rose and toppled.

In the great age of acquisition men everywhere were outdoing
each other in elegant pretentiousness. Other men of fortune were
protecting themselves against change by constructing great
fortresses of wealth about them. Others, too, were buying power
with their dollars, and courting popular favor by their largesse. He
even lived to see wealth prosecuted at the bar of public opinion.

But his man stood out above the scramble. Not grandeur, not
power, not rights, but duty was his all-consuming care. Modesty
kept him from making known the extent of his gifts; he did not seek
credit for his generosity. Not how to hold, but how to justify his
wealth was the concern of his life. In his life the world may read
the lesson of a man with a rare appreciation of the public obligation
of private property.

A world too often cynical may find inspiration in a man of whom
it may be said with all sincerity: "He loved his fellow-men."

In October, 1895, Charles F. Thwing, President of Western Reserve
University, published a piece in *The Forum* entitled, "Well-Meant But
Futile Endowments: The Remedy." He begins by presenting the "six
rules for benevolence" from the book *Endowed Charities* by Courtney
Stanhope Kenny:

1. Of two ways of palliating an evil, we must choose the more
powerful.

2. Relief which removes the causes of the evil is better than that
which palliates or increases it.

3. If we must choose among forms of relief that only assuage the

evil without removing its cause, those—if of equal potency—are to be preferred which produce least new evil.

4. The graver the evil, the more desirable is the charity that relieves it.

5. An inevitable evil is more deserving of relief than an avoidable one.

6. An unexpected evil is more deserving of relief than one that could be foreseen.

Mr. Thwing's article is generally critical of foundations that "try too hard to perpetuate the interests of the original benefactor; they are generally too inflexible by policy and administration to address the problems of subsequent generations." Thwing wrote: "It is not wise for a founder to say exactly what men shall believe, or in what terms they should express their belief a hundred years, or two hundred years, or five thousand years, after he is dead. He would better entrust his general purpose, without specific conditions, to the men of the future." To make his point he quotes from John Stuart Mill's "Dissertations and Discussions":

At the head of the foundations which existed in the time of Turgot was the Catholic heirarchy, then almost effete; which had become irreconcilably hostile to the progress of the human mind, because that progress was no longer compatible with belief of its tenets; and which, to stand its ground against the advance of incredulity, had been driven to knit itself closely with the temporal despotism, to which it had once been a substantial, and the only existing, impediment and control. After this came monastic bodies, constituted ostensibly for the purpose, which derived their value chiefly from superstition, and now not even fulfilling what they professed; bodies of most of which the very existence had become one vast and continued imposture. Next came universities and academical institutions, which had once taught all that was then known; but, having ever since indulged their ease by remaining stationary, found it for their interest that knowledge should do so too—institutions for education, which kept a century behind the community they affected to educate; who, when Descartes appeared, publicly censured him for differing from Aristotle; and, when Newton appeared, anathematized him for differing from Descartes. There were hospitals which killed more of their unhappy patients than they cured; and charities of which the superintendents, like the licentiate in "Gil Blas," got rich by taking care of the affairs of the poor; or which at best made twenty beggars by giving or pretending to give a miserable and dependent pittance to one.

The foundations, therefore, were among the grossest and most conspicuous of the familiar abuses of the time; and beneath their shade flourished and multiplied large classes of men by interest and habit the protectors of all abuses whatsoever. What wonder that a life spent in practical struggle against abuses should have strongly prepossessed Turgot against foundations in general! Yet the evils existed, not because there were foundations, but because those foundations were perpetuities, and because provision was not made for their continual modification to meet the wants of each successive age.

Thwing ends on a similar but slightly more positive note:

This review brings us to certain rather important conclusions; for the number of people in the United States who desire to make the noblest and most lasting use of their wealth is already large and is constantly increasing. One conclusion is, that it is not the part of wisdom to surround a foundation with very specific conditions. A second conclusion is, that if a gift is surrounded with very specific conditions, a means of relief should be afforded in a general permission to use the gift in the promotion of a general purpose. A third conclusion is that a founder should trust the men of the future to carry out his general purpose. He should not lay down certain narrow methods or merely technical rules for their following. The good men of A. D. 3895 will have more wisdom for administering a trust made two thousand years before than any man living in 1895 can suggest to them. . . .

After all this study and analysis, my own profile for effective philanthropy would look like this:

Independence. If the philanthropic organization—and indeed philanthropy in general—cannot make independent decisions, then it loses its quintessential characteristic and value. The sector is so minute compared with the other sectors—even the larger foundations are so comparatively small—that its principal purpose must be to represent a different way of looking at things. That can only happen if the freedom exists to be different.

In *A Philosophy for a Foundation*, Raymond B. Fosdick of the Rockefeller Foundation said:

If wisely designed, a foundation enjoys a freedom of actions possessed by few other organizations. It has no stockholders to satisfy and no constituents to appease. It has no alumni, no faculty, and no student body whose conflicting views must be harmonized. It represents no particular interests—religious, political, or private;

its responsibility is to the public as a whole. It can be free of entanglements and restrictions, and while it is often under pressure from those who are seeking its grants, these pressures can generally be resolved in a spirit of good will.

For Fulton Cutting, William H. Allan, and Mary Harrison to take on the bosses of Tammany Hall, to begin to put citizens in charge of their cities, and to be farsighted enough to establish public administration as a career, took many qualities, but especially independence from almost all the countervailing forces.

Leadership. Money is only one form of leadership. Philanthropic organizations have an opportunity to exercise influence far beyond the dollars they can spend. They should leverage all their assets, including their independence, the reputation of their board members, their relative objectivity, their perceived power, and their capacity to influence other donors and leaders.

The Rockefeller Foundation learned very early that finding the causes of disease and premature death was only half the battle. Putting the solutions to work was the other half. The foundation's efforts to establish the U.S. Sanitary Commission and similar commissions in many southern states as the vehicles for applying what the foundation had helped to discover about the relationship of hookworm to many serious disabilities is one of thousands of examples of foundations exercising leadership far beyond dollars.

An Intelligence Function. Good funders have an extraordinary capacity to know their areas of specialty, their communities, and the people in them, and they have a capacity to network, finding out what they don't know when they need to know it.

The "community involvement teams" of the Levi Strauss Company, which encourage employee volunteers to identify local community needs, design projects to meet those needs and provide funding for the projects, represent that kind of community intelligence and effective application of total corporate philanthropy.

Flexibility. The best funders have the ability to make exceptions—sometimes to make lots of them—to change programs, and to work with all kinds of people and organizations. To be sure, flexibility can be unattractive in the extreme when grantmakers zigzag following the "in" topics. But, if a funder is dealing with a real problem, the situation is likely to require a combination of tenaciousness and flexibility.

Surely, the Gannett Foundation wasn't overjoyed to fund the Yaddo Retreat's costs for hooking up to the county water system—and most foundations would have exercised the conditioned response that "it's outside our program"—but Gannett was flexible and realistic enough to realize that without the input of clean water there wasn't going to be much output of artistic creativity.

Innovation, Daring, Boldness, Responsiveness. In a 1985 speech to INDEPENDENT SECTOR, David Rockefeller observed that one thing philanthropy needs most is "boldness."

There's a new "Giraffe Project" that honors people "who stick their necks out to try to make a difference in their communities."

The New York Community Trust developed a "Windmill Project" to support and honor those who may appear to be foolishly pursuing an illusory goal—to be tilting at windmills—but who are making a daring effort to try something different.

The Seaver Fund of California, a growing foundation, makes relatively few grants but puts a lot of money behind "big gambles" though they know most of them won't pay off.

The Chairman of General Electric, John Welch, believes that people in that corporation should be rewarded for "taking the big swing" even if they miss, and he expects that principle to be applied to GE's philanthropy as well. The boards of too many foundations want to be on the "cutting edge" only so long as the operation is "fail-safe." They can't have it both ways. One of the unique opportunities *and* obligations of grantmakers is to gamble.

Certainly Daniel Guggenheim's support of "Moon Man" Goddard was a daring gamble bordering on foolishness and Lady Gregory must have funded a lot of awfully bad literature between rare finds of the likes of James Joyce.

Enthusiasm. Oliver Wendell Holmes observed that: "Philanthropists are commonly grave, occasionally grim, and not very rarely morose."

When David Rockefeller talked about boldness, he coupled it with such words as "fun" and "exciting." I attend a lot of board meetings, and rarely do I have the sense that the board is having the fun of "the big swing" or the excitement of being in on a gamble that could pay off. Granted, most of the business of foundations, like that of all organizations, is somewhat routine, but making grants is one area where spiritedness should be more common. Thornton Wilder provided this counsel:

> It's your business not to be eager about the thousand and one things in the night-sky of knowledge, but to be enthusiastic about the one or two constellations that you have marked down for your own. . . . Count that month lost in which you have not been swept up in an enthusiasm.

Ralph Waldo Emerson put it even more definitely when he said: "Nothing was ever accomplished without enthusiasm."

Anna T. Jeanes contributed gladly because she believed that giving was not a sacrifice but the happy extension of a generous diety, Peter Cooper found it exhilarating to provide an opportunity for young people through his Cooper Clinics and other charities; and D. K. Pearsons had to be enthusiastic when he pinned his farewell note to the fifty thousand dollars he contributed to Montpelier Seminary.

In his book, *The Golden Donors*, Waldemar Nielsen urges foundations to achieve what he calls "maximum feasible function":

> . . .there are four criteria that depict excellence for large foundations by the standard of maximum feasible function:

> • *First, they should concentrate their efforts on matters of a scope and significance proportionate to their resources and their special capabilities as foundations.* They should avoid doing those things that other foundations and sources of funding can do, not only to avoid duplication but, of greater importance, to avoid leaving a most dangerous gap in the spectrum of national issues that receive the benefit of diverse, disinterested ideas and criticism. Only the large foundations command sufficient maneuverable social capital in the nonprofit sector to be able to finance a competent private contribution to the discussion of such problems as the adequacy of government regulation of the safety of the airlines or of nuclear power reactors, or the improvement of public secondary education, or the control of health-care costs. If the big foundations do not make possible a pluralistic monitoring, stimulative, or evaluative function at the higher levels of national problems, then those matters will be abandoned to special-interest groups, government, and "solution" by the horse trading of politics.

> • *Second, large foundations should maintain staffs of a competence comparable to the best institutions in other fields and should possess the intellectual vigor to take initiatives in their grant making rather than being purely reactive.* This is neither arrogance nor presumption but rather simply the utilization of their situational advantage. A foundation is a crossroads, a marketplace of information and ideas. Heads of individual schools or hospitals from their vantage point can see the needs of their institutions with particular clarity; foundation officers from their vantage point and with a wider scan can sometimes see with special clarity opportunities that can benefit whole groups of institutions or fields of educational, scientific, or other activity. They are also in a position to assemble advisers, commission research, and attract the cooperation of other relevant institutions in an enterprise in a way that persons differently situated cannot. Responsiveness to the felt needs of others is a virtue in

philanthropy; but creative action that may relate to needs not yet
perceived by others can be an even greater virtue, and some of the
most important contributions of major foundations in the past have
derived from just such actions.

- *Third, a large foundation should be open, interactive, and collaborative with all kinds of other private institutions relevant to its purposes.* These include not only other foundations but all nonprofit
agencies, not only its own grantees. These hundreds of thousands of
institutions are not only the clientele of foundations but are the
instruments of action through which grant-making foundations must
work. Collaboration with business corporations is not only a relatively new departure for foundations, but also a most promising one.
The large private foundations can play a valuable role in helping
improve the work of corporate foundations, a rapidly growing ele-
ment in philanthropy, and in encouraging major business firms to
expand their programs of social investment in housing, education,
and job creation, for example. The kind of isolation and encapsula-
tion that characterized the behavior of many foundations in the past
is a serious impediment to the achievement of optimum
effectiveness.

- *Fourth, and of crucial importance, a major foundation must keep
itself well informed about governmental policies and programs in its
fields of interest, must make its grant decisions in full awareness of
their relationship to the activities of government, and must have a
conscious and carefully formulated posture toward the role and policies of government in the area of its work.* Government, at the federal, state, and local levels, has for the past half-century been a
factor of rapidly increasing importance in every field except religion
in which foundations operate. It is now overwhelmingly the pre-
dominant source of funding in nearly all those fields. Its presence
must therefore be carefully taken into account. In some cases a
foundation may simply want to avoid duplication of effort; sometimes it may choose to form a joint venture with government; and
sometimes it may devote itself to trying to persuade government to
alter what it is doing.

There remains a still larger role and responsibility of major foundations vis-a-vis government. This relates to the problem of the
growing incompetence, or breakdown, of the means by which the
citizenry have traditionally been aided in exercising their critical
and evaluative function over government policies and programs.
Under the impact not only of the growing scale but also of the
growing complexity of many new areas of government action, legislative bodies are less and less capable of overseeing and controlling

government economic, social, scientific, and military programs. The newspapers and mass media keep a critical eye on government, but they have been more effective in connection with relatively simple problems such as scandals and graft than in appraising such questions as the effectiveness of government regulation of mass communications or the defects of federal programs for the training and employment of minority youth. Similarly, for even the most intelligent and informed citizens, many areas of government activity, such as the work of the National Institutes of Health or the Department of Energy, are simply beyond their technical competence and experience.

The large foundations offer one of the few possibilities for subjecting such matters to competent private assessment and for the formulation of meaningful recommendations. A number of foundation-supported public commissions and policy research projects have in fact been extremely useful in this way. Such initiatives are a particularly crucial contribution by the big foundations to the effective functioning of the American democratic system under modern conditions.

Nielsen also speaks of the power of foundations as "role models" and suggests that when major grantmakers take on a topic, it has a "locomotive effect, [for] example the influence of a role model like Robert Wood Johnson increases as knowledge of what it is doing and how it is doing it circulates among others in philanthropy, and as the inevitable comparisons are made with their own policies and programs." He also speaks of a "fifth, and metaphysical criterion. . .":

It is a waste of important potential if foundations do not make use of the special freedoms they have been given: to take the long view; to back the promising but unproven idea, individual, or institution; to take an unpopular or unorthodox stand; to facilitate change rather than automatically endorsing the status quo (a reflex that could be called knee-jerk conservatism); to act and not merely react; to initiate even to gamble and dare . . . .
. . . In this sphere they have an obligation of standard setting, of lifting hearts and hopes. As in the case of great concert artists, it is not sufficient that they arrive at the performance on time, play on key, and remember to thank their accompanist. More is and should be expected of them: high aspiration, dedication, and inspiration to others. They must believe in something, stand for something, and with conviction.

Robert L. Payton, President of the Exxon Education Foundation offers his own prescription in a paper, "Philanthropic Values," prepared for a Wilson Center Colloquium in 1982:

- The integrity of philanthropic activity rests on the primacy of concern for others. To practice philanthropy is to engage in a constant struggle with the claims of self-interest. Our skill at rationalizing those claims threatens our philanthropic integrity.

- To achieve and maintain a high level of philanthropy requires effort of intellect and effort of will. As individuals and as institutions we have still not accepted how difficult it is to do the right thing. We tend to be guided by an easy sentiment or by narrow rationalism. We will improve our performance only if we seek to understand how philanthropy works—and why, so often, it doesn't.

- Philanthropic activity at its best is then an informed discipline, a habit of mind and behavior infused with value. Such habits are acquired by socialization and education, especially in the early years. We should pay more attention to the way that philanthropy is taught.

- Philanthropy enlists only a small portion of our resources, and this operates at the margin of the economy. Yet the leverage of change is found at the margin, and private philanthropic initiatives have been the source of improvements in every aspect of our lives.

- Philanthropy thus becomes a sort of First Amendment right, and we should protect the philanthropic entrepreneurs who presume to make our lives better. We should not let our legitimate concern about some silliness or even fraud to obscure the enormous value of charitable activity dispersed throughout the population.

- It is argued here that private initiatives supported or even originated by philanthropy have shaped the social role of government. As "public altruism" has emerged, those initiatives have been seized by bureaucrats drawing on public funds. Governments have proved to be inept as philanthropic agents. The need to increase the magnitude of funds available for social and cultural purposes has led us to rely on governments to take over philanthropic responsibilities. The answer to our dilemma appears to lie in tax incentives and in public funds administered by private agencies.

- Finally, the habit of philanthropy seems to be best acquired in a social *ethos* that encourages attention to matters of ultimate concern—to religious values. The material and the spiritual values of our society are tested in the matrix of philanthropy, and we cannot treat intelligently of the one without the other. Our secular prefer-

ence for focussing on the material is not sufficient. We must come
to grips with our religious values as well, and philanthropy forces
us to do that. Whether we like it or not.

In his summary chapter, "The Consensus," from *U.S. Philanthropic
Foundations*, Warren Weaver writes:

There are some activities of philanthropic foundations that have
concrete, measurable, and indisputable value. In the twenty years
following 1943, when the Rockefeller Foundation effectively began
its agricultural program in Mexico, the population of that country
increased by 75 percent; but the production of their basic foods
increased by 300 percent. This kind of accomplishment is easy to
measure and to appreciate. There are many other foundation
activities that are less easy to assess, and there are activities that
are really impossible to assess in any provable way. When dealing
with this last category, one simply has to have faith in the ultimate
value of sincere, honest, dedicated, well-intentioned and ably-
manned attempts. However difficult assessment is, the fact remains
that competent persons, expert and experienced in a wide variety
of fields, have in these preceding contributed chapters borne clear
witness to their own convictions that foundations are serving society
well.

In fact and in summary, what is the over-all evidence furnished
by the authors of the preceding eighteen chapters? It is that
foundations have freed large parts of the world from the curse of
diseases such as malaria and yellow fever; have brought enjoyment
of the arts to millions of people; have created and helped support
universities and research institutes; have clarified and otherwise
served the law; have in many practical ways promoted international
understanding and have encouraged the cause of peace; have
shown how population can be controlled and people fed; have
helped develop broadly trained leadership for business and
government; have significantly aided the emerging nations; have
importantly contributed to our growing knowledge of physical and
living nature; have been alert in aiding new fields of activity; have
helped to clarify the goals of present-day humanistic scholarship;
have made possible the development of important new scientific
instruments for studying the atom, the cell, and the star; have, in
language and area studies, anticipated and provided for some of the
pressing needs of our country in its new worldwide responsibility;
have created multi-million-dollar free funds for basic research; have
recently developed and supported several projects to extend the
opportunities of higher education to qualified Negroes; and have

liberated thousands of gifted individuals from the limitations of inadequate education, thus freeing them for greater service to society.

What it all seems to come down to is that even though philanthropic dollars are very small compared to the expenditures of government and commerce, when these dollars have been targeted independently and creatively, the leadership value has been tremendous. In turn that comes down to a prescription for the future of even more of the best of philanthropy in action.

BIBLIOGRAPHY

The preparation of this bibliography paralleled the development of the similar reference list, *Philanthropy and Voluntarism: An Annotated Bibliography,* compiled by Daphne Niobe Layton of the Association of American Colleges (AAC) and published by The Foundation Center in June, 1987. Indeed, at times there was almost monthly checking to see what each was uncovering to help future researchers and writers.

We hasten to acknowledge that theirs is by far the more definitive reference work. The narrower focus of our book and bibliography is to provide information on the impact of specific grants rather than of philanthropy in general.

We ended the introduction to the bibliography for *America's Voluntary Spirit* (published by The Foundation Center in 1983) with the statement "We hope the reader will view this list as a starting point for larger efforts, hopefully soon to come." The work of the AAC and of an increasing number of others is our greatest encouragement.

Brian O'Connell
Ann Brown O'Connell

"A Giver Who Gave All." *Literary Digest* 44 (May 11, 1912):1003–1005.

Abell, Aaron I. *The Urban Impact on American Protestantism, 1865–1900.* Hamden, Conn.: Archon Books, 1962.

Abrams, Burton A., and Schitz, Mark D. "The Crowding-Out Effect of Governmental Transfers on Private Charitable Contributions." *Public Choice* 33 (1978):29–40.

Adams, David W. "Philanthropists, Progressives, and Southern Black Education." *History of Education Quarterly* 23 (1983):99–111.

Adams, James Luther. *On Being Human Religiously.* Boston: Beacon Press, 1976.

Addams, Jane. *My Friend, Julia Lathrop.* New York: Macmillan Co., 1935.

Addams, Jane; Woods, Robert A.; Huntington, Father J. O. S.; Giddings, Franklin H.; and Bosanquet, Bernard. *Philanthropy and Social Progress: Seven Essays.* Delivered before the School of Applied Ethics, 1892. Freeport, N.Y.: Books for Libraries Press, 1893.

Alchon, Guy. *The Invisible Hand of Planning: Capitalism, Social Science and the State in the 1920's.* Princeton, N.J.: Princeton University Press, 1985.

Alexander, John K. *Render Them Submissive: Responses to Poverty in Philadelphia, 1760–1800.* Amherst: University of Massachusetts Press, 1980.

Allen, Kerry Kenn; Chapin, Isolde; Keller, Shirley; and Hill, Donna. *Volunteers from the Workplace.* Washington, D.C.: VOLUNTEER: The National Center for Voluntary Action, 1979.

Allen, Kerry Kenn; Keller, Shirley; and Vizza, Cynthia. *A New Competitive Edge: Volunteers from the Workplace.* Arlington, Va.: VOLUNTEER: The National Center for Voluntary Action, 1986.

Allen, Peter C. *Stanford From the Beginning.* Stanford, Calif.: Office of Public Affairs, Stanford University, 1984.

Allen, William H. *Modern Philanthropy.* New York: Dodd, Mead & Co., 1912.

Alperovitz, Gar, and Faux, Jeff. *Rebuilding America.* New York: Pantheon, 1984.

Alumni Association of the Cooper Union. "Peter Cooper: A Tribute in Commemoration of the 100th Anniversary of His Birth."

American Association of Fund-Raising Counsel, Inc. *Giving USA: Annual Report, 1985 (Facts and Trends on American Philanthropy for the year 1984).* New York: American Association of Fund-Raising Counsel, Inc., 1985

"American Millionaires and Their Recent Benefactions." *The Review of Reviews* 7 (February 1893):48–60.

Anderson, James D. "Northern Foundations and the Shaping of Southern Black Rural Education, 1902–1935." *History of Education Quarterly* 18 (1978): 371–396.

Anderson, Joyce Meeks. "Otto H. Kahn: An Analysis of His Theatrical Philanthropy in the New York City Area From 1909 to 1934." Ph.D. Dissertation, Kent State University, 1983.

Andrews, F. Emerson. *Corporation Philanthropy*. New York: Russell Sage Foundation, 1953.

Andrews, F. Emerson. "Growth and Present Status of American Foundations." *Proceedings* (of the American Philosophical Society) 105 (April 21, 1961): 141–161.

Andrews, F. Emerson. "Foundation Influence on Education." *Educational Record*, Winter 1972, pp. 23–29.

Andrews, F. Emerson. *Foundation Watcher*. Lancaster, Pa.: Franklin and Marshall College, 1973.

Andrews, F. Emerson. *The Legal Instruments of Foundations*. New York: Russell Sage Foundation, 1958.

Andrews, F. Emerson. "New Trends in Corporation Giving." In *Social Welfare Forum* (Official Proceedings of the National Conference of Social Work), 1952, pp. 251–261.

Andrews, F. Emerson. *Patman and the Foundations: Review and Assessment*. New York: The Foundation Center, 1968.

Andrews, F. Emerson. *Philanthropic Foundations*. New York: Russell Sage Foundation, 1956.

Andrews, F. Emerson. *Philanthropy in the United States: History and Structure*. New York: The Foundation Center, 1974.

Andrews, Frank M. *A Study of Company-Sponsored Foundations*. New York: Russell Sage Foundation, 1960.

Anheier, Helmut K. "Indigenous Voluntary Associations, Nonprofits, and Development in Africa." In *Handbook on Nonprofit Organizations*. Edited by W. Powell. New Haven, Conn.: Yale University Press, 1986.

Antler, Joyce. "Female Philanthropy and Progressivism in Chicago." *History of Education Quarterly* 21 (1981):461–469.

Aquinas, St. Thomas. "Charity." *Summa Theologiae*, Vol. 34, 2a2ae: 23–33. New York: McGraw Hill, 1975.

Aramony, William. *The United Way: The Next 100 Years*. New York: Donald I. Fine, Inc., 1987.

Arbuthnot, Thomas S. *Heroes of Peace: A History of the Carnegie Hero Fund Commission*. New York: Carnegie Hero Fund Commission, 1935.

Arey, Henry W. The Girard College and Its Founder. Philadelphia: C. Sherman, Printer, 1852.

Arlow, Peter, and Gannon, Martin J. "Social Responsiveness, Corporate Structure, and Economic Performance." *Academy of Management Review* 7 (1982):235–241.

Arnove, Robert. "The Ford Foundation and 'Competency-Building' Overseas: Assumptions, Approaches, Outcomes." *Studies in International Development* 12 (1977):100–126.

Arnove, Robert. "The Ford Foundation and the Transfer of Knowledge: Convergence and Divergence in the World System." *Compare* 13 (1983):7–24.

Arnove, Robert S., ed. *Philanthropy and Cultural Imperialism: Foundations at Home and Abroad.* Bloomington: Indiana University Press, 1982.

Arrow, Kenneth J. "Gifts and Exchanges." *Philosophy and Public Affairs* 1 (1975):343–362.

Axinn, June, and Levinn, Herman. *Social Welfare: A History of the American Response to Need.* New York: Dodd, Mead, & Co., 1975.

Ayres, Leonard. *Seven Great Foundations.* New York: Russell Sage Foundation, 1911.

Banner, Lois W. *Elizabeth Cady Stanton: A Radical for Women's Rights.* Boston: Little, Brown & Co., 1980.

Barlow, Robin; Brazer, Harvey E.; and Morgan, James N. *Economic Behavior of the Affluent.* Washington, D.C.: Brookings Institution, 1966.

Barzun, Jacques. "The Folklore of Philanthropy." In *The House of Intellect.* New York: Harper & Bros., 1959.

Bauer, Yehuda. *My Brother's Keeper: A History of the American Jewish Joint Distribution Committee, 1929–1939.* Philadelphia: The Jewish Publication Society of America, 1974.

Baumol, William J.; Likert, Renis; Wallich, Henry G.; and McGowan, John J., eds. *A New Rationale for Corporate Social Policy.* New York: Committee for Economic Development, 1970.

Beard, Charles A., and Beard, Mary R. *The Rise of American Civilization.* Vol. 2. New York: Macmillan Co., 1927.

Beckman, Margaret; Langmead, Stephen; and Black, John. *The Best Gift: A Record of the Carnegie Libraries in Ontario.* Toronto: Dundurn Press, 1984.

Bellah, Robert N.; Sullivan, William M.; Madsen, Richard; Swidler, Ann; and Tipton, Steven M. *Habits of the Heart: Individualism and Commitment in American Life.* Berkeley: University of California Press, 1985.

Belles, A. Gilbert. "The NAACP, the Urban League and the Julius Rosenwald Fund." *Crisis* 86 (1979):97–106.

Berger, Peter, and Neuhaus, Richard John. *To Empower People: The Role of*

Mediating Structures in Public Policy. Washington, D.C.: American Enterprise Institute for Public Policy Research, 1977.

Berman, Edward H. "American Philanthropy and African Education: Toward an Analysis." *African Studies Review* 20 (1977):1.

Berman, Edward H. "The Extension of Ideology: Foundation Support for Intermediate Organizations and Forums." *Comparative Education Review* 26 (1982): 48–68.

Berman, Edward H. *The Ideology of Philanthropy: The Influence of the Carnegie, Ford and Rockefeller Foundations on American Foreign Policy.* Albany: State University of New York Press, 1983.

Berner, Carl W. *Power of Pure Stewardship.* St. Louis: Concordia Publishing House, 1970.

Bernhard, Virginia. "Cotton Mather and the Doing of Good: A Puritan Gospel of Wealth." *New England Quarterly* 49 (1976):225–241.

Bernstein, Philip. *To Dwell in Unity: The Jewish Federation Movement in America Since 1960.* Philadelphia: The Jewish Publication Society of America, 1983.

Biebel, Charles. "Private Foundations and Public Policy: The Case of Secondary Education During The Depression." *History of Education Quarterly* 16 (1976): 3–33.

Blaine, Mrs. Emmons. "Can Citizenship Be Fullfilled by Philanthropy?" *The Survey,* July 2, 1910, pp. 542–547. The Charity Organization Society of the City of New York, publisher.

Blandin Foundation. *Annual Report, 1982.* Grand Rapids, Minn. Blandin Foundation.

Blendon, Robert J. "The Changing Role of Private Philanthropy in Health Affairs." In *Research Papers of the Commission on Private Philanthropy and Public Needs.* Vol. 2. Washington, D.C.: Department of Treasury, 1977.

Blitzer, Wolf. "Who Gives, Who Doesn't—And Why." *Present Tense* 10 (1983):21–22.

Bobinski, George S. *Carnegie Libraries: Their History and Impact on American Public Library Development.* Chicago: American Library Association, 1969.

Bogen, Boris D. *Jewish Philanthropy.* Montclair, N.J.: Patterson Smith, 1969.

Bolling, Landrum R. *Private Foreign Aid: U.S. Philanthropy for Relief and Development.* Boulder, Colo.: Westview Press, 1982.

Bolling, Landrum R. "Private Philanthropy and International Activities in the Decade After the Filer Report." In *Working Papers for Spring Research Forum: Since the Filer Commission.* Washington, D.C.: Independent Sector, 1983.

Bolton, Sarah K. *Famous Givers and Their Gifts*. New York/Boston: T. Y. Crowell & Co., 1896.

Boorstin, Daniel J. "From Charity to Philanthropy." In *The Decline of Radicalism*. New York: Random House, 1963.

Boorstin, Daniel J. "Missions and Momentum." In *The Americans: The Democratic Experience*. New York: Random House, 1973.

Boorstin, Daniel J. *The Americans: The Colonial Experience*. New York: Random House/Vintage Books, 1958.

Boudreaux, Julianna Liles. "A History of Philanthropy in New Orleans, 1835–1862." Ph.D. dissertation no. 61–6706, Tulane University 1961. Ann Arbor, Michigan: University Microfilms, Inc., 1985.

Boulding, Kenneth E. "Notes on a Theory of Philanthropy." In *Philanthropy and Public Policy*. Edited by Frank G. Dickinson. Washington, D.C.: National Bureau of Economic Research, 1962.

Boulding, Kenneth E. *Towards a Pure Theory of Foundations*. Danbury, Conn.: Nonprofit Report, Inc., 1972.

Boyd, George Adams. *Elias Boudinot: Patriot and Statesman 1740–1821*. Princeton, N.J.: Princeton University Press, 1952.

Brawley, Benjamin. *Doctor Dillard of the Jeanes Fund*. Freeport, N.Y.: Books for Libraries Press, 1971.

Bremner, Robert H. *American Philanthropy*. Chicago: University of Chicago Press, 1960.

Bremner, Robert H. *From the Depths: The Discovery of Charity in the United States*. New York: New York University Press, 1964.

Bremner, Robert H. "The Impact of the Civil War on Philanthropy and Social Welfare." *Civil War History* 12 (1966):293–303.

Bremner, Robert H. "Private Philanthropy and Public Needs: Historical Perspective." In *Research Papers of the Commission on Private Philanthropy and Public Needs*. Vol. 1. Washington, D.C.: Department of Treasury, 1977.

Bremner, Robert H. *The Public Good*. New York: Alfred A. Knopf, 1980.

Bremner, Robert H. "'Scientific Philanthropy', 1873–1893." *Social Service Review* 30 (1956):168–173.

Brockett, Linus Pierpont. *The Philanthropic Results of the War in America. By an American Citizen*. New York: Press of Wynkoop, Hallenbeck, and Thomas, 1863.

Brooks, Harvey; Liebman, Lance; and Schelling, Corinne S., eds. *Public–Private Partnership: New Opportunities for Meeting Social Needs*. Cambridge, Mass.: Ballinger, 1984.

Broughton, Walter. "Religiosity and Opposition to Church Social Action: A Test of a Weberian Hypothesis." *Review of Religious Research* 19 (1978):154–166.

Brown, E. Richard. *Rockefeller Medicine Men: Medicine and Capitalism in America.* Berkeley: University of California Press, 1980.

Brown, E. Richard. "Public Health in Imperialism: Early Rockefeller Programs at Home and Abroad." *American Journal of Public Health* 66 (September 1976): 897–903.

Browne, Robert S. "Developing Black Foundations: An Economic Response to Black Community Needs." *Black Scholar* 9 (1977):25–28.

Bullock, Mary Brown. *An American Transplant: The Rockefeller Foundation and Peking Union Medical College.* Berkeley: University of California Press, 1980.

Bulmer, Martin, and Bulmer, Joan. "Philanthropy and Social Science in the 1920's: Beardsley Ruml and the Laura Spelman Rockefeller Memorial, 1922–1929." *Minerva* 19 (1981):347–407.

Bulmer, Martin. "Philanthropic Foundations and the Development of the Social Sciences in the Early Twentieth Century: A Reply to Donald Fisher." With Fisher, "A Response to Martin Bulmer." *Sociology* 18 (1984):572–587.

Bundy, McGeorge. "The President's Review." In *The Ford Foundation Annual Report for 1977.* Review delivered on February 24, 1978.

Butler, Nicholas Murray. "The Carnegie Endowment and International Peace." *Advocate of Peace,* July 1911, pp. 152–157. Also, *The Independent* 76 (November 27, 1913):396–400.

Carey, Sarah C. "Philanthropy and the Powerless." In *Research Papers of the Commission on Private Philanthropy and Public Needs.* Vol. 2. Washington, D.C.: Department of Treasury, 1977.

Carnegie, Andrew. *Autobiography of Andrew Carnegie.* New York: Houghton Mifflin, 1920.

Carnegie, Andrew. *The Gospel of Wealth: And Other Timely Essays.* New York: The Century Co., 1900.

Carter, Richard. *The Gentle Legions.* Garden City, N.Y.: Doubleday & Co., Inc., 1961.

Chamber of Commerce of the United States. *Community Foundations.* Washington, D.C.: Chamber of Commerce of the United States, 1921.

Chamberlain, Neil W. *The Limits of Corporate Responsibility.* New York: Basic Books, 1973.

Chambers, M. M. *Charters of Philanthropies: A Study of Selected Trust Investments, Charters, By-laws, and Court Decisions.* New York: Carnegie Foundation for the Advancement of Teaching, 1948.

The Charitable Impulse in 18th Century America: Collected Papers. Advisory Editor, David J. Rothman. New York: Arno Press, 1971.

Cheit, Earl F., and Lobman, Theodore E., III. "Private Philanthropy and Higher Education: History, Current Impact, and Public Policy Considerations." In *Research Papers of the Commission on Private Philanthropy and Public Needs.* Vol. 2. Washington, D.C.: Department of Treasury, 1977.

"Cigar Man Gives $4 Million To City." *New York Times,* September 24, 1964, pp. 1, 18.

Cleveland, Harlan. "The Internalization of Domestic Affairs." *The Annals of the American Academy of Political and Social Science* (January) 1979.

Cochrane, Robert, ed. *Beneficent and Useful Lives.* London: W. and R. Chambers, Ltd., 1910.

Coffman, Harold Coe. *American Foundations: A Study of Their Role in the Child Welfare Movement.* New York: Association Press, 1936.

Cohen, Jules. *Conscience of the Corporations: Business and Urban Affairs, 1967–1970.* Baltimore: Johns Hopkins University Press, 1971.

Cohen, Steven M. "Will Jews Keep Giving? Prospects for the Jewish Charitable Community." *Journal of Jewish Communal Service* 55 (1978):59–71.

Colton, Joel, and Richardson, Malcolm I. *The Humanities and the Well-Being of Mankind: A Half-Century of the Humanities at the Rockefeller Foundation.* New York: Rockefeller Foundation, 1982.

Colwell, Mary Anna Culleton. "Philanthropic Foundations and Public Policy: The Political Role of Foundations." Ph.D. dissertation, University of California at Berkeley, 1981.

Commonwealth Fund. *The Commonwealth Fund: Historical Sketch, 1912–1962.* New York: The Commonwealth Fund, 1963.

Commission on Private Philanthropy and Public Needs. *Donee Group Report and Recommendations—Private Philanthropy: Vital and Innovative? or Passive and Irrelevant?* Washington, D.C.: Department of Treasury, 1977.

Commission on Private Philanthropy and Public Needs. *Giving in America: Report of the Commission on Private Philanthropy and Public Needs.* Washington, D.C.: Department of Treasury, 1975.

Conference Board. *Annual Survey of Corporate Contributions.* New York: The Conference Board, annual.

Connecticut Mutual Life Insurance Company. *The Connecticut Mutual Life Report on American Values in the '80s: The Impact of Belief.* Hartford, Conn.: Connecticut Mutual Life Insurance Company, 1981.

Coon, Horace. *Money to Burn: What the Great American Philanthropic Foundations Do With Their Money.* Freeport, N.Y.: Books for Libraries Press, 1972.

Corben, Edward. *Philanthropy in America.* New York: Associated Press, 1950.

Cornuelle, Richard C. *Reclaiming the American Dream.* New York: Random House, 1965.

"Corporate Philanthropy—An Integral Part of Corporate Social Responsibility." *Business Roundtable,* March 1981.

Coser, Lewis. "Foundations as Gatekeepers of Contemporary Intellectual Life." In *Men of Ideas.* Lewis Coser, ed. New York: Free Press, 1965, pp. 337–348.

Council on Foundations. *Corporate Philanthropy.* Washington, D.C.: Council on Foundations, 1982.

Council on Foundations. "The Philanthropy of Organized Religion." *Foundation News* 25 (September/October 1984).

Cousins, Norman. "New Directions for American Foundations." *Saturday Review* 35 (September 13, 1952):24.

Cox, June; Daniel, Neil; and Boston, Bruce O. *Educating Able Learners: Programs and Promising Practices.* Austin: University of Texas Press, 1985.

Cranston, Alan, and Pifer, Alan. *Foundations on Trial.* New York: Council on Foundations, 1970.

Crothers, Rev. Samuel. "The Art of Philanthropy." *Survey,* 1905, pp. 872–873.

Cuninggim, Merrimon. "The Foundations: Sources of Educational Variety or Constraint?" *Liberal Education* 59 (1973):166–175.

Cuninggim, Merrimon. *Private Money and Public Service: The Role of Foundations in American Society.* New York: McGraw-Hill, 1972.

Curti, Merle E. *American Philanthropy Abroad: A History.* New Brunswick, N.J.: Rutgers University Press, 1963.

Curti, Merle E. "American Philanthropy and the National Character." *American Quarterly* 10 (Winter 1958):420–437.

Curti, Merle E. "Creative Giving: Slogan or Reality?" *Foundation News* 3 (November 1962):7–10

Curti, Merle, and Nash, Roderick. *Philanthropy in the Shaping of American Higher Education.* New Brunswick, N.J.: Rutgers University Press, 1965.

Curti, Merle E. "The History of American Philanthropy as a Field of Research." *American Historical Review* 62 (January 1957):352–363.

Curti, Merle E. "Tradition and Innovation in American Philanthropy." *Proceedings of the American Philosophical Society* 105 (April 1961):145–156.

Curti, Merle; Green, Judith; and Nash, Roderick. "Anatomy of Giving: Millionaires in the Late 19th Century." *American Quarterly* 15 (1963):415–435.

Dahlberg, Jane S. *The New York Bureau of Municipal Research: Pioneer in Government Administration.* New York: New York University Press, 1966.

Dain, Norman. *Clifford W. Beers: Advocate for the Insane*. Pittsburgh: University of Pittsburgh Press, 1980.

Danforth Foundation. "The Danforth and Kent Fellowships: A Quinquennial Review." St. Louis: The Danforth Foundation, 1976.

Dass, Ram, and Gorman, Paul. *How Can I Help?: Stories and Reflections on Service*. New York: Knopf, 1985.

Davis, Keith. "The Case for and Against Business Assumption of Social Responsibilities." *Academy of Management Journal* 16 (1973):312–322.

Dawkins, Richard. *The Selfish Gene*. New York: Oxford University Press, 1976.

Desmore, Abe James Bourne. *Torch Bearers in Darkest America*. Pretoria, South Africa: The Carnegie Corporation Visitors' Grant, 1937.

Dickinson, Frank G. *The Changing Position of Philanthropy in the American Economy*. Occasional paper, no. 110. New York: National Bureau of Economic Research, 1970.

Dickinson, Frank G., ed. *Philanthropy and Public Policy*. New York: National Bureau of Economic Research, 1962.

Doll, Eugene E. *Twenty-Five Years of Service: 1930–1955*. Philadelphia: Carl Schurz Memorial Foundation, Inc., 1955.

Douglas, James. *Why Charity? The Case for a Third Sector*. Beverly Hills, Calif.: Sage, 1983.

Douglas, James, and Wildavsky, Aaron. "Big Government and the Private Foundations." *Policy Studies Journal* 9 (1980–1981):1175–1190.

Duke Endowment. *The First Fifty Years, 1924–1974*. New York: The Duke Endowment, 1974.

Eastman Kodak Company. *Joint Ventures*. Rochester, N.Y.: Corporate Communications Department, Eastman Kodak Company, 1979.

Eells, Richard. *The Corporation and the Arts*. New York: Macmillan Co., 1967.

Eells, Richard. *Corporation Giving in a Free Society*. New York: Harper & Bros., 1956.

Eells, Richard, ed. *International Business Philanthropy*. New York: Macmillan Co., 1979.

Eells, Richard. "A Philosophy for Corporate Giving." *The Conference Board Record*, January 1968, pp. 14–18.

Eisenberg, Pablo. "The Voluntary Sector: Problems and Challenges." In *Research Papers of the Commission on Private Philanthropy and Public Needs*. Vol. 2. Washington, D.C.: Department of the Treasury, 1977.

Elliott, Charles. *"Mr. Anonymous": Robert W. Woodruff of Coca-Cola.* Atlanta: Cherokee Publishing Company, 1982.

Elliott, Edward C., and Chambers, M. M. *Charters of Philanthropies: A Study of The Charters of Twenty-Nine American Philanthropic Foundations.* New York: Carnegie Foundation for the Advancement of Teaching (with Purdue University), 1939.

Embree, Edwin R. "The Business of Giving Away Money." *Harper's Magazine,* August 1930, pp. 320–329.

Embree, Edwin R., and Waxman, Julia. *Investment in People: The Story of the Julius Rosenwald Fund.* New York: Harper & Bros., 1949.

Ettling, John. *The Germ of Laziness. Rockefeller Philanthropy and Public Health in the New South.* Cambridge, Mass.: Harvard University Press, 1981.

Faris, N. A. *The Mysteries of Almsgiving.* Beirut: Kazi Publications, 1966. Lahore: Kazi Publications, 1974.

Fenn, Dan H., Jr. "Executives as Community Volunteers." *Harvard Business Review,* March/April 1971, pp. 4–13.

Ferguson, Clyde. "The Political and Social Ideas of Andrew Carnegie and John D. Rockefeller: A Study in Conservatism." Thesis Abstract, Urbana: University of Illinois, 1951.

Filer, John H. "The Social Goals of a Corporation." In *Corporations and Their Critics: Issues and Answers to the Problems of Corporate Responsibility.* Edited by Thornton Bradshaw and David Vogel. New York: McGraw-Hill, 1982.

Finn, David. "The Public Invisibility of Corporate Leaders." *Harvard Business Review* 58, no. 6, 1980.

Fisch, Edith L. *The Cy-Pres Doctrine in the United States.* New York: Matthew Bender & Co., 1950.

Fisher, Donald. "The Role of Philanthropic Foundations in the Reproduction and Production of Hegemony: Rockefeller Foundations and the Social Sciences," *Sociology* 17 (1983):206–233.

Flexner, Abraham. *Funds and Foundations: Their Policies Past and Present.* New York: Arno Press, 1976 (1952).

Flexner, Abraham. *I Remember. The Autobiography of Abraham Flexner.* New York: Simon & Schuster, 1940.

Flexner, Abraham. "Private Fortunes and the Public Future." *The Atlantic Monthly,* no. 156 (August 1935), pp. 215–224.

Flexner, Eleanor. *Century of Struggle.* New York: Atheneum, 1973.

Florance, Howard. "Distributing Conrad Hubert's Millions." *Review of Reviews* 533 (April 1931):64–65.

Fosdick, Raymond B. *Adventure in Giving: The Story of the General Education Board.* New York: Harper & Row, 1962.

Fosdick, Raymond B. *Chronicle of a Generation: An Autobiography.* New York: Harper & Row, 1958.

Fosdick, Raymond B. *John D. Rockefeller, Jr.: A Portrait.* New York: Harper & Bros., 1956.

Fosdick, Raymond B. *A Philosophy for a Foundation: On the Fiftieth Anniversary of the Rockefeller Foundation, 1913–1963.* New York: Rockefeller Foundation, 1963.

The Foundation Directory. 10th ed. New York: The Foundation Center, 1985.

Foundation News. "Social Policy in Foundation Investments." *Bulletin of the Foundation Library Center* 8 (July 1967):61–64.

Foundations, Private Giving, and Public Policy: Report and Recommendations of the Commission on Foundations and Private Philanthropy. Chicago: University of Chicago Press, 1970.

Fox, Daniel M. *Engines of Culture: Philanthropy and Art Museums.* Madison: State Historical Society of Wisconsin, 1963.

Fremont-Smith, Marion R. *Philanthropy and the Business Corporation.* New York: Russell Sage Foundation, 1972.

Friedrich, Carl J. "Foundations and the World of Science and Scholarship." *Polity* 4 (1970):526–532.

Fry, Louis W.; Keim, Gerald; and Meiners, Roger E. "Corporate Contributions: Altruistic or For Profit?" *Academy of Management Journal* 25 (1982):94–106.

Fuller, Reginal H., and Rice, Brian. *Christianity and the Affluent Society.* Grand Rapids, Mich.: William B. Eerdmans Publishing Co., 1967.

Furst, Clyde. "Wealth Grows Generous." *World's Work,* November 1929, pp. 56–60.

Galaskiewicz, Joseph. *Social Organization of an Urban Grants Economy: A Study of Business Philanthropy and Nonprofit Organizations.* Orlando, Fla.: Academic Press, 1985.

Gallup Organization, Inc. *Americans Volunteer, 1985.* Washington, D.C.: Independent Sector, 1986.

Gallup Organization, Inc. *Public Awareness of and Attitudes Toward Philanthropic Foundations.* Washington, D.C.: Council on Foundations, 1972.

Gamwell, Franklin I. *Beyond Preference: Liberal Theories of Independent Association.* Chicago: University of Chicago Press, 1984.

Gardner, John W. "Private Initiative for the Public Good." In *Annual Report of the Carnegie Corporation of New York.* 1964.

Gates, Frederic Taylor. *Chapters in My Life.* New York: Free Press, 1977.

Gaylin, Willard; Glasser, Ira; Marcus, Steven; and Rothman, David. *Doing Good: The Limits of Benevolence.* New York: Pantheon Books, 1978.

Gettleman, Marvin E. "Philanthropy and Radicalism." *Science and Society* 29 (1965):448–453.

Gettleman, Marvin E. "Philanthropy and Social Control in Late Nineteenth-Century America: Some Hypotheses and Data on the Rise of Social Work." *Societas* 5 (1975):49–59.

Gilman, Daniel Colt. "Five Great Gifts." *Outlook* 86 (1907): 648–657.

Gingrich, Arnold. *Business and the Arts: An Answer to Tomorrow*. New York: P. S. Eriksson, 1969.

Gladden, Washington. "Tainted Money." *Outlook* 52 (1895):886–887.

Glenn, John M.; Brandt, Lilian; and Andrews, F. Emerson. *Russell Sage Foundation, 1907–1946*. 2 vols. New York: Russell Sage Foundation, 1947.

Goff, Frederick H. *Community Trusts*. Cleveland: The Cleveland Trust Co., 1919.

Goodale, Frances A., ed. *The Literature of Philanthropy*. New York: Harper & Bros., 1893.

Goodpaster, Kenneth E., and Matthews, John B., Jr. "Can a Corporation Have a Conscience?" *Harvard Business Review*, January–February 1982.

Gordon, C. Wayne, and Babchuk, Nicholas. "A Typology of Voluntary Associations." In *The Government of Associations*. Edited by William A. Glaser and David L. Sills. Totowa, N.J.: The Bedminster Press, 1966.

Goulden, Joseph C. *The Money Givers*. New York: Random House, 1971.

Gray, B. Kirman. *A History of English Philanthropy*. London: P. S. King & Son, 1905.

Greenleaf, William. *From These Beginnings: The Early Philanthropies of Henry and Edsel Ford, 1911–1936*. Detroit: Wayne State University Press, 1964.

Grossman, David M. "American Foundations and The Support of Economic Research, 1913–1929. *Minerva* 20 (Spring/Summer 1982):59–82."

Gulick, Luther. *The National Institute of Public Administration: A Progress Report*. New York: NIPA, 1928.

Hall, Edward K. *Richard Drew Hall, 1904–1924*. Boston: privately printed, 1926.

Hall, Peter Dobkin. "The Model of Boston Charity: A Theory of Charitable Benevolence and Class Development." *Science and Society* 38 (1974–1975): 464–477.

Hall, Peter Dobkin. *The Organization of American Culture, 1700–1900: Private Institutions, Elites, and the Origins of American Nationality*. New York: New York University Press, 1982.

Hall, Peter Dobkin. "Philanthropy as Investment." *History of Education Quarterly* 22 (1982):185–203.

Hallion, Richard P. "Philanthropy and Flight: Guggenheim Support of Aeronautics, 1925–1930." *Aerospace History* 28 (1981):10–21.

Hammond, Charles A. *Gerritt Smith: The Story of a Noble Man's Life.* Geneva, N.Y.: Press of W. F. Humphrey, 1900.

Handlin, Oscar, and Handlin, Mary. *The Dimensions of Liberty.* Cambridge, Mass: Harvard University Press/Belknap Press, 1961.

Hands, A. R. *Charities and Social Aid in Greece and Rome.* Ithaca, N.Y.: Cornell University Press, 1968.

Hardee, Covington. "Philanthropy and the Business Corporation, Existing Guidelines—Future Policy." In *Philanthropy and Public Policy.* New York: National Bureau of Economic Research, 1962.

Hardin, John R. *The Marcus L. Ward Home at Maplewood, New Jersey.* Newark, N.J.: Osborne Co., 1928.

Hardy, Robert T. *The Social Gospel in America, 1870–1920.* New York: Oxford University Press, 1966.

Harris, James F., and Klepper, Anne. "Corporate Philanthropic Public Services Activities." In *Research Papers of the Commission on Private Philanthropy and Public Needs.* Vol. 3. Washington, D.C.: Department of Treasury, 1977.

Harrison, Shelby M. "Foundations and Public Service." *American Journal of Economics and Sociology* 9 (1949):107–115.

Havighurst, Robert J. "Philanthropic Foundations as Interest Groups." *Education and Urban Society* 13 (1981):193–218.

Haygood, Atticus G. "Slater Fund Beginnings." *Journal of Southern History* 5 (1939):223–245.

Heale, M. J. "Patterns of Benevolence: Associated Philanthropy in the Cities of New York, 1830–1860." *New York History* 57 (1976):53–79.

Heimann, Fritz, ed. *The Future of Foundations.* (Background papers for the 41st American Assembly, 1972.) Englewood Cliffs, N.J.: Prentice-Hall, 1973.

Hellman, Geoffrey. *Bankers, Bones and Beetles: The First Century of the American Museum of Natural History.* Garden City, N.Y.: Natural History Press, 1969.

Hellman, Geoffrey T. "The First Great Cheerful Giver." *American Heritage* 17 (June 1966):28–33, 76.

Hendrick, Burton J., ed. *Miscellaneous Writings of Andrew Carnegie.* Garden City, N.Y.: Doubleday, Page and Co., 1933.

Hersch, Burton. *The Mellon Family.* New York: Morrow, 1978.

Higginson, Thomas Wentworth. "The Word Philanthropy." In *Freedom and Fellowship in Religion.* Boston: Roberts Bros., 1875, pp. 323–327.

"The History of American Philanthropy as a Field of Research." *American Historical Review* 62 (January 1957):352–363.

Hijiha, James A. "Four Ways of Looking at a Philanthropist: A Study of Robert Weeks De Forest." *Proceedings of the American Philosophical Society* 124 (1980):404–418.

Hollis, Ernest V. *Philanthropic Foundations and Higher Education.* New York: Columbia University Press, 1938.

Hoover, Herbert Clark. *An American Epic.* Vol. 1. Chicago: Henry Regnery Co., 1959.

Hopkins, Charles H. *The Rise of the Social Gospel in American Protestantism, 1865–1915.* New Haven, Conn.: Yale University Press, 1940.

Hopkins, Charles. *History of the YMCA in North America.* New York: Association Press, 1951.

Horowitz, Irving Louis, and Horwitz, Ruth Leonora. "Tax-Exempt Foundations: Their Effects on National Policy." *Science* 168 (April 10, 1970):220–228.

Hoskins, Lewis M. "Voluntary Agencies and Foundations in International Aid." *Annals of the American Academy of Political and Social Science* 329 (1960):57–68.

Howard, Nathaniel R. *Trust for all Time: The Story of the Cleveland Foundation and the Community Trust Movement.* Cleveland: Cleveland Foundation, 1963.

Howe, Barbara. *The Emergence of the Philanthropic Foundation as an American Social Institution, 1900–1920.* Unpublished dissertation, Cornell University, 1976.

Huch, Ronald K. "Patriotism Versus Philanthropy: A Letter From Gerritt Smith to Frederick Douglass." *New York History* 49 (1968):327–335.

Human Resources Network. *The Handbook of Corporate Social Responsibility: Profiles of Involvement.* Durham, N.C.: Duke Graduate School of Business, 1975.

Human Resources Network. *Managing Social Performance in a Changing Business Environment.* Durham, N.C.: Duke Graduate School of Business, 1980.

Huntington, Father James, O. J. "Philanthropy: Its Success and Failure." In *Philanthropy and Social Progress.* Henry C. Adams, ed. Freeport, N.Y.: Books for Libraries Press, 1893, 1969.

Hutchins, Robert Maynard. *Freedom, Education, and the Fund: Essays and Addresses, 1946–1956.* New York: Meridian Books, 1956.

Iles, George. "The Art of Large Giving." *The Century Illustrated Monthly Magazine* 53 (March 1897):767–781.

Institute of Educational Affairs. *The Future of Private Philanthropy.* Foundation Officers Forum, Occasional Paper no. 5. New York: The Institute of Educational Affairs, 1982.

International Institute of Tropical Agriculture. "Sowing the Green Revolution." Ibadan, Nigeria. New York: Ford Foundation, April 1970.

Ireland, Thomas R., and Johnson, David B. *The Economics of Charity*. Blacksburg, Va.: Center for the Study of Public Choice, 1970.

Ise, John. *Our National Park Policy: A Critical History*. Baltimore: Johns Hopkins Press, 1961.

Jackson, Robert. "New Means for New Music." *Saturday Review* 5 (September 28, 1968):57–71.

Jackson, Philip. "Black Charity in Progressive Era Chicago." *Social Service Review* 52 (1978):400–417.

Jacoby, Neil H. *Corporate Power and Social Responsibility: A Blueprint for the Future*. Studies of the Modern Corporation. New York: Macmillan Co., 1973.

James, Estelle. "Comparisons of Nonprofit Sectors Abroad." In *Working Papers for Spring Research Forum: Since the Filer Commission*. Washington, D.C.: Independent Sector, 1983.

James, Estelle. "How Nonprofits Grow: A Model." *Journal of Policy Analysis and Management*, Spring 1983.

James, Estelle. "The Nonprofit Sector in Comparative Perspective." In *The Nonprofit Sector: A Research Handbook*. Edited by W. Powell. New Haven, Conn.: Yale University Press, 1986.

Jameson, Anna. *Sisters of Charity, Catholic and Protestant and the Communion of Labor*. Westport, Conn.: Hyperion Press, 1976.

Jarchow, Merrill E. *Amherst H. Wilder and His Enduring Legacy to Saint Paul*. St. Paul, Minn.: The Amherst H. Wilder Foundation, 1981.

Jenkins, Edward C. *Philanthropy in America*. New York: Association Press, 1950.

Jennings, Walter Wilson. *A Dozen Captains of American Industry*. New York: Vantage Press, Inc., 1954.

Johnson, Grace. "Corporate Philanthropy: An Analysis of Corporate Contributions." *Journal of Business*, October 1966, pp. 489–504.

Jones, Gareth H. *History of the Law of Charity, 1532–1827*. New York: Cambrige University Press, 1969.

Jones, John Price. *The American Giver: A Review of American Generosity*. New York: Inter-River Press, 1954.

Jones, John Price. *American Giving in the Field of Higher Education*. New York: John Price Jones, 1955.

Jordan, Wilbur K. "The Development of Philanthropy in England in the Early Modern Era." *Proceedings of the American Philosophical Society* 105 (April 1961).

Jordan, Wilbur K. *Philanthropy in England, 1480–1660*. New York: Russell Sage Foundation, 1959.

Joseph, James A. *Private Philanthropy and the Making of Public Policy.* Washington, D.C.: The Council on Foundations, 1985.

Joseph, Samuel. *History of the Baron de Hirsch Fund: The Americanization of the Jewish Immigrant.* Fairfield, N.J.: A. M. Kelley, 1978.

Josephson, Matthew. *The Robber Barons: The Great American Capitalists, 1861–1901.* New York: Harcourt, Brace, 1934.

Kammen, Michael. "The Philanthropic Impulse and the Democratization of Traditions in America." Proceedings Research Forum. Washington, D.C.: Independent Sector, 1986.

Karl, Barry D. "Corporate Philanthropy: Historical Background." In *Corporate Philanthropy.* Washington, D.C.: Council on Foundations, 1982.

Karl, Barry D. "Donors, Trustees, Staffs: An Historical View, 1890–1930." New York: Rockefeller Archives Center, 1977.

Karl, Barry D. "Philanthropy, Policy Planning and the Bureaucratization of the Democratic Ideal." *Daedalus* 105 (Fall 1976): 129–150.

Karl, Barry D., and Katz, Stanley N. "The American Private Philanthropic Foundation and the Public Sphere, 1890–1930." *Minerva* 19 (Summer 1981): 236–270.

Karp, Abraham. *To Give Life: The UJA in the Shaping of the American Jewish Community.* New York: Schocken, 1981.

Katz, Milton. *The Modern Foundation: Its Dual Character, Public and Private.* New York: The Foundation Library Center, 1968.

Keele, Harold M., and Kiger, Joseph C., eds. *Foundations.* Greenwood Encyclopedia of American Institutions. Westport, Conn.: Greenwood Press, 1984.

Keim, Gerald D. "Corporate Social Responsibility: An Assessment of the Enlightened Self-Interest Model." *Academy of Management Review* 3 (1978):32–39.

Kellogg (W. K.) Foundation. *W. K. Kellogg Foundation: The First Half Century, 1930–1980.* Battle Creek, Mich.: W.K. Kellogg Foundation, 1980.

Kelly, Frank K. *Court of Reason: Robert Hutchins and the Fund for the Republic.* New York: Free Press London, Collier Macmillan Publishers, 1981.

Keppel, Frederick P. *The Foundation: Its Place in American Life.* New York: Macmillan Co., 1930.

Keppel, Frederick Paul. *Philanthropy and Learning.* New York: Columbia University Press, 1936.

Kiger, Joseph C. "Foundation Support of Educational Innovation by Learned Societies, Councils and Institutes." In *Innovations in Education.* Edited by Matthew Miles. New York: Teachers College Press, 1964.

Kiger, Joseph C. *Operating Principles of the Larger Foundations*. New York: Russell Sage Foundation, 1954.

King, Cornelia S., ed. *American Philanthropy, 1731–1860*. New York: Garland Publishing, Inc., 1984.

Kiser, Clyde W. *The Milbank Memorial Fund: Its Leaders and Its Work, 1905–1974*. New York: Milbank Memorial Fund, 1975.

Klein, Philip. *From Philanthropy to Social Welfare: An American Cultural Perspective*. San Francisco: Jossey-Bass, 1968.

Knauft, Edwin B. *Profiles of Effective Corporate Giving Programs*. Washington, D.C.: Independent Sector, 1985.

Knauft, Edwin B. "A Research Agenda for Corporate Philanthropy." In *Corporate Philanthropy*. Washington, D.C.: Council on Foundations, 1982.

Knowles, Louis. "Alternative Investments: Helping Communities The Old Fashioned Way." *Foundation News*, May/June 1985, pp. 18–23.

Koch, Frank. *Corporate Giving: Policy and Practice*. New York: President's Association, 1978.

Koch, Frank. *The New Corporate Philanthropy*. New York: Plenum Press, 1979.

Kohler, Robert E. "A Policy for the Advancement of Science: The Rockefeller Foundation, 1924–1929." *Minerva* 16 (1978):480–515.

Koskoff, David E. *The Mellons*. New York: Crowell, 1978.

Kresge Foundation. *The Kresge Foundation: Fifty Years, 1924–1974*. Detroit: Kresge Foundation, 1974.

"Lady Philanthropist." *New Yorker* 33 (June 8, 1957):26–27.

Lageman, Ellen Condliffe. *Private Power for the Public Good: A History of the Carnegie Foundation for the Advancement of Teaching*. Middletown, Conn.: Wesleyan University Press, 1983.

Landis, Bernard, and Tauber, Edward S., eds. "The Protestant Ethic with Fewer Tears." In *In the Name of Life: Essays in Honor of Erich Fromm*. New York: Holt, Rinehart and Winston, 1971.

Lane, James B. "Jacob A. Riis and Scientific Philanthropy During the Progressive Era." *Social Service Review* 47 (1963):32–48.

Lankford, John Errett. *Congress and the Foundations in the Twentieth Century*. River Falls: Wisconsin State University Press, 1964.

Lankford, John Errett. *Protestant Stewardship and Benevolence, 1900–1941: A Study in Religious Philanthropy*. Ph.D. dissertation no. 62–1183, University of Wisconsin, 1962. Ann Arbor, Mich.: University Microfilms, Inc., 1985.

Lawson, Ellen Nickenzie. *Mary Elizabeth Johnston, 1913–1937*. Oberlin, Ohio: Oberlin College, 1982.

Leavell, Ullin Whitney, *Philanthropy in Negro Education.* Westport, Conn.: Negro Universities Press, 1970.

Lester, Robert M. "The Philanthropic Endowment in Modern Life." *South Atlantic Quarterly* 34 (1935):1–14.

Letwin, William. "The American Foundations: Fairy Godmothers or Avenging Angels?" *Encounter* 41 (1973):53–56.

Levy, Ferdinand K., and Shatto, Gloria M. "The Evaluation of Corporate Contributions." *Public Choice* 33 (1978):19–28.

Levy, Reynold, and Nielsen, Waldemar. "An Agenda for the Future." In *Research Papers of the Commission on Private Philanthropy and Public Needs.* Vol. 2. Washington, D.C.: Department of Treasury, 1977.

Lick, Rosemary. *The Generous Miser: The Story of James Lick of California.* Los Angeles: Ward Ritchie Press, 1967.

Lindeman, Eduard C. *Wealth and Culture.* New York: Harcourt, Brace, 1936.

Link, Terry. "The Radical Philanthropists: Foundations That Fund For Social Change." *San Francisco Monthly,* March 1971, pp. 34–35.

Loch, C. S. *How to Help Cases of Distress.* London: Charity Organization Society, 1895.

Lomask, Milton. *Seed Money: The Guggenheim Story.* New York: Farrar, Straus and Co., 1964.

Long, J. C., and Carmichael, Leonard. *James Smithson and the Smithsonian Story.* New York: G. P. Putnam's Sons, 1965.

Loomis, Frank Denman. *The Chicago Community Trust: A History of its Development, 1915–1962.* Chicago: Chicago Community Trust, 1962.

Lousteau, Nicolie Roscoe. "Corporate Philanthropy and Art Museums." *Curator* 20 (1977):215–226.

Lowell, Josephine Shaw. *Public Relief and Private Charity.* New York: G. P. Putnam's Sons, 1884.

Lyman, Richard W. "In Defense of the Private Sector." *Daedalus* 104 (Winter 1975):156–159.

Lyman, Richard W. *What Kind of Society Shall We Have?* Occasional Papers Series. Washington, D.C.: Independent Sector, 1980.

MacDowell, Marian Griswold. *The First Twenty Years of the MacDowell Colony.* Peterborough, N.H.: Transcript Printing Company, 1951.

McGuire, Joseph W. *Business and Society.* New York: McGraw-Hill, 1963.

Mack, Edward C. *Peter Cooper: Citizen of New York.* New York: Columbia University Press, 1949.

Macy, Josiah, Jr., Foundation. *The Josiah Macy, Jr. Foundation, 1930–1955: A Review of its Activities.* New York: Josiah Macy, Jr., Foundation, 1955.

Magat, Richard. *The Ford Foundation at Work.* New York: Plenum Press, 1979.

Maguarrie, John. *Dictionary of Christian Ethics.* London: Westminster Press, 1967.

Mann, Arthur. *Yankee Reformers in an Urban Age: Social Reform in Boston, 1880–1900.* New York: Harper Torchbooks, 1954.

McCarthy, Kathleen D. *Noblesse Oblige: Charity and Cultural Philanthropy in Chicago, 1849–1929.* Chicago: University of Chicago Press, 1982.

McCarthy, Kathleen D., ed. *Philanthropy and Culture: The International Foundation Perspective.* Philadelphia: University of Pennsylvania Press, 1984.

MacDonald, Dwight. *The Ford Foundation: The Men and the Millions.* New York: Reynal & Co., 1956.

Marts, Arnaud C. *The Generosity of Americans.* Englewood Cliffs, N.J.: Prentice-Hall, 1966.

Marts, Arnaud C. *Philanthropy's Role in Civilization: Its Contribution to Human Freedom.* New York: Harper & Bros., 1973.

Mather, Cotton. "Bonifacius—Essays to Do Good." In *The American Puritans: This World and the Next.* Edited by Perry Miller. Garden City, N.Y.: Anchor Books, 1956.

Matthews, William H. *Adventures in Giving.* New York: Dodd, Mead & Co., 1939.

Maus, Marcel. *The Gift: Forms and Functions of Exchange in Archaic Societies.* New York: W. W. Norton & Co., Inc. 1967.

Mavity, Jane H., and Ylvisaker, Paul N. "Private Philanthropy and Public Affairs." In *Research Papers of the Commission on Private Philanthropy and Public Needs.* Vol. 2. Washington, D.C.: Department of Treasury, 1977.

Mayer, Robert A. "The Role of Philanthropic Foundations." *American Archivist* 35 (April 1972):183–192.

Meehan, Mary. "Foundation Power." *Human Life Review,* Fall 1984, pp. 42–60.

Meier, Elizabeth G. *A History of the New York School of Social Work.* New York: Columbia University Press, 1954.

Merrill, Charles. *The Checkbook: The Politics and Ethics of Foundation Philanthropy.* Boston, Ma.: Oelgeschlager, Ginn and Hain Publishers, Inc., 1986.

Miller, Howard S. *Dollars for Research: Science and its Patrons in 19th Century America.* Seattle: University of Washington Press, 1970.

Miller, Lillian B. *Patrons and Patriotism: The Encouragement of the Fine Arts in the United States, 1790–1860.* Chicago: University of Chicago Press, 1966.

Miller, Perry. "Do Good." In *The New England Mind: From Colony to Province*, Cambridge, Mass.: Harvard University Press, 1953.

Moe, Henry Allen. "Notes on the Origin of Philanthropy in Christendom." *Proceedings of the American Philosophical Society* 105 (1961):141.

Mount, May Wilkinson. "New York Women in Philanthropic Work." *Municipal Affairs* 2 (September 1898):447–457.

Murphy, E. Jefferson. *Creative Philanthropy: Carnegie Corporation and Africa, 1953–1973*. New York: Teachers College Press, Columbia University, 1976.

Myrdal, Gunnar. *An American Dilemma*. New York: Harper & Bros., 1944.

Nagel, Thomas. *The Possibility of Altruism*. New York: Oxford University Press, 1970.

Nason, John W. *Trustees and the Future of Foundations*. New York: Council on Foundations, 1977.

Nelson, Ralph L. *Economic Factors in the Growth of Corporation Giving*. New York: Russell Sage Foundation, 1970.

Nevins, Allan, and Hill, Frank E. *Ford: Decline and Rebirth, 1933–1962*. New York: Scribner, 1963.

"New Trends in Corporation Giving." *Social Welfare Forum*. Official Proceedings of the National Conference of Social Work, 1952, pp. 251–261.

New York University. *Proceedings of New York University First Through Tenth Biennial Conferences on Charitable Foundations*. New York: Matthew Bender, 1972.

Nielsen, Waldemar A. *The Big Foundations*. New York: Columbia University Press, 1972.

Nielsen, Waldemar A. *The Endangered Sector*. New York: Columbia University Press, 1979.

Nielsen, Waldemar A. *The Golden Donors*. New York: Truman Talley Books/E. P. Dutton, 1985.

Nielsen, Waldemar A. "How Solid Are the Foundations?" *New York Times Magazine*, October 21, 1962, p. 27.

Nielsen, Waldemar A. *The Third Sector: Keystone of a Caring Society*. Occasional Paper, no. 1. Washington, D.C.: Independent Sector, 1980.

"No One Need Give." *Fortune*. November 1933, pp. 58–102.

O'Connell, Brian, ed. *America's Voluntary Spirit: A Book of Readings*. New York: The Foundation Center, 1983.

O'Connell, Brian. *Effective Leadership in Voluntary Organizations*. New York: Association Press, 1976.

O'Connell, Brian. *Finding Values That Work.* New York: Walker and Company, 1978.

O'Connell, Brian. "From Service to Advocacy to Empowerment." *Social Casework* 59 (April 1978): 195–202.

O'Connell, Brian. "Voluntary Agencies Must Ask: What Price Independence?" *Foundation News* 17 (July/August 1976):16–20

Odendahl, Teresa J., ed. *America's Wealthy and the Future of Foundations.* New York: The Foundation Center, 1987.

Owen, David Edward. *English Philanthropy, 1660–1960.* Cambridge, Mass.: Harvard University Press, Belknap Press, 1964.

Park, Charles Francis. *A History of the Lowell Institute School, 1903–1928.* Cambridge, Mass.: Harvard University Press, 1931.

Palmer, George H. *Altruism: Its Nature and Varieties.* Westport, Conn.: Greenwood Press, Inc., reprint (1919).

Parker, Franklin. *Philanthropic Foundations: A Research Report and Partially Annotated Bibliography.* Tulsa: University of Oklahoma, 1964.

Parker, Franklin. *George Peabody: A Biography.* Nashville, Tenn.: Vanderbilt University, 1971.

Parrish, Thomas. "The Foundation: A Special American Institution." In *The Future of Foundations.* Edited by Fritz Heimann. Englewood Cliffs, N.J.: Prentice-Hall, 1973.

Patman, Wright. *Tax-Exempt Foundations and Charitable Trusts: Their Impact on our Economy. Chairman's Report to the Select Committee on Small Business.* House of Representatives, 87th Congress. Washington, D.C.: Government Printing Office, 1962.

Patterson, David S. "Andrew Carnegie's Quest for World Peace." *Proceedings of the American Philosophical Society,* October 20, 1970.

Payton, Robert L. *Major Challenges to Philanthropy.* Washington, D.C.: Independent Sector, 1984.

Payton, Robert L. "Philanthropic Values." Paper presented at the Wilson Center Colloquium, October 2–3, 1982.

Peeps, J. M. Stephen. "Northern Philanthropy and the Emergence of Black Higher Education: Do-Gooders, Compromisers, or Co-conspirators?" *Journal of Negro Education* 50 (1981):251–269.

Pekkanen, John. "The Great Givers." *Town and Country* 133 (December 1979):141–148 (part 1); 134 (January 1980):37–44 (part 2).

Penfield, Wilder. *The Difficult Art of Giving: The Epic of Alan Gregg.* Boston: Little, Brown & Co., 1967.

Perry, William Graves, ed. *The Rotch Traveling Scholarship: A Review of its History 1883–1963.* Boston: Rand Press, 1963.

Pessen, Edward. *Riches, Class and Power Before the Civil War.* Lexington, Mass.: Heath, 1974.

"Philanthropy, Patronage, Politics." *Daedalus* 116 (Winter 1987).

Pifer, Alan. *The Foundation in the Year 2000.* New York: The Foundation Library Center, 1968.

Pifer, Alan. "Foundations and Public Policy Formation." In *Carnegie Corporation Annual Report.* New York: 1974.

Pifer, Alan. "Foundations and the Unity of Charitable Organizations." In *Carnegie Corporation Annual Report.* New York: 1968.

Pifer, Alan. "The Jeopardy of Private Institutions." In *Carnegie Corporation Annual Report.* New York: 1970.

Pifer, Alan. "The Nongovernmental Organization at Bay." In *Carnegie Corporation Annual Report.* New York: 1966.

Pifer, Alan. *Philanthropy in an Age of Transition.* N.Y.: The Foundation Center, 1984.

Pifer, Alan. "The Quasi Nongovernmental Organization." In *Carnegie Corporation Annual Report.* New York: 1967.

Pifer, Alan. *Speaking Out: Reflections on Thirty Years of Foundation Work.* Washington, D.C.: Council on Foundations, 1984.

Plino, Alex, and Scanlon, Joanne. *Resource Raising: The Role of Non-Cash Assistance in Corporate Philanthropy.* Washington, D.C.: Independent Sector, 1986.

Polsky, Richard M. *Getting to Sesame Street: Origins of the Children's Television Workshop.* New York: Praeger Publishers, Inc., 1974.

Powell, Daniel. *John Hay Whitney Foundation.* Vol. 2, The John Hay Fellows. New York: The John Hay Whitney Foundation, 1972.

President's Task Force on Private Sector Initiatives. *Corporate Community Involvement.* New York: Citizens Forum on Self-Government/National Municipal League, 1982.

Pumphrey, Ralph E. "Compassion and Protection: Dual Motivations in Social Welfare." *Social Service Review* 33 (March 1959):21–29.

Raushenbush, Esther. *John Hay Whitney Foundation.* Vol. 1, Opportunity Fellows —Fullbright and Visiting Professors. New York: The John Hay Whitney Foundation, 1972.

Reeves, Thomas C. *Freedom and the Foundation.* New York: Alfred A. Knopf, 1969.

Reeves, Thomas C., ed. *Foundations Under Fire*. Ithaca, N.Y.: Cornell University Press, 1970.

Rein, Richard. "PRI: Will Its Time Ever Come?" *Foundation News*, November/December 1973, pp. 13–23.

Rhinelander, William Stewart. *The Philanthropic Work of Josephine Shaw Lowell*. New York: Macmillan Co., 1911.

Richards, William C., and Norton, William J. *Biography of a Foundation: The Story of the Children's Fund of Michigan 1929–1954, a Terminal Philanthropic Foundation*. Detroit: Children's Fund of Michigan, 1957.

Richman, Saul. "Down the Highways and Byways With American Philanthropy." *Foundation News*, January/February 1980, pp. 13–37.

Rockefeller, John D. "The Difficult Art of Giving." *The World's Work*, 1908.

Rockefeller, John D., 3rd. "In Defense of Philanthropy." *Business and Society Review*, no. 25 (Spring 1978).

Rockefeller, John D. *Random Reminiscences of Men and Events*. New York: Doubleday Page, 1909.

Rockefeller, John D., 3rd. "The Third Sector." *Across the Board*, March 1978.

Rogers, William Garland. *Ladies Bountiful*. New York: Harcourt, Brace, & World, 1968.

Rosenwald, Julius. "Principles of Public Giving." *Atlantic Monthly*, May 1929.

Russell, K., and Tooke, J. *Learning to Give*. Elmsford, N.Y.: Pergamon Press, Inc., 1968.

Russell Sage Foundation. *Report of the Princeton Conference on the History of Philanthropy in the United States*. New York: Russell Sage Foundation, 1956.

Safran, Claire. "Mama Hale and Her Little Angels." *Reader's Digest*, September 1984, pp. 49–56.

Sanford, Terry. *Foundations: Their Role in Our American Pluralistic System*. Grass Roots Guides on Democracy and Practical Politics, booklet no. 52. Washington, Conn.: The Center for Information on America, 1974.

Sarnoff, Paul. *Russell Sage: The Money King*. New York: Ivan Obolensky, Inc., 1965.

Saunders, Charles B., Jr. *The Brookings Institution*. Washington, D.C.: Brookings Institution, 1966.

Savage, Howard J. *Fruit of an Impulse: Forty-five Years of the Carnegie Foundation, 1905–1950*. New York: Harcourt, Brace, 1953.

Saveth, Edward N. "Patrician Philanthropy in America: The Late Nineteenth and Early Twentieth Centuries." *Social Service Review* 54 (1980):76–91.

Sayers, Elliseva. "The Greatest Day of My Life." *Philanthropy*, November 19, 1952, pp. 8, 9, 17.

Schad, Robert Oliver. *Henry Edwards Huntington: The Founder and the Library.* San Marino, Calif.: Henry E. Huntington Library and Art Gallery, 1931.

Schlossman, Steven L. "Philanthropy and the Gospel of Child Development." *History of Education Quarterly* 21 (1981):275–299.

Schonberg, Harold C. "Alice Tully Looks Back On A Busy Life in Music." *New York Times*, October 24, 1982, pp. 1, 17.

Sears, Jesse B. *Philanthropy in the History of American Higher Education.* Washington, D.C.: U.S. Bureau of Education, 1922.

Seeley, John R; Junker, Buford H.; Jones, R. Wallace; Jenkins, N. C.; Haugh, M. T.; and Miller, I. *Community Chest: A Case Study in Philanthropy.* Toronto: University of Toronto Press, 1957.

Shakeley, Jack. "Community Foundations." *Grantsmanship Center News* (March/April) 1976: 29–52.

Shankland, Robert. *Steve Mather of the National Parks.* New York: Knopf, 1970.

Shaplen, Robert. *Toward the Well-Being of Mankind: Fifty Years of the Rockefeller Foundation.* Garden City, N.Y.: Doubleday & Co., 1964.

Shaw, Albert. "American Millionaires and Their Public Gifts." *Review of Reviews* 7 (1893):48–60.

Shaw, George Bernard. *Socialism for Millionaires.* London: Fabian Society, 1902.

Sheehan, Bernard W. *Seeds of Extinction: Jeffersonian Philanthropy and the American Indian.* New York: W. W. Norton & Co., 1974.

Sheen, Fulton J. "The Philosophy of Charity." In *Old Errors and New Labels.* New York: The Century Co., 1931, pp. 233–253.

Sherry, Paul H. "Voluntary Associations and Public Policy." *Journal of Current Social Issues*, Autumn 1971.

Shryock, Richard H. *American Medical Research Past and Present.* New York: The Commonwealth Fund, 1947.

Shuman, Edwin L. "Broad Scope of American Philanthropy." *Current History* 33 (1931):702–707.

Simon, John G. "Research on Philanthropy." Speech delivered at the 25th Anniversary Conference of the National Council on Philanthropy, Denver, Colorado, November 8, 1979. Reprinted as a Research Report for Independent Sector, July 1980.

Simon, Louis M. *A History of the Actors' Fund of America.* New York: Theatre Art Books, 1972.

Smith, David Horton. "The Philanthropy Business." *Society* 15 (1978):8–15.

Smith, David Horton. "Values, Voluntary Action and Philanthropy: The Appropriate Relationship of Private Philanthropy to Public Needs." In *Research Papers of the Commission on Private Philanthropy and Public Needs.* Vol. 2. Washington, D.C.: Department of Treasury, 1977.

Smith, Hayden. "Profile of Corporate Contributions Since the Filer Commission." In *Working Papers for Spring Research Forum: Since the Filer Commission.* Washington, D.C.: Independent Sector, 1983.

Smith, Timothy L. "Biblical Ideals in American Christian and Jewish Philanthropy, 1880–1920." *American Jewish History* 74 (1984–1985):3–26.

Sorrell, Walter. "American Foundations: Their Origins and Achievements." Swissair Gazette, 2 (1978):1–3.

Southern Regional Council. *New South: The Southern Regional Council 1944–1964.* Atlanta: Southern Regional Council, 1964.

Stewart, Harry A. "I Believe In Shooting Square With Man and God." *American Magazine* 100 (July 1925):16–18.

Stewart, William Rhinelander. *The Philanthropic Work of Josephine Shaw Lowell.* New York: Macmillan Co., 1911 (Reprint—Montclair, N.J.: Patterson Smith, 1974.)

Strickland, Tamara G., and Strickland, Stephen P. *The Markle Scholars: A Brief History.* New York: Prodist, 1976.

Swain, Donald C. *Wilderness Defender: Horace M. Albright and Conservation.* Chicago: University of Chicago Press, 1970.

Taylor, Jeremy. *The Rules and Exercises of Holy Living and Holy Dying.* London: John Henry Parker 1650–51 (1849).

Tebbel, John. *The Inheritors: A Study of America's Great Fortunes and What Happened to Them.* New York: G. P. Putnam's Sons, 1962.

"The Rotch Traveling Scholarship." *The American Architect* 132 (May 5, 1920):538–541.

Thomas, Lewis. "Altruism: Self-Sacrifice for Others." *The Saturday Evening Post,* May/June, 1982.

Thompson, Jacqueline. *The Very Rich Book: America's Supermillionaires and Their Money—Where They Got It, How They Spend It.* New York: William Morrow and Co., Inc., 1981.

Thwing, Charles P. "Well-Meant but Futile Endowments: The Remedy." *The Forum* (October 1895): 133–144.

Titmuss, Richard Morris. *The Gift Relationship.* London: George Allen & Unwin, Ltd., 1963.

Tjerandsen, Carl. *Education for Citizenship: A Foundation's Experience.* Santa Cruz, Calif.: Emil Schwarzhaupt Foundation, Inc., 1980.

Troy, Kathryn. *The Corporate Contributions Function.* New York: The Conference Board, 1982.

"True and False Philanthropy." *Newly Revised Eclectic Reader.* Edited by William W. McGuffey. Cincinnati, Ohio, 1844.

Turnbaugh, Douglas. "The Rise of the House of Harkness." *The Atlantic* 222 (November 1968):137–139.

U.S. Congress, House Select Committee to Investigate Foundations and Other Organizations. *Final Report.* 82nd Congress, 2nd session. House Report 2524. Washington, D.C.: Government Printing Office, 1953.

U.S. Congress Committee on Ways and Means. *Hearings.* 98th Congress, Committee on Ways and Means, Part 1 and 2, June 27, 28, 30, 1983. Tax Rules Governing Private Foundations. Washington, D.C., 1983.

Virgadamo, Peter R. "Charity for a City in Crisis: Boston, 1740–1775." *Historical Journal of Massachusetts* 10 (1982):22–33.

"Voluntary Health and Welfare Agencies in the United States." An exploratory study by an ad hoc citizens committee. Robert H. Hamlin, study director. New York: The Schoolmasters' Press, 1961.

Walker, John. "The Founding Benefactors." In *The National Gallery of Art.* New York: Abrams, 1975, pp. 30–50.

Walter, Claire. *Winners: The Blue Ribbon Encyclopedia of Awards.* New York: Facts on File, 1978.

Walzer, Michael. *Spheres of Justice, A Defense of Pluralism and Equality.* New York: Basic Books, 1983.

Warner, Amos G. *American Charities.* Revised by Mary Coolidge. New York: Russell Sage Foundation, 1971.

Warner, Amos G; Queen, Stuart A.; and Harper, Ernest B. *American Charities and Social Work.* New York: Thomas Y. Cromwell, 1930.

Washington, Booker T. "Raising Money." *Up From Slavery.* Garden City, N.Y.: Harper & Row, 1963, chapter 12.

Weaver, Warren. *Alfred P. Sloan, Jr., Philanthropist.* Occasional Paper. New York: Alfred P. Sloan Foundation, 1975.

Weaver, Warren. *U.S. Philanthropic Foundations: Their History, Structure, Management, and Record.* New York: Harper & Row, 1967.

Weeks, Edward. *The Lowells and Their Institute.* Boston: Little, Brown & Co., 1966.

Whitaker, Benjamin. *The Foundations: An Anatomy of Philanthropic Societies.* New York: Penguin Books, 1979.

Whitaker, Ben. *The Philanthropoids: Foundations and Society.* New York: William Morrow & Co., Inc. 1974.

Widdemer, Margaret. *Golden Friends I Had.* Garden City, N.Y.: Doubleday, 1964.

Wilhelm, Marion. "Voluntary Foreign Aid: 25 Years of Partnership." In *War on Hunger.* Washington, D.C.: Agency for International Development, 1971.

Winthrop, John. "A Model of Christian Charity." In *The American Puritans.* Edited by Perry Miller. Garden City, N.Y.: Anchor Books, 1956.

Wolfenden Committee Report. *The Future of Voluntary Organizations.* London: Croom Helm, 1978.

"Women and Charitable Work." *The Cornhill Magazine* 30 (July/December 1874):417–427.

Woodring, Paul. *Investment in Innovation.* Boston: Little, Brown, & Co., 1970.

Wooster, James W. *Edward Stephen Harkness: 1874–1940: A Biography.* New York: Harper Brothers, 1949.

Wright, Arthus Davis. *The Negro Rural School Fund, Inc.* (Anna T. Jeanes Foundation) 1907–1933. Washington, D.C.: The Negro Rural School Fund, Inc., 1933.

Wyllie, Irving. "The Reputation of the American Philanthropist." *Social Service Review* 32 (1958):215–222.

Yarmolinsky, Adam. "The Foundation as an Expression of a Democratic Society." In *Proceedings of the Fifth Biennial Conference on Charitable Foundations.* Edited by Henry Sellin. Albany, N.Y.: Matthew Bender, 1961.

Yarmolinsky, Adam. "Philanthropic Activity in International Affairs." In *Research Papers of the Commission on Private Philanthropy and Public Needs.* Vol. 2. Washington, D.C.: Department of Treasury, 1977.

INDEX